MW00861128

POESIA
FIRST ANTHOLOGY

FERNANDO PESSOA

BILINGUAL EDITION
PT | EN

POESIA
FIRST ANTHOLOGY

FERNANDO PESSOA

Selection and introduction
Adolfo Casais Monteiro

Edition of the source text
Andrea Ragusa

Translation
Austen Hyde

Preface
George Monteiro

with an essay by **Eduardo Lourenço**

SHANTARIN

TITLE
Poesia. First Anthology

AUTHOR
Fernando Pessoa

SELECTION AND INTRODUCTION
Adolfo Casais Monteiro

EDITION OF THE SOURCE TEXT
Andrea Ragusa

TRANSLATION
Austen Hyde

TRANSLATION REVISION
Leonor Simas-Almeida

ILLUSTRATIONS
Kleber Sales

GRAPHIC DESIGN
Teresa Matias

FONTS
Aria Text G1, by Rui Abreu
Sabon, by Jan Tschichold
Usual, by Rui Abreu

PUBLISHING DIRECTOR
João Pedro Ruivo

SERIES
Litteraria

PUBLISHER
SHANTARIN

First edition: January 2022
Lisboa, Portugal
Printed by Guide – Artes Gráficas, Lda.
ISBN 978-989-53422-2-8 | Dep. legal 493310/21

shantarin.com
shantarin@shantarin.com

© Antiga Shantarin, Lda.
All rights reserved. No part of this publication may
be reproduced in any form or by any means without
prior permission in writing from the publisher.

MIX
Paper from
responsible sources
FSC® C153240

ACKNOWLEDGEMENTS

In 1942, the first major anthology of Fernando Pessoa's orthonymous and heteronymous work was published thanks to the initiative of Adolfo Casais Monteiro, a poet and critic from the literary movement of the journal *Presença*. An admirer and friend of Pessoa's, to whom Pessoa recounted in a letter the origin of his heteronyms, Casais Monteiro offered Portuguese-language readers a fine selection of poems and introduced the volume.

As part of a project of disseminating the works of Portuguese poets in other languages, this publishing house has undertaken to share this classic anthology—working from the definitive, expanded selection of poems from its second edition, from 1945—with the growing readership of Fernando Pessoa all over the world.

This book is one in a set of bilingual editions entitled *Poesia. Primeira Antologia* [First Anthology], which, to some extent, expand on and pay homage in several languages to Casais Monteiro's pioneering initiative in disseminating Fernando Pessoa's poetic work.

The realization of this idea has involved the support of Adriano Lourenço, Ana Maria Almeida Martins, António Cardiello, Guilherme d'Oliveira Martins, João Rasteiro, Maria Beatriz Nizza da Silva, and Pedro Sepúlveda.

Collaborators on this English-language edition have included, with professionalism and dedication, Andrea Ragusa, who edited and annotated the source text, Austen Hyde, who translated, Leonor Simas-Almeida, who edited the translations, George Monteiro, who prefaced the volume, and Kleber Sales, who illustrated it.

This house is grateful to every individual involved, as well as to the National Library of Portugal, to the Casa da Escrita de Coimbra [Coimbra Writing House], and to the Calouste Gulbenkian Foundation.

Lastly, a particular note of thanks goes to Eduardo Lourenço, who has graciously allowed the translation and publication of his essay "Casais Monteiro's *Pessoa*," sealing this work with a golden key.

CONTENTS

ADOLFO CASAIS MONTEIRO

(1908–1972)

Adolfo Casais Monteiro was born in Porto, where he earned a degree in History and Philosophy. Beginning in the 1930s he was a collaborator on, and later director of, *Presença*, a journal that played a pioneering role in the critical analysis and dissemination of the work of Fernando Pessoa. As a poet, he debuted with *Confusão* [Confusion] (1929), publishing in his lifetime more than ten anthologies, including *Voo sem Pássaro Dentro* [Birdless Flight] (1954). In 1945 he published his first novel, *Adolescentes* [Adolescents]. In the scope of his wide essayistic output, particularly relevant are the volumes dedicated to Pessoa, to *Presença*, and to literary theory. An objector to the *Estado Novo* regime, he was detained and persecuted and was forbidden to practice teaching in Portugal. In 1954 he moved to Brazil, where he remained until his death. He lectured at UNESP (São Paulo) and other universities, and collaborated with various literary journals, never abandoning his activity as a critic and writer.

CONTRIBUTORS TO THIS EDITION

Andrea Ragusa, a researcher in Portuguese and Brazilian language and translation at the University of Parma and member of the IELT – Instituto Estudos de Literatura e Tradição (FCSH – Universidade Nova de Lisboa), is particularly dedicated to studies on translation, linguistics and Portuguese literature. He has translated into Italian works by various Portuguese-speaking authors, including Antero de Quental, Fernando Pessoa and José de Almada Negreiros. In 2019, he published the essay *Como exilados de um céu distante. Antero de Quental e Giacomo Leopardi.*

Austen Hyde is a translator based in Austin, Texas. He studied Portuguese and Brazilian Studies and Comparative Literature at Brown University, specializing in Portuguese translation. In addition to translating, he has been a Shakespeare instructor, theater company manager, actor, director, musician, and writer.

Kleber Sales, born in Brasília, studied Visual Arts, specialization in Design, at the University of Brasilia (UnB). He is illustrator for Correio Braziliense since 1997 and collaborates with the newspapers *Estado de São Paulo*, *Folha de São Paulo*, and *Bild am Sonntag*, the periodicals *Piaui*, *Quatro Rodas*, *Playboy Brasil*, and *Runners Brasil* and with other communication media in Brazil and abroad. He has received various awards, including from the Society for News Design and from the Salão Internacional de Desenho de Imprensa.

Leonor Simas-Almeida has a PhD in Comparative Literature from Brown University. She is a Senior Lecturer in Portuguese and Lusophone African literatures in the Department of Portuguese and Brazilian Studies at the same university, where she is also Director of Graduate Studies. She has published extensively in the areas of her teaching, with a theoretical focus on postcolonial studies and the construction of emotions in literature.

Once, in Brazil, I was told that Jorge de Sena's problem was that he had always wanted to be Adolfo Casais Monteiro but, sadly, wasn't. One might well add to this characterization the further speculation that Sena, the poet-critic, could just as readily have longed to have been one of those men who, in 1927, launched what turned out to be a ground-breaking journal. With Branquinho da Fonseca, João Gaspar Simões and José Régio as editors, *presença* presented itself as the first journal in Portugal devoted to "art and criticism." The editors also projected their bravura by deliberately de-capitalizing its title. The journal lasted until 1940.

Soon after its inception two of *presença*'s founding editors left their posts and were replaced by Adolfo Casais Monteiro and Adolfo Rocha (Miguel Torga). Of those editors in the early years, it was Adolfo Casais Monteiro who most took the aims of the journal to heart, mainly to promote what is now commonly called the second wave of Portuguese modernism. In doing so, he also came to be recognized as one of Pessoa's most perceptive critics.

While it was not Casais Monteiro who first called Fernando Pessoa "Mestre" in print, he nevertheless seems to have assumed early on the delicate task of courting the Master and attracting his work to the pages of *presença*. In this vein, I would point to two major Casais Monteiro initiatives that to this day have had considerable influence on the way scholars have looked at the Master.

The earlier of Casais Monteiro's two initiatives in the matter of Pessoa's work stemmed from was the discomfort he felt in 1934 when he discovered that Pessoa had permitted the publication of *Mensagem*. In a letter to the poet, Casais Monteiro voiced his opinion that by so doing Pessoa had damaged his literary reputation. He would have done himself and his work greater service, argued Casais Monteiro, had he collected and published as his first book, for example, a collection of the verse he attributed to one of his major poetic creations—heteronyms, he called them—or the best of the lyrical verse he assigned to himself. Pessoa answered as best he could by describing the circumstances of an offer that he chose not to refuse. Casais Monteiro was right, of course, for reviewers misread *Mensagem* as a suite of poems celebrating Portugal's exalted historical past and enabling the notion that the country's best days lay ahead. In Mensagem, concluded those readers, Pessoa had embraced the 'reality' of the myth they called Sebastianism. No surprise, then, that the book's second edition appeared, in 1941, under the aegis of the Agência Geral das Colónias. Patriotic readings of *Mensagem* have continued to this day.

The second of Casais Monteiro's major initiatives on Pessoa studies is the critical (and biographical) question he posed to Pessoa early in 1935. His question pertained to the origins and circumstances surrounding the creation (the "birth," so to speak) of his three most important individualized voices—heteronyms, the poet called them. Casais Monteiro's curiosity about the origins of Alberto Caeiro, Ricardo Reis and Álvaro de Campos sparked Pessoa's memory and, undoubtedly, his imagination. He answered Casais Monteiro's question in full, perhaps even fulsomely. Manipulating dates, collapsing facts and inserting questionable details, Pessoa created an original foundation narrative that, since his letter's publication in *presença* in June 1937, has been accepted as a faithful autobiographical account by scores upon scores of readers, critics and scholars. Taken as utterly factual in its details and dates, Pessoa's account has shaped and directed much of the criticism of Pessoa's work, Casais Monteiro's not excepted.

Casais Monteiro could not do much about the tide of mis-readings of *Mensagem*. But it was another matter when it came to the publication of an anthology of the verse Pessoa attributed to himself, not to heteronyms. No such collection had ever appeared. So, in 1942, he collected the poems himself and published his selection under a simple and unimposing title—*Poesia*.

George Monteiro
Brown University

NOTE ON THE SOURCE TEXT

This edition maintains the poetic anthology of Fernando Pessoa edited by Adolfo Casais Monteiro and published by Editorial Confluência in 1945 (the second edition of this book which had been first released in 1942). The sources used by the editor are respected, even in cases where the chosen source does not match the last version published by the author during his lifetime.

The original texts have been corrected from imprecisions in transcription through comparison with their sources, proceeding, when necessary, to consultation of the manuscripts, of genetic editions or of other notable editions, to which references are provided in the bibliography.

The spelling of the original texts follows the norm previous to the Orthographic Agreement of 1990, wherever it does not alter the meter of the verse or the phonological characteristics of words. In cases of syncope and/or apheresis (*'sp'rito, 'sp'rança, 'splenda,* etc.), when the metrics so demand, the apostrophe is utilized, as prescribed in the same norm.

We have followed the order of the poems proposed by Casais Monteiro, with one exception: Pessoa's translation of Aleister Crowley's "Hymn to Pan" ["Hino a Pã"] has been incorporated in the translations section, alongside poems by Edgar Allan Poe. This section of the anthology has been kept in order to show a lesser known, nonetheless important dimension of Fernando Pessoa's works: that of literary translator.

Two texts of an autobiographical nature by Fernando Pessoa have been translated in full—the "Letter on the Genesis of the Heteronyms" and the "Bibliographical Table"—, which Casais Monteiro, for reasons well founded at the time, transcribed only partially.

The composition dates of the poems (where present) and the original sources indicated by Casais Monteiro are cited on a page at the end of the poems. I am responsible for the endnotes, as well as for the footnotes in the appendices, except when otherwise noted.

Andrea Ragusa
University of Parma

POESIA

FIRST ANTHOLOGY

FERNANDO PESSOA

Introduction

Along the highest ridgeline of Portuguese poetry, the heights signified by four poets form unto themselves a distinct chain and, with the subsidiary figures prolonging them, we might call them, still using geographical vocabulary, a true orographic system. And such a "system" shall we see standing out in greater relief above the general landscape of our literature if we take into account that these four poets are precisely, if not the greatest, at least four of the greatest born among us: Camões, Antero, Pascoais, and Fernando Pessoa.

In proving that these are in fact our four greatest poets, and that this particular nexus does exist among their poetic oeuvres, we will pave the way to be able eventually to attempt a determination of the foundational values of Portuguese poetry that is no longer based solely on vague affinities, vague "constants" which more often than not do not even broach the issue, leaving untouched the mystery of a possible unity. A unity that would connect unto themselves the highest expressions attained by our poetry, a unity that would define that poetry, no longer only in terms of the individual greatness of poets but as an affirmation of a common base, of a latent philosophy, of a coherent sense, albeit out of these poets only the latter two intended to be recognized as participants in a common base—and those latter two, as I take it, in seeking a common base of Portuguese poetry, were led, as was only natural, to accentuate more what was unique to them and to their contemporaries than such supra-temporal bonds.

It has often been said that between English poetry and ours have existed certain affinities, although this idea has never yet, as far as I am aware, been elaborated upon, remaining still a mere observation. Neither can I venture into the issue, as the occasion is not opportune and I am not equipped with the tools to attempt to do so. For here, what is important is the fact that, as in English poetry, some of the highest expressions of our poetry have revealed themselves in that area which might be termed the "trans-human"—the area where poetry, although not abandoning the expression of the properly human, seeks a prolongation thereof beyond immediate life, and at every moment craves some transcendent *more*. Let us say that it is a search for the human in the transcendent, in a meta-human that nevertheless does not lose sight of earthly man. A meta-human whose condition for validity would be that it is not abstract. It may help us better situate this trend to compare it with a strong current in French poetry—so strong that to many all French poetry is defined by it—whose most typical expression is given to us by the work of Racine, and which is characterized by the substitution for real man of an ideal being, a poetry in which, in sum, the abstract is substituted for the concrete.

In this brief sketch I have barely gestured toward what would doubtless demand larger development, and, in the first place, proof. My objective is not however to prove anything, but, in speaking of Fernando Pessoa, to begin by situating him—something which has not been attempted—among his peers. And his peers can be no other but the poets who only sang of life in order to seek its "other side," to speak of it but at the same time of that other side as well. And, if we ought to avoid calling them "intellectual," which indeed would approximate them to the idealistic attitude of that current in French poetry to which I referred, perhaps we ought not to leave off using a different term, though risky: "metaphysical."

Indeed, how else to determine Fernando Pessoa's place in our literature, except taking into account that his work is, above all, that of a poet for whom the immediate never existed as a value of poetic expression? But this can only be fully understood in light of what was said earlier with respect to that *more* that certain of our poets have sought beyond the actual, without abandoning it altogether. Pessoa's case is not, however, that of any other of the aforementioned poets; and, obviously, it could not be: a great poet's "case" is always his own, and only "afterwards" will it also be something common to him and to others. Pessoa is in fact so uniquely different that to this day there has almost exclusively been discussion of what differentiates him, as though nothing could approximate him to any other poets.

There is no reason to state: "Pessoa did not care about life at all"; we do not know that, or rather: we do know enough to state that, at least, it is not quite so. To make such a statement would be to infer unfairly about his life from his work. For his work, indeed, Pessoa did never cared at all about life, in the sense already specified that he never "sang" his life. Pessoa's work is clearly a work of divorce from immediate life, from present reality.

Of his contemporaries, some were artists because they lived, or else because they wished to live and could not, like the tormented Sá-Carneiro; others were artists *against* life, for the sake of aestheticism—but Fernando Pessoa was an artist *in spite* of life. Shall we say then that his work was a product of culture, one of those works whose roots seek out the minimum of blood they need in a literary tradition and are constructions built upon previous constructions? This is well known not to be true at all. Anyone who reads him with passion knows that. And one does not read with passion the intricate art aforementioned. Only art whose foundations are common to itself and to our lives can really be felt. Rooted in some intuition of life, of the living.

What, then, is this poet's secret? It is that he transformed, so to speak, his thoughts into emotions, sensitized the cerebral, gave roots of existence to the absolute. We may say, in other words, that for I'm the human was precisely that which is customarily considered outside the human; not strictly because such a thing can be affirmed, but because we know that, in speaking of the *human*, concerning literature, we tend to designate that which gets its virtue from immediate life. Now Fernando Pessoa, as it seems, nowhere in his poetry spoke of his own life except in "lying." Let us remember that passage from a letter to João Gaspar Simões in which he says: "The church-bell of my village... is the Igreja dos Mártires, right in the Chiado. The village where I was born was the Largo de São Carlos...", having already said before that "artistically" he can do nothing "but lie." And it is understandable that many are scandalized because, having felt great emotion from that poem that begins "O church-bell of my village," they came to hear from the poet's own mouth that he never felt any of it himself. But if reacting this way they will commit the injustice of expecting more from art than art. In fact, Fernando Pessoa responded in a curious poem to all those who might make such censure. There, he goes indeed much farther than in his statement from the letter:

The poet is a feigner.
So fully does he feign
that even pain he truly feels,
he must pretend is pain.

And those who read his poems
feel, in the pain they've read,
not those same two the poet bore,
but one they never had.

The crux of this poem is the line "Not those same two the poet bore," and here would not be the place for the analysis of what Pessoa meant to be taken as far as would be necessary. But suffice it to point out that even Pessoa does not take this feigning of his to be incompatible with feeling, establishing on the contrary a doubling of it: the feeling borne and the feeling expressed. The poet may not have felt what he speaks of, but can give anything an emotion, wherever it comes from, that in any case he does have. But on how he has it, we are far from able to use any Romantic interpretation assimilating the expression of feelings with the very feeling experienced. For a case like Pessoa's it must be admitted that he *bore* those feelings—but that he may well have never *used* them.

This brings us to approach now the issue of depersonalization. Let us hear him, still in the letter cited to João Gaspar Simões: "The central point of my personality as an artist is that I am a dramatic poet; I have continually, in everything I write, the inward exaltation of the poet and the depersonalization of the playwright. I fly as someone else—that is all... The critic knows that, as a poet, I feel; that, as a dramatic poet, I feel by detaching myself from myself; that, as a (non-poet) dramatist, I automatically transmute what I feel into an expression alien to what I felt, constructing in the emotion a nonexistent person who would truly feel it, and therefore feel, by derivation, other emotions which I, as purely myself, have forgotten to feel." Exactly so, when speaking of the works signed by his heteronyms, he defined them as "by the author outside of his own person, by a complete self fabricated by him, as would be the speeches of any character in any drama of his."

If we take this last statement too literally, without correcting it with the one transcribed before, as well as the others he left, we would be led to conclude that the poetry of Fernando Pessoa is pure artifice. But even he himself, through the mouth of his heteronym Álvaro de Campos, once let slip this aphorism: "Pretending is knowing oneself." And indeed, although obviously it can reveal nothing to us about his life, his work is no less "true" for that. But, as the least Romantic of any we know, in it everything is transposed and deformed—his art at no moment imitates or echoes life.

Fernando Pessoa did not believe, or at least he feigned not to believe, in pure inspiration, in the spontaneity of artistic expression: in him, even the spontaneous was "born" lucid, that is, we cannot imagine him as a poet except immediately redoubling himself as a spectator. In this man was such lucidity that it is impossible to imagine him as anything but conscious of what he was writing. And it seems to me that he would be no less so when writing one of the impeccable odes of Ricardo Reis than an apparently spontaneous poem of Álvaro de Campos. And if there really is a drama of man in Fernando Pessoa's poetry, it is one of merciless lucidity: the immense richness of this work, which has no equal in our poetry for the depth of its intelligence, the genius of its transposition of the psychological universe into plastic images, is not a lyrical richness in the common sense, and is really quite far from our sentimental tradition—and that was the very reason I approximated him to a Camões, an Antero, and a Pascoais.

*

If one thing seems certain among the many that lead us to designate certain poets as "great," it is without a doubt the fact that their poetry has a solid foothold, not only as a form, but as an essence, in the spiritual physiognomy of the poet. This is not the case, for instance, with an António Nobre or a Sá-Carneiro, nor with a Cesário or a Gomes Leal. In any of those, poetry arises from a series of incursions, which at times lead them quite far, into the uncharted regions from which there bring us those intuitions that give life to their potery; they are short clefts in the darkness, dazzling illuminations, brusque and brief descents to the bottomless well of the worlds within man's reach. But the poetry of the truly great—of the Shakespeares, the Goethes, the Baudelaires, to cite only three of the greatest—we may say constitutes something like a luminous mist within that darkness, and is not made merely of flashes that cut through it only then to vanish; I mean that it possesses a unity that in the others' is lacking.

Such a unity seems to me to exist in the poetry of Fernando Pessoa. Let the multiplicity of planes not delude us: what does it matter how much the various heteronyms may contradict themselves, if in the end we are left with an impression of totality? If indeed, as though summarizing all paths in himself, Fernando Pessoa presents himself to us as at once both classic and modern, if he is now Celtic, now mystic, if he contains a materialist, a spiritualist, and a pantheist, but leaves for us a final impression of totality, why should the apparent contradictions matter to us? Given what I have just stated, clearly it will not be in the conciliation of the various attitudes avowedly manifested by him and in each of his heteronyms that I search for that unity. Certainly it cannot be in the poet's *statements*, or in one of the various philosophies we might extract from each of these "rooms" in his work, but in some inner recess, not expressly confessed, not rendered in verses or poems whose meaning can be transposed into philosophical affirmations. The unity lies in the very structure of any of his work's senses, in a fundamental orientation that lies in its being an uninterrupted chain of efforts to establish man's contact with the universe. From a man interested— seriously and deeply interested—in problems of astrology and occultism, to the Whitmanian singer of "Maritime Ode," Fernando Pessoa's whole oeuvre is a search for reality beyond the fleeting forms of appearance. The Nobres, the Sá-Carneiros, the Gomes Leals (despite the efforts of this last to attain a philosophical synthesis of which he sensed the necessity, but which he lacked the framework to raise), all react to the world as the world offers itself to them. On the other hand, in the poetry of Fernando Pessoa, as in the set of statements about his personality that are known to us, there is nothing resembling a string of reactions to a string of moments—on the contrary, we are faced with a perfect example of a lack of time in his work, for, although each of us may place any moment from his time within any manifestation of that work, the work, for its own part, does not live by that moment, and for this very reason can one make about his work, as we shall soon see, this unusual observation: at any moment in Pessoa's poetry it is impossible to situate it as a before or an after to any other part.

Nothing is farther, however, from being "philosophical poetry" than this, if by "philosophical poetry" we understand that which lays out a philosophical system or in some manner *treats of* philosophical problems. Even a great poet, he or any other, could not defeat the didacticism into which similar attempts fall to their death. It is quite a different thing that goes on with Fernando Pessoa's poetry, which is a poetry pregnant with "philosophical content," if we wish so to say. It is a poetry that frequently springs from the "life" which in the poet has certain *problems*; from the reality so intimate that it has become life; from various ideas, various views, various apprehensions of reality fixed according to their objective value, but transformed into the subjectivity necessary for the poetry to arise from them. What is philosophical about his poems is not that they treat of *problems*, but that they constitute expressions of the dramas of the spirit which philosophy takes as problems— or rather, classical philosophy.

Indeed, the poetry of Fernando Pessoa sets out from a central node; from there, its tentacles stretch through tunnels hollowed by man's anxiety in every direction, takes a thousand forms according to the "drama" it embodies, and leaps over the greatest or least vivacity of any forms of man's experience; the poets of lesser greatness with whom I have compared him leap from the moment into eternity; a Pessoa descends from "within" that eternity to the moments in time, which he "feigns" in order to express himself.

Occasionally there resounds in his poetry that high, pure note of a song liberated from contingency to which the pure lyricism of the individual is structurally bound. Far be it from me, I repeat once more, to think that for this note's height and purity timelessness is an indispensable condition. On the contrary, it is the temporal that is indispensable to it, because only "within" the temporal is it able to assert itself. In this there is none of the "spiritualism" of that poetry which finds in abstract pseudo-unity the solution to all dilemmas that cannot be solved in the concrete. Here, on the contrary, the voice resounds so high and pure because it has the timbre of the concrete, because it is molded in forms of existence. The song is dispersed and various—it is the voice that has unmistakably in its most bitter or most tender accents, most melancholic or most resigned—broadly speaking, most human—the continuous hum of a meaning that upholds it above circumstance and fortuity.

*

Several times now I have referred to Fernando Pessoa's heteronyms. Whatever attitude each of us may take regarding this division of personality, and it being admitted that this issue may itself not present the slightest interest to many readers, who will read undistinguishingly Ricardo Reis or Caeiro, Fernando Pessoa "himself" or Álvaro de Campos, not caring about their respective authorships, interested in them merely as "one" or "another," simply as poetry by Fernando Pessoa, it is certain that for others, if not the solution, at least the investigation of what this means may offer the greatest interest. Not to mention those readers of this *Anthology* who are making contact with Pessoa's personality for the first time, to whom my earlier references to one or another of the heteronyms will on their own be cause for confusion—and more than sufficient justification for the relative breadth with which I will next engage with the issue.

Before anything else, I will transcribe what Fernando Pessoa's "bibliographical table," published by *Presença* in its seventeenth issue and written by him, that addresses the heteronyms:

> What Fernando Pessoa writes belongs to two categories of works, which we may call orthonymous and heteronymous. It cannot be said that they are anonymous or pseudonymous, because they truly are not. Pseudonymous work is by the author in his own person, except the name assigned; heteronymous work is by the author outside his own person, from an individual completely fabricated by him, as would be the speeches of any character in any play he wrote.

> The heteronymous works of Fernando Pessoa are written under, so far, three people's names—Alberto Caeiro, Ricardo Reis, Álvaro de Campos. These individuals

ought to be considered as distinct from their author. Each one forms a kind of drama; and all of them together form another drama. Alberto Caeiro, who is considered to have been born in 1889 and died in 1915, has written poems with one certain orientation. He has had as disciples—coming, as such, from various aspects of that orientation—the other two: Ricard Reis, considered to have been born in 1887, who isolated in his work, stylizing it, the intellectual and pagan side; Álvaro de Campos, born in 1890, who in his work isolated the emotional side so to speak, which he called "sensationist," and which—linking it to various influences, among which predominates, although below that of Caeiro, that of Walt Whitman—produced various complications, generally of scandalous and provocative character, especially for Fernando Pessoa, who in any case has no remedy but to write them and publish them, however much he disagrees with them. The works of these three poets form, as stated, a dramatic set; and the intellectual interaction of their personalities has been duly studied, as well as their personal relationships. All this will appear in biographies yet to be written, accompanied, when they are published, by horoscopes and, perhaps, photographs. It is a drama in people, instead of acts.

(Whether these three individuals are more or less real than Fernando Pessoa himself—that is a metaphysical problem, which he, absent from the secret of the Gods, and ignoring therefore what reality is, will never be able to solve.)

Despite the ironic tone—so characteristic of Pessoa's human personality—there is already in this text some number of elements that, together with those occasionally indicated so far and completed with those I will use following, are a sufficient basis to proceed.

I think it legitimate to venture this hypothesis: to view the *birth* of the heteronyms as, ultimately, one of Fernando Pessoa's poetic works; indirect poetic creation, it may be said, but nonetheless poetic creation. "Works" of poetry are not merely those that are written; and for a man who, like Pessoa, experienced so much *inwardly*, the presence of poetry, the creation of poetry by the very act of living, is, it may be said, constant. Let us read this passage from the letter he addressed to me about the heteronyms, which I published in issue 49 of *Presença*:

Alberto Caeiro having appeared, I then attended to finding him—*instinctively and subconsciously*[1]—some disciples. I pulled out of his false paganism the latent Ricardo Reis, discovered his name, and adjusted him to himself, for at this point I now *saw* him. And, suddenly, by an opposite derivation from that of Ricardo Reis, a new individual came to me impetuously. In a burst, at the typewriter, without interruption or emendation, out came the *"Ode Triunfal"* ["Triumphal Ode"] of Álvaro de Campos—the Ode with that name and the man with the name he has.

I formed, then, a nonexistent coterie. I cast it all in molds of reality. I graded their influences, learned of their friendships, heard within myself their arguments and differences of opinion, and in all this it seemed that I, the creator of it all, was the one least there. It all seemed to take place independently of me. And it seems that it still does. If I ever am able to publish the aesthetic argument between Ricardo Reis and Álvaro de Campos, you will see how they are different, and how I am not in the material at all.

Hence we are not speaking, as with the heteronyms, merely of *expressed* poetry. We are not speaking merely of aesthetic creations (this "merely" is not meant depreciatively, of course!) but in some form of that which A. Borel and G. Robin[2] have called *rêve éveillé*. Now, by his confession, and from what we know about his life, Fernando Pessoa is an abulic. And not only do his letters say so. So do his poems, and especially "Deferral":

The day after tomorrow, yes, not until the day after tomorrow...
I shall spend tomorrow thinking ahead to the next day,
and then that day will do; but not today...
No, none of it today; I can't today.
The addled persistence of my objective subjectivity,
the intercalated sleep of my real life,
the infinite expectant weariness,
worlds of weariness over catching a streetcar...

---

1. The emphasis is mine. Later I will utilize this and other statements by Pessoa, very important to combat the idea, which the clarity of his expression may provoke, that the heteronyms are "inventions of the intellect."
2. A. Borel and G. Robin. *Les Rêveurs Éveillés*. Paris: Gallimard, 1925.

In Fernando Pessoa, the lack of will allied itself to a truly shocking power of imagination; an imagination that did not take the usual forms of imagination, because it belonged to a genius—and not merely to a poet of genius: the genius of his imagination was *beyond any literary expression thereof*. And the creation of his heteronyms is a phase of his creation of companions, situations, lives... The creations of his "waking dream"[3] demanded of him at a certain point in his life an aesthetic transposition; not—and here begins the unusual—that he communicate them as dramatic characters, in poems or novels, but that he give them a poet's voice.

I would rather quote myself than repeat myself: I have written on this subject (in my commentary on Pessoa's letter, likewise in issue 49 of *Presença*): "Fernando Pessoa is a *novelist in poets*: after all, as a novelist can only bring the characters in his work to life when they are in some way himself, so too the heteronymous works of Fernando Pessoa are like monologues from characters in a novel." Might there have passed through Pessoa's imagination the possibility of actually writing a novel, or novels, that would be the lives of his heteronyms? Indeed, the man who "feels by detaching himself from himself" may be a novelist. But... perhaps Pessoa was missing the possibility of executing, perhaps even of dreaming of executing a longer work, to say nothing of other potential obstacles that at first blush may seem the most natural and likely consequence of his tendencies. At any rate, and definitively, what matters most for us is not what might have been, but what really was; and if the result of the *processus* whose effervescence led Pessoa, "since childhood," to create "a fictitious world," to "surround himself with friends and acquaintances who never existed" (his own phrases, from the letter cited), was eventually the appearance of various poets, each with a distinct message of his own, it is this that ought to engage us; it is these poets and their respective messages whose meaning matters for us to determine.

When faced with the work of a major poet, one who is not a pure lyricist, in whom poetry is not mere spontaneity that breaks through the crust of the social man, but leaves it intact; when faced, as I was saying, with the work

---

3. This is the meaning of the French phrase "rêve éveillé," cited above. (Translator's note)

of a major poet, in whom expression is more than a momentary reaction against his own day-to-day self, who has poetry integrated into his very life, who experiences in its full dimensions the drama of his poetry—in such a case the poet is never a simple being, unilateral, complete in only direction. And therefore, the figure of Pessoa that begins to be drawn when, to *seek* it, we follow the path of, let us say, literal interpretation his psychological problem, will suffice to raise difficulties that may become dangerous when we come to face the work of the poet in its nakedness. Effectively, that first path referred will lead us almost fatally to single out in the poet whatever is or seems to be, on the one hand, pretense, and predominantly cerebral creation, on the other, in his poetry. "Intellectual poet," as we have said, is a vague expression but one that nonetheless represents justly enough one opinion that may form about Pessoa's poetry—that it is not properly false, but excessively incomplete, so incomplete that presented on its own it will give a totally wrongheaded view of his work.

While Fernando Pessoa says that "the poet is a feigner," he says no less that might appear contradictory to that: for example (in the letter about the heteronyms), when telling how Ricardo Reis was born, how he had sketched out a few things in irregular verse and given them up. "However, there had been sketched for me, in a *barely pictured half-light*, a faint portrait of the person who was writing them. (*Unbeknownst to me*, Ricardo Reis had been born.)" (The emphasis is mine.) And soon afterward, this passage that will be even more elucidating to us:

> A year and a half, or two years, later I decided one day to play a joke on Sá-Carneiro—to invent a bucolic poet, a complicated type, and introduce him to him, I no longer remember how, in some sort of reality. I spent several days developing the poet *but nothing came of it*. One day when I had finally given up—it was the 8th of March, 1914—I ensconced myself in a high room, and, taking a pen, began to write, standing, the way I write whenever I can. And I wrote thirty-some poems in a row, *in a kind of ecstasy whose nature I will never be able to define*. It was the triumphal day of my life, and I will not ever get another like it. I opened with a title, "The Keeper of Flocks." *And what followed* was the appearance of someone in me, to whom right away I gave the name Alberto Caeiro.

(The emphasis is mine.) Let us attend to the elements these passages offer us; and in the first place it will be noted that all of the phrases I have emphasized show us on the one hand that Fernando Pessoa did not create his heteronyms when he wished, but when he was able, and on the other that the creation of those works through which his heteronyms first asserted themselves came prior to the establishment of their biographies. I believe that each of these observations is of the greatest importance. But we will see in the second place that the character of that creation, at least in the case of Alberto Caeiro's appearance, assumed characteristics that would leave us least able to surmise in his origin a determination by will. I will draw the conclusions that I find necessary:

Fernando Pessoa, who since his childhood lived surrounded by a world of figures he only called unreal with that ironic hesitation he always used when needing to comply with habitual distinctions, simply transposed into his work the atmosphere that had always encircled him. We cannot speak of simulation or mystification—except in a certain very special sense: understanding thereby a way of realizing his personality in artistic expression seated, like a primordial dado, not on a transposition of social reality, of fellowship, of relation, but on the transposition of what might have been a work by those figures who accompanied him. Rather: to simulate is here merely to make up or imagine—yet we do not tend to call novelists simulators or mystifiers. Let us recall now the analysis cited above, and Pessoa's self-classification as "essentially a dramatic poet"; what he feels is not what he communicates to us (not always; ahead we will see how far we can accept this lack of Pessoa the man in his work), but it is upon what he feels that he constructs "a nonexistent person who would truly feel it." It is thus as an artist who gives himself up to what is another's, who is transported to the core of other lives, who recreates and renews them—hence, like a novelist—that we should begin to consider Fernando Pessoa. We have seen why it is understandable that he was not *in fact* a novelist; but what matters now is to agree his family was that of the latter, as was the orientation of his creative work.

Here we must introduce a new element: the anti-Romantic Pessoa. By this I do not mean that he was classical; rather, it is with respect to his refusal to be sentimental, in the most general sense of the word, that that phrase to me seems appropriate. Pessoa, in fact, realizes like no one else that concept of Rainer Maria Rilke, applied, I believe, to a character in a novella, but which, it seems, suits Rilke himself: "*C'était un poète, et il haïssait l'à peu près*"[4] (I am quoting from memory and cannot guarantee the accuracy of the phrase—but it suffices that the meaning has not been betrayed). Now, the current notion is that being a poet and loving precision are incompatible notions—at least that is the current notion in Portugal. Imprecision, however, may lie in what is expressed, and yet the expression not be imprecise at all. In any case, what is certain is that, like to no other, this concept applies felicitously to Fernando Pessoa. Love of precision in both his imaginary and his expression are without a doubt two characteristics that at a glance may seem strange in a man of such *unruly* imagination. But let it not be forgotten that Pessoa's imagination is indeed unusual, unique, an imagination that, rather than diluted and vague, possesses a rigor at times even hallucinatory. Fernando Pessoa's imagination is in fact something *monstrous*: monstrous in its meticulousness and no less monstrous in its *exactness*. Which leads us to classify it as an intelligent imagination or, better yet, an imagination developed with intellect. Pessoa's anti-Romanticism, I see precisely in his exactness in expressing anything, and in the control constantly achieved by him over the creations of his mind. Given this, nothing is more explicable than that Fernando Pessoa may be conceived as a poet with full mastery of his art, that is, *who simply does as he wishes*. Nothing is more explicable—when explained by those who forget that poetry is not *created* by the intellect.

There are human types who seem to delegate to others the life that they can only dream of, or yet, who intervene in others' destinies by provoking contact, encounters or clashes, and remaining outside, like spectators who do not dare take part in the action—to this sort belong all troublemakers, for instance, who are such by psychic fatality. Fernando Pessoa went one better; if every artist is a being who frees himself through his art, who by means of it realizes, by transposing them to another plane, the destinies, the actions, the feelings, and the passions that for whatever reason he does not practice

---

4. "He was a poet, and he hated the approximate." (Translator's note)

and experience—in Fernando pessoa this projection takes on unheard-of proportions, strange even, since it was not lives, destinies, that were *realized* and projected into his work, but the creations of artists imaginary in their own right. Thus there is in Pessoa a double movement of the imagination, that of creating these imaginary figures, and that of them in turn... imagining! It is here that, in my opinion, we must make great allowances for some of Pessoa's statements. There is, in fact, nothing that leads us to establish a real connection between the works of Alberto Caeiro, Ricardo Reis, and Álvaro de Campos and the imaginary "people" who existed to Pessoa. It is to Pessoa himself that we must link each of their works. That is to say: the reality of their works does not *create* that of the authors. Nothing could be more natural, since we are dealing, in all those cases, with poets who, like Fernando Pessoa himself, are dramatic poets, that is, who "feel by detaching themselves from themselves, automatically transmuting what they feel into an expression alien to what they felt." Poets, then, who speak of feelings and of passions, of life and of things, but by hiding, disguising, transporting the true emotion of one moment into other *possible* emotions. Non-lyric poets. But do such poets exist? Or what existence do they have? Well, they do not exist, and the problem lies precisely, now, in knowing whether Fernando Pessoa would have written works authored by them in the case of their nonexistence. It is worth noting that none of them gives us testimony, in the poems they authored, of any time whose passage the work reflects, any evolution it witnesses. On this character of immobility I once wrote to Pessoa, and from the letter in which he answered me two paragraphs seem to me almost as important as the letter about the heteronyms already quoted several times. Here is that passage:

Your observation about the absence in me of what I might legitimately be called any evolution is extraordinarily well made. There are poems of mine, written twenty years ago, that are equal in worth—as well as I can assess—to those I write today. I do not write any better than I did then, except in my knowledge of the Portuguese language. I write differently. Perhaps the solution to the matter lies in the following.

What I essentially am—behind the involuntary masks of the poet, the reasoner, and all the rest—is a playwright. The phenomenon of my instinctive depersonalization, to which I alluded in my earlier letter to explain the existence of the heteronyms, leads naturally to that definition. Being so, I do not evolve: I JOURNEY (due to a slippage of the capitals key, this word came out all capitalized, without my intention. It looks right, and I will let it stay that way). I change personalities, I go about (here there may be evolution) enriching myself in my capacity to create new personalities, new types of feigning that I understand the world, or, rather, of feigning that it can be understood. That is the reason I gave this going in me as comparable not to an evolution, but to a journey: I have not risen from one story to another; I have moved, on a plain, from one place to another. I have lost, to be sure, some simpleness and ingenuity that was there in my poems from adolescence; that, however, is not evolution, but aging.

Journeying from personality to personality—can we yet doubt that Fernando Pessoa himself was each one of them? That is, can we believe in a total depersonalization, especially with regard to the three heteronymous poets? I have a vague sense that I wrote to Pessoa more or less in this vein: that his work seemed to me to testify to a near-absolute atemporality, there being no past or future in it, but only an eternal-present that is the true *time* in which great imaginers ought to live, *rêveurs éveillés* or whatever they be, to whose family he belonged. Now the case of depersonalization and that of the absence of evolution are closely connected. The former thus takes on a coherent aspect with what we know about Pessoa: it appears to us, not so much as resulting from the necessity of *delegating* to other imaginary beings an activity not exercised by the social man, but mainly as a requirement of the mind of a creative artist who, due to the fact of needing to feign, would not dare be in his own name the author of the deranged strophes of Álvaro de Campos or the anti-metaphysical metaphysics of Alberto Caeiro. Note: I do not mean to say that this "not daring" was socially rooted; I simply see at stake Pessoa's own spirit vis-à-vis himself; it would be vis-à-vis himself that he would not dare to write certain poems, had they not imposed on him those imaginary personalities. Does he not say so himself in his "bibliographic table"?

A great mystery nevertheless persists at the center of Pessoa's personality, and this mystery is not that, or those, of the heteronyms: it is the utmost mystery of the birth of his poetry. Nothing, after all, should be less conducive to the expression of a great poetic work—so it seems, at least—than such a scattered personality, than a mind so thoroughly conscious of itself, to say nothing now of his hunger for intelligibility in his expression. But we are faced with the brutal, inviolable fact: the poetry of Fernando Pessoa and of his heteronyms is that of a great poet. And on this point at least—here is an argument against the thesis that accepts the total separation of the various heteronymous personalities—there is absolute unanimity among Fernando Pessoa himself, Álvaro de Campos, Alberto Caeiro, and Ricardo Reis: the equal genius of their respective creations.

*

I have spoken thus far of poetry and of Fernando Pessoa's personality without considering its significance within his time and nearly without reference to the fundamental role he exercised in the literary reformation to which was attached the unfortunate name of "modernism." But this introduction is reaching decidedly inadmissible proportions, and I find myself forced to abbreviate. This aspect is however the one which gained the most public prominence, due to the scandal of the first expressions of "modernism"— and it may be said that most of the public knew little more about Fernando Pessoa, when he died, than that scandalous account spun around his name by the vulgar mentality of inept journalists and "intellectuals" jealous to keep their honorific titles as *glories of the moment*.

Hence I will refrain from expanding on the properly reformative aspect of Pessoa's work, under which he does not offer an easy physiognomy to sketch, either, for on many points Pessoa was *ardently* traditionalist—a classicist at the same time as the most daring revolutionary. These "contradictions" are of the same root as all those offered to us by the study of his heteronyms. To clear up whether, out of all the directions in which he projected his multiple and contradictory activity, some ought to be held as more real and more profound, is a question that only knowledge of his work in the whole could permit—if that...

The revolutionary aspect of Fernando Pessoa's work today belongs to literary history. Admitted even into anthologies, as noted by José Régio in his

Pequena História da Moderna Poesia Portuguesa [Brief History of Modern Portuguese Poetry], Fernando Pessoa is no longer intimidating to our so easily spooked national sensibility. Even schoolchildren, when reciting the names of great poets, indeed recite his in the mix with those of other sanctioned glories. For the danger, now, is different: with the doors of consecration opened, we must beware of the title he is wanted for. A mutilated Fernando Pessoa is not Fernando Pessoa. That only in the whole of his work, in the totality of his various aspects, does it matter if his work reaches the greater public. To read, for example, *Message* and ignore the "Eighth Poem by the Keeper of Sheep" or the "Maritime Ode," would be as much as to reduce him to too small a stature to pass through the doorway of immortality. And it is such a reduced stature that we might fear they intend to reduce him, with a compunctious silence on what is most important.

*

These pages make no intention whatsoever of "explaining" Fernando Pessoa's poetry. Any critical commentary of a work still largely unpublished, can have no other ambition but to clear provisional paths, seeking in the known elements what can clarify as of now the meanings of the work and situate it properly.

Pessoa died in 1935, and when the first edition of this *Anthology* came out, there was only one book of his published: *Message*. This *Anthology* therefore came to the aid of an undelayable necessity: that of making available to the public, who cannot go rummaging through collections of journals from a period of twenty-five years, most of them difficult to obtain, the essentials of what work of his Pessoa himself made public. And yet, notwithstanding all the difficulties, notwithstanding the fragmentary character of the published portion of his work, Fernando Pessoa already held, at least in the minds of younger generations, a place which few could give him in his life. And there remains no doubt that it was not on his single published book of Portuguese verse that his renown rested, but on some dozens of poems, which people collected here and there, which many copied with fervor. What has been gathered in this volume is the most significant part of that Pessoa's scattered work. From *Mensagem* itself a few poems have been selected, in order for the whole to encompass every facet of his work. Included for the same reason are the unpublished sonnets "At the Tomb of Christian Rosenkreutz," the transmission of which I owe to the kindness of Almada Negreiros, with whom Pessoa entrusted them to be published in *Sudoeste*. They are, in Pessoa's poetry, what I know most completely to reveal the occultist.

The first volume of this Anthology having been edited when the poems of Fernando Pessoa "himself" still remained uncollected, which now make up the first volume of *Obras Completas de Fernando Pessoa* [Complete Works of Fernando Pessoa], published by Editorial Ática under the direction of Luís de Montalvor and João Gaspar Simões, our selection was therefore limited to texts published by the poet, along with a few more that became public posthumously, with the exception of the sonnets titled "At the Tomb of Christian Rosenkreutz." In preparing this new edition, we have been able to expand it with a few poems revealed by the referred first and second volumes of the *Obras Completas*. Generally speaking, it seems to us that Fernando Pessoa "himself," as revealed in the *Obras Completas*, does not alter the picture we had of him courtesy of the partial knowledge we had until then. We have therefore selected, to expand this reedition, only this or that poem which seemed to us to express better some facet less stressed in the previous selection.

Additionally, the reader will find here a few poems published in journals, by the poet or after his death, which were not collected in that of the *Obras Completas*, and which, in our view, are too exquisite for the public to wait for a distant volume of *Dispersos* [Dispersed Works] to read them, as is the intent of the editors of the *Obras Completas*.

Adolfo Casais Monteiro

FERNANDO PESSOA

Ó NAUS FELIZES, QUE DO MAR VAGO
Volveis enfim ao silêncio do porto
Depois de tanto nocturno mal —
Meu coração é um morto lago,
E à margem triste do lago morto
Sonha um castelo medieval...

E nesse, onde sonha, castelo triste,
Nem sabe saber a, de mãos formosas
Sem gesto ou cor, triste castelã
Que um porto além rumoroso existe,
Donde as naus negras e silenciosas
Se partem quando é no mar manhã...

Nem sequer sabe que há o, onde sonha,
Castelo triste... Seu 'sp'rito monge
Para nada externo é perto e real...
E enquanto ela assim se esquece, tristonha,
Regressam, velas no mar ao longe,
As naus ao porto medieval...

O HAPPY SHIPS, FROM UPON THE DIM SEA
returning at last to the haven's silence
after your long nocturnal toil—
my heart is a lifeless lake,
and by the sad shore of the lifeless lake
stands a medieval castle in dream...

And there in the dreamed-of dreary castle,
unknowing is, with beauteous hands
unmoving and hueless, the glum chatelaine,
unaware that a haven lies loud beyond,
whence the black and silent vessels
part when the morning breaks at sea...

Nor knows she even that there is the dreamed-of
dreary castle... Her monklike spirit
to nothing outward is near and real...
And as she muses so, in her gloom,
the ships, but sails in the distant sea,
to the medieval haven repair...

Impressões do crepúsculo

I

Ó SINO DA MINHA ALDEIA,
Dolente na tarde calma,
Cada tua badalada
Soa dentro da minh'alma,

E é tão lento o teu soar,
Tão como triste da vida,
Que já a primeira pancada
Tem um som de repetida.

Por mais que me tanjas perto
Quando passo triste e errante,
És para mim como um sonho —
Soas-me sempre distante...

A cada pancada tua,
Vibrante no céu aberto,
Sinto mais longe o passado,
Sinto a saudade mais perto.

Twilight Impressions

I

O CHURCH-BELL OF MY VILLAGE,
your every mournful toll
across the stilly evening
rings out within my soul,

And so slow is your tolling,
so grieved, as it were, with life,
that even the first knolling
sounds as if sounded twice.

However near you strike from
when past I sadly stray,
yet you to me sound dreamlike—
forever far away…

And with each peal vibrating
across the open sky,
I feel the past more distant,
And longing closer by.

II

Pauis de roçarem ânsias pela minh'alma em ouro...
Dobre longínquo de Outros Sinos... Empalidece o louro
Trigo na cinza do poente... Corre um frio carnal por minh'alma...
Tão sempre a mesma, a Hora!... Balouçar de cimos de palma!...
Silêncio que as folhas fitam em nós... Outono delgado
Dum canto de vaga ave... Azul esquecido em estagnado...
Oh que mudo grito de ânsia põe garras na Hora!
Que pasmo de mim anseia por outra coisa que o que chora!
Estendo as mãos para além, mas ao estendê-las já vejo
Que não é aquilo que quero aquilo que desejo...
Címbalos de Imperfeição... Ó tão antiguidade
A Hora expulsa de si-Tempo!... Onda de recuo que invade
O meu abandonar-me a mim próprio até desfalecer,
E recordar tanto o Eu presente que me sinto esquecer!...
Fluido de aureola, transparente de Foi, oco de ter-se...
O Mistério sabe-me a eu ser outro... Luar sobre o não conter-se...
A sentinela é hirta — a lança que finca no chão
É mais alta do que ela... Pra que é tudo isto?... Dia chão...
Trepadeiras de despropósito lambendo de Hora os Aléns...
Horizontes fechando os olhos ao espaço em que são elos de erro...
Fanfarras de ópios de silêncios futuros... Longes trens...
Portões vistos longe... através das árvores... tão de ferro!

II

Marshes of rustling yearnings across my golden soul...
Far-off knell of Other Bells... The blond wheat pales
in the grey ash of the west... Through my soul runs a carnal chill...
How ever the same, the Hour!... Swinging of palm-crests!...
Silence the leaves fix on us... Subtle autumn
of a faint bird's song... Azure left stagnant, forgotten...
Oh what a mute cry of yearning sinks its talons into the Hour!
What self-wonder in me yearns for something besides what it mourns!
I reach my hands beyond, but reaching them out I see
that what I long for is not what I wish...
Cymbals of Imperfection!... O too ancient
the Hour banished from Time-itself!... Retreating wave that assails
my abandonment of myself to myself till I grow faint,
and so remember my present Self that I sense myself forgetting!...
Fluid as a halo, transparent as Was, hollow as holding oneself...
The Mystery smacks of me as another... Moonlight over nonrestraint...
The sentinel stands stiff—the spear he plants in the ground
is taller than he... Wherefore all this?... Dull day...
Senseless vines lapping at the Beyonds with the Hour...
Horizons shutting their eyes to the space where they are bonds of error...
Opium fanfares of silences yet to be... Distant trains...
Gates viewed afar off... through the trees... so ironbound!

Hora absurda

O teu silêncio é uma nau com todas as velas pandas...
Brandas, as brisas brincam nas flâmulas, teu sorriso...
E o teu sorriso no teu silêncio é as escadas e as andas
Com que me finjo mais alto e ao pé de qualquer paraíso...

Meu coração é uma ânfora que cai e que se parte...
O teu silêncio recolhe-o e guarda-o, partido, a um canto...
Minha ideia de ti é um cadáver que o mar traz à praia..., e entanto
Tu és a tela irreal em que erro em cor a minha arte...

Abre todas as portas e que o vento varra a ideia
Que temos de que um fumo perfuma de ócio os salões...
Minha alma é uma caverna enchida pla maré cheia,
E a minha ideia de te sonhar uma caravana de histriões...

Chove ouro baço, mas não no lá-fora... É em mim... Sou a Hora,
E a Hora é de assombros e toda ela escombros dela...
Na minha atenção há uma viúva pobre que nunca chora...
No meu céu interior nunca houve uma única estrela...

Hoje o céu é pesado como a ideia de nunca chegar a um porto...
A chuva miúda é vazia... A Hora sabe a ter sido...
Não haver qualquer coisa como leitos para as naus! Absorto
Em se alhear de si, teu olhar é uma praga sem sentido...

Todas as minhas horas são feitas de jaspe negro,
Minhas ânsias todas talhadas num mármore que não há,

Absurd Hour

Your silence is a ship with every sail full-blown...
Softly, the breezes play about the pennons, your smile...
And your smile in your silence is the stairway and the stilts
I stand on to feign I am taller and close to some paradise...

My heart is an amphora that falls and breaks to pieces...
Your silence gathers it up and keeps it, broken, in a corner...
My idea of you is a corpse that washes ashore..., and yet
you are the unreal canvas where I miscolor my art...

Open all the doors and let the wind sweep out
the idea we have that a smoke scents the halls with idleness...
My soul is a cavern filled up by the risen tide,
and my idea of dreaming you a troupe of players...

It rains dull gold, but not outside... In me... I am the Hour,
and the Hour is of dismay and is all debris of itself...
In my attention is a poor widow who never weeps...
In my internal sky has never hung one star...

Today the sky sags like the idea of never reaching a harbor...
The thin rain is empty... The Hour smacks of having been...
There ought to be something like beds for ships! Engrossed
in absentness from itself, your gaze is a senseless plague...

All of my hours are fashioned out of black jasper,
my yearnings all are hewn in a marble that is not,

Não é alegria nem dor esta dor com que me alegro,
E a minha bondade inversa não é nem boa nem má...

Os feixes dos lictores abriram-se à beira dos caminhos...
Os pendões das vitórias medievais nem chegaram às cruzadas...
Puseram in-fólios úteis entre as pedras das barricadas...
E a erva cresceu nas vias férreas com viços daninhos...

Ah, como esta hora é velha!... E todas as naus partiram!...
Na praia só um cabo morto e uns restos de vela falam
Do Longe, das horas do Sul, de onde os nossos sonhos tiram
Aquela angústia de sonhar mais que até para si calam...

O palácio está em ruínas... Dói ver no parque o abandono
Da fonte sem repuxo... Ninguém ergue o olhar da estrada
E sente saudades de si ante aquele lugar-outono...
Esta paisagem é um manuscrito com a frase mais bela cortada...

A doida partiu todos os candelabros glabros,
Sujou de humano o lago com cartas rasgadas, muitas...
E a minha alma é aquela luz que não mais haverá nos candelabros...
E que querem ao lado aziago minhas ânsias, brisas fortuitas?...

Porque me aflijo e me enfermo?... Deitam-se nuas ao luar
Todas as ninfas... Veio o sol e já tinham partido...
O teu silêncio que me embala é a ideia de naufragar,
E a ideia de a tua voz soar a lira dum Apolo fingido...

neither joy nor grief is this grief that overjoys me,
and my inverted goodness is neither good nor ill...

The lictors' fasces came unbound along the roadsides...
The medieval victory banners never reached the crusades...
Folios, useful ones, were stuffed between barricade-stones...
And the weeds came up on the railways with a noxious health...

Ah, how old is this hour!... And all the ships have gone!...
Only a stranded, fraying line and some sail-scraps tell
of Afar, of the Southerly hours, from where our dreams derive
their anguish of dreaming more than they hush even from themselves...

The palace stands in ruin... Sore sight, the neglect of the jetless
fountain in the park... No one lifts an eye from the road
and feels an old self-longing before that autumn-place...
This scene is a manuscript with the loveliest phrase cut out...

The madwoman broke every one of the glossy candelabras,
stained the lake human with torn-up letters, piles of them...
And my soul is the light that the candelabras hold no more...
And what do my yearnings, stray breezes, want from the ill-omened side?...

Why do I trouble and sicken myself?... Naked in the moonlight
lie all the nymphs... The sun came up and they had gone...
Your silence rocking me is the idea of foundering,
and of your voice strumming a false Apollo's lyre...

Já não há caudas de pavões todas olhos nos jardins de outrora...
As próprias sombras estão mais tristes... Ainda
Há rastos de vestes de aias (parece) no chão, e ainda chora
Um como que eco de passos pela alameda que eis finda...

Todos os ocasos fundiram-se na minha alma...
As relvas de todos os prados foram frescas sob meus pés frios...
Secou em teu olhar a ideia de te julgares calma,
E eu ver isso em ti é um porto sem navios...

Ergueram-se a um tempo todos os remos... Pelo ouro das searas
Passou uma saudade de não serem o mar... Em frente
Ao meu trono de alheamento há gestos com pedras raras...
Minha alma é uma lâmpada que se apagou e ainda está quente...

Ah, e o teu silêncio é um perfil de píncaro ao sol!
Todas as princesas sentirem o seio oprimido...
Da última janela do castelo só um girassol
Se vê, e o sonhar que há outros põe brumas no nosso sentido...

Sermos, e não sermos mais!... Ó leões nascidos na jaula!...
Repique de sinos para além, no Outro Vale... Perto?...
Arde o colégio e uma criança ficou fechada na aula...
Porque não há-de ser o Norte o Sul?... O que está descoberto?...

E eu deliro... De repente pauso no que penso... Fito-te
E o teu silêncio é uma cegueira minha... Fito-te e sonho...
Há coisas rubras e cobras no modo como medito-te,
E a tua ideia sabe à lembrança de um sabor de medonho...

Gone are the peacocks' tails all eyes in the gardens of yore…
Even the shadows have grown sadder… There are still trails
of chambermaids' garments (so it appears) on the ground, and still
a kind of footstep-echo weeps down the mall that ends here…

All of the sinking suns fused together in my soul…
The swards of every meadow were cool under my cold feet…
The idea of deeming yourself calm has dried up in your gaze,
and my seeing this in you is a harbor with no ships…

The oars were lifted all at once… Through the gold of the wheat-fields
passed a longing not to be the sea… Before
my throne of absentness are motions are made with gems…
My soul is a lamp that has been put out and still is warm…

Ah, and your smile is the profile of a peak in the sun!
Every princess feeling her bosom oppressed… From the farthest
window of the castle only one sunflower
is seen, and to dream that there are others fogs our sense…

We are, and are no more!… O lions born encaged!…
Chiming of bells beyond, in the Other Valley… Nearby?…
The school burns up and a child is locked inside a classroom…
Why should the North not be the South?… What has been discovered?…

And I muse… Of a sudden I pause in thought… I stare at you,
and your silence is a blindness of mine… I stare and dream…
There are red glows and snakes in the way I ponder you,
and your idea smacks of recalling of a dreadful taste…

Para que não ter por ti desprezo? Porque não perdê-lo?...
Ah, deixa que eu te ignore... O teu silêncio é um leque —
Um leque fechado, um leque que aberto seria tão belo, tão belo,
Mas mais belo é não o abrir, para que a Hora não peque...

Gelaram todas as mãos cruzadas sobre todos os peitos...
Murcharam mais flores do que as que havia no jardim...
O meu amar-te é uma catedral de silêncios eleitos,
E os meus sonhos uma escada sem princípio mas com fim...

Alguém vai entrar pela porta... Sente-se o ar sorrir...
Tecedeiras viúvas gozam as mortalhas de virgens que tecem...
Ah, o teu tédio é uma estátua de uma mulher que há-de vir,
O perfume que os crisântemos teriam, se o tivessem...

É preciso destruir o propósito de todas as pontes,
Vestir de alheamento as paisagens de todas as terras,
Endireitar à força a curva dos horizontes,
E gemer por ter de viver, como um ruído brusco de serras...

Há tão pouca gente que ame as paisagens que não existem!...
Saber que continuará a haver o mesmo mundo amanhã — como nos
                                                    desalegra!...
Que o meu ouvir o teu silêncio não seja nuvens que atristem
O teu sorriso, anjo exilado, e o teu tédio, auréola negra...

Suave, como ter mãe e irmãs, a tarde rica desce...
Não chove já, e o vasto céu é um grande sorriso imperfeito...
A minha consciência de ter consciência de ti é uma prece,
E o meu saber-te a sorrir é uma flor murcha a meu peito...

Wherefore should I not scorn you? Why not let it go?...
Ah, let me pay you no mind... Your silence is a fan—
a fan shut tight, that if opened would be so lovely, so lovely,
but lovelier still is to keep it shut, lest the Hour sin...

All of the hands crossed over every breast were frozen...
More flowers wilted than there had been flowers in the garden...
My loving you is a cathedral of chosen silences,
and my dreams a stairway with no beginning but with an end...

Someone's about to come in at the door... I feel the air smile...
Weaving widows treasure the maidens' shrouds they weave...
Ah, your tedium is a statue of a woman yet to be,
The scent chrysanthemums would have, if they had any...

The purpose warranting every bridge must be destroyed,
The landscapes of every land dressed up in absentness,
the curves of the horizons all must be forced straight,
and we must moan over having to live, like whining saws...

There are so few people who love landscapes that do not exist!...
How heartbreaking, to know the same world will still be here
                                                    tomorrow!...
Let my listening to your silence not be clouds that sadden
your smile, a banished angel, and your tedium, a dark halo...

Sweetly, like having a mother and sisters, the rich dusk falls...
The rain has stopped, and the sky is a great uneven smile...
My consciousness that I am conscious of you is a prayer,
and my knowing you to be smiling, a wilted flower at my breast...

Ah! se fôssemos duas figuras num longínquo vitral!...
Ah! se fôssemos as duas cores de uma bandeira de glória!...
Estátua acéfala posta a um canto, poeirenta pia baptismal,
Pendão de vencidos tendo escrito ao centro este lema — *Vitória*!

O que é que me tortura?... Se até a tua face calma
Só me enche de tédios e de ópios de ócios medonhos!...
Não sei... Eu sou um doido que estranha a sua própria alma...
Eu fui amado em efígie num país para além dos sonhos...

Ah, if we two were stained-glass figures in a far window!...
Ah, if we both were the colors in a flag of glory!...
An overlooked headless statue, a dusty baptismal font,
a banner of the conquered, this motto written at its center—*Victory*!

What is it that torments me?... If even your calm face
only fills me with tediums and opiums and dreadful idleness!...
I do not know... I'm a madman who wonders at his own soul...
I was beloved in effigy once in a land beyond dreams...

Chuva oblíqua
Poemas interseccionistas

I

ATRAVESSA ESTA PAISAGEM O MEU SONHO DUM PORTO INFINITO
E a cor das flores é transparente de as velas de grandes navios
Que largam do cais arrastando nas águas por sombra
Os vultos ao sol daquelas árvores antigas...

O porto que sonho é sombrio e pálido
E esta paisagem é cheia de sol deste lado...
Mas no meu espírito o sol deste dia é porto sombrio
E os navios que saem do porto são estas árvores ao sol...

Liberto em duplo, abandonei-me da paisagem abaixo...
O vulto do cais é a estrada nítida e calma
Que se levanta e se ergue como um muro,
E os navios passam por dentro dos troncos das árvores
Com uma horizontalidade vertical,
E deixam cair amarras na água pelas folhas uma a uma dentro...

Não sei quem me sonho...
Súbito toda a água do mar do porto é transparente
E vejo no fundo, como uma estampa enorme que lá estivesse desdobrada,
Esta paisagem toda, renque de árvores, estrada a arder em aquele porto,
E a sombra duma nau mais antiga que o porto que passa
Entre o meu sonho do porto e o meu ver esta paisagem
E chega ao pé de mim, e entra por mim dentro,
E passa para o outro lado da minha alma...

Slanting Rain

Intersectionalist Poems

I

ACROSS THIS LANDSCAPE RUNS MY DREAM OF AN INFINITE HARBOR
and the color of the flowers is transparent as the sails of great ships
that set out from the wharf towing through the waters in shadow
the sunlit bulks of those ancient trees...

The harbor I dream is shadowy and pale
while this landscape is filled with sunlight on this side...
But in my spirit the sunshine of this day is a shadowy harbor
and the ships that leave the port are these sunlit trees...

Doubly freed, I have abandoned myself down from the landscape...
The figure of the wharf is the quiet, sunny street
that rises and stands like a wall,
and the ships pass through the trunks of the trees
in vertically horizontal motion,
and drop hawsers into the water one by one in amongst the leaves...

I do not know who I dream that I am...
Suddenly all the seawater in the harbor is transparent
and at the bottom I see, like a massive print spread open there,
this entire landscape, trees in a row, street shimmering there in the harbor,
as the shadow of a ship more ancient than the harbor passes
between my dream of the harbor and my view of this landscape
and sails up to me, and enters into me,
and passes on across my soul...

IV

Que pandeiretas o silêncio deste quarto!...
As paredes estão na Andaluzia...
Há danças sensuais no brilho fixo da luz...

De repente todo o espaço pára...,
Pára, escorrega, desembrulha-se...,
E num canto do tecto, muito mais longe do que ele está,
Abrem mãos brancas janelas secretas
E há ramos de violetas caindo
De haver uma noite de primavera lá fora
Sobre o eu estar de olhos fechados...

IV

How jangling the silence in this room!…
Its walls are in Andalusia…
There are sensual dances in the steady glow of light…

At once all space stops…,
stops, slips off, clears away…,
and up in a corner, much farther away than the ceiling,
secret windows unclasp white hands
and there are bouquets of violets falling
from the existence of a spring night outside
down onto my eyes' being shut…

VI

O MAESTRO SACODE A BATUTA,
E lânguida e triste a música rompe...
Lembra-me a minha infância, aquele dia
Em que eu brincava ao pé dum muro de quintal
Atirando-lhe com uma bola que tinha dum lado
O deslizar dum cão verde, e do outro lado
Um cavalo azul a correr com um *jockey* amarelo...

Prossegue a música, e eis na minha infância
De repente entre mim e o maestro, muro branco,
Vai e vem a bola, ora um cão verde,
Ora um cavalo azul com um *jockey* amarelo...

Todo o teatro é o meu quintal, a minha infância
Está em todos os lugares, e a bola vem a tocar música
Uma música triste e vaga que passeia no meu quintal
Vestida de cão verde tornando-se *jockey* amarelo
(Tão rápida gira a bola entre mim e os músicos...)

Atiro-a de encontro à minha infância e ela
Atravessa o teatro todo que está aos meus pés
A brincar com um *jockey* amarelo e um cão verde
E um cavalo azul que aparece por cima do muro
Do meu quintal... E a música atira com bolas
À minha infância... E o muro do quintal é feito de gestos
De batuta e rotações confusas de cães verdes
E cavalos azuis e *jockeys* amarelos...

VI

THE MAESTRO WAVES HIS BATON,
and the music breaks out languid and mournful…
It reminds me of my childhood, of that day
when I played by a backyard wall,
tossing a ball against it that had on one side
the gliding of a green dog, and on the other
a blue horse running with a yellow jockey…

The music continues, and here in my childhood
suddenly between the maestro—a white wall—and me,
the ball goes to and fro, now a green dog,
now a blue horse with a yellow jockey…

The whole theater is my backyard, my childhood
is in every seat, and the ball comes back playing music,
a sad, faint music that strolls through my backyard
dressed in a green dog turning into a yellow jockey
(so quickly does the ball spin between me and the musicians…)

I throw it against my childhood and it
spans across the whole theater that lies at my feet
playing with a yellow jockey and a green dog
and a blue horse that appears on top of the wall
in my backyard… and the music tosses balls
at my childhood… And the backyard wall is made of motions
with the baton and the jumbled spinning of green dogs
and blue horses and yellow jockeys…

Todo o teatro é um muro branco de música
Por onde um cão verde corre atrás da minha saudade
Da minha infância, cavalo azul com um *jockey* amarelo...

E dum lado para outro, da direita para a esquerda,
Donde há árvores e entre os ramos ao pé da copa
Com orquestras a tocar música,
Para onde há filas de bolas na loja onde a comprei
E o homem da loja sorri por entre as memórias da minha infância...

E a música cessa como um muro que desaba,
A bola rola pelo despenhadeiro dos meus sonhos interrompidos,
E do alto dum cavalo azul, o maestro, *jockey* amarelo tornando-se preto,
Agradece, pousando a batuta em cima da fuga dum muro,
E curva-se, sorrindo, com uma bola branca em cima da cabeça,
Bola branca que lhe desaparece pelas costas abaixo...

The whole theater is a white wall of music
through which a green dog runs after my longing
for my childhood, a blue horse with a yellow jockey...

And from side to side, from right to left,
from where there are trees, through the branches near the treetops
with orchestras playing music,
to where there are rows of balls in the store where I bought mine
and the man in the store smiles through my childhood memories...

And the music cuts out like a wall collapsing,
the ball rolls over the precipice of my interrupted dreams,
and from atop a blue horse, the maestro, a yellow jockey turning
black,
gives his thanks, resting his baton on the disappearance of a wall,
and bows with a smile, balancing a white ball on his head,
a white ball that vanishes down his back...

COMO A NOITE É LONGA!
Toda a noite é assim...
Senta-te, ama, perto
Do leito onde esperto.
Vem pr'ao pé de mim...

Amei tanta coisa...
Hoje nada existe.
Aqui ao pé da cama
Canta-me, minha ama,
Uma canção triste.

Era uma princesa
Que amou... Já não sei...
Como estou esquecido!
Canta-me ao ouvido
E adormecerei...

Que é feito de tudo?
Que fiz eu de mim?
Deixa-me dormir,
Dormir a sorrir
E seja isto o fim.

How LONG IS THE NIGHT!
Every night is so bleak…
Come sit by me, nurse,
come up and sit close
to the bed where I wake…

I once loved so much…
Now everything's gone.
Here by my bedside,
sing to me, nursemaid,
sing me a sad song.

There once was a princess
who loved… I don't know…
I can't remember!
Sing into my ear,
and to sleep I'll go…

What's become of everything?
What's become of me?
Let me fall asleep,
let me smile in my sleep
and let nothing else be.

BATE A LUZ NO CIMO
Da montanha, vê...
Sem querer, eu cismo
Mas não sei em quê...

Não sei que perdi
Ou que não achei...
Vida que vivi,
Que mal eu a amei!...

Hoje quero tanto
Que o não posso ter.
De manhã há o pranto
E ao anoitecer.

Tomara eu ter jeito
Para ser feliz...
Como o mundo é estreito,
E o pouco que eu quis!

Vai morrendo a luz
No alto da montanha...
Como um rio a flux
A minha alma banha,

Mas não me acarinha,
Não me acalma nada...
Pobre criancinha
Perdida na estrada!...

LOOK, THE LIGHT IS GLOWING
upon the mountaintop...
Aimlessly I ponder
upon I know not what...

What I have lost I know not,
or what stayed always hid...
Oh me, oh me, how little
have I loved the life I've lived!...

Today I long for so much more
than ever can be mine.
In the morning come my tears
and at evening-time.

I wish I could be merry,
like some that are so skilled...
How small this little world is,
and the little I have willed!

Now upon the mountain
the light begins to fade...
As in a rushing river,
my soul in it is bathed,

but it does not soothe me,
nor ease my deep dismay...
Oh, poor little wandering child
lost along the way!...

SABER? QUE SEI EU?
Pensar é descrer.
— Leve e azul é o céu —
Tudo é tão difícil
De compreender!...

A ciência, uma fada
Num conto de louco...
— A luz é lavada —
Como o que nós vemos
É nítido e pouco!

Que sei eu que abrande
Meu anseio fundo?
Ó céu real e grande,
Não saber o modo
De pensar o mundo!

Know? What do I know?
To think is not to trust it true.
—The sky is airy and blue—
How difficult is anything
at all to construe!…

Knowledge, why, a fairy
from a madman's tale…
—The light shines clear and pale—
Everything that we can see
is so plain and small!

What do I know to soften
my deep longing urge?
O sky real and large,
how I wish I knew the way
to think out the world!

VAI REDONDA E ALTA
A lua. Que dor
É em mim um amor?...
Não sei que me falta...

Não sei o que quero,
Nem posso sonhá-lo...
Como o luar é ralo
No chão vago e austero!...

Ponho-me a sorrir
Pra a ideia de mim...
E tão triste, assim
Como quem está a ouvir

Uma voz que o chama
Mas não sabe donde
(Voz que em si se esconde)
E só a ela ama...

E tudo isto é o luar
E a minha dor
Tornado exterior
Ao meu meditar...

Que desassossego!
Que inquieta ilusão!
E esta sensação
Oca, de ser cego

Round and high glides the moon.
What is in me, this ache
that feels like a love?...
I don't know what I lack...

I don't know what I'd like,
cannot dream of so knowing...
On the bleak ground, how feebly
the moonlight is glowing!...

I break into a smile
at the thought of myself...
So gloomy, like someone
who loves nothing else

but a voice he keeps hearing
that calls him by name,
but can't tell where it comes from
(it's hidden in him)...

And this is all moonlight,
and this is my aching
made manifest outside
of my sullen sulking...

Oh, such a disquiet!
Such tricks in my mind!
And this hollow sensation
that I must be blind

No meu pensamento,
Na minha vontade...
Ah, a suavidade
Do luar sem tormento

Batendo na alma
De quem só sentisse
O luar, e existisse
Só pra a sua calma.

in my thoughts, in my will…
Ah, how sweet it would be
to take in the moonlight
untroubled and free,

let it shine on my soul
and quite simply admire it,
existing for nothing
but my own peace and quiet.

CHOVE? NENHUMA CHUVA CAI...
Então onde é que eu sinto um dia
Em que o ruído da chuva atrai
A minha inútil agonia?

Onde é que chove, que eu o ouço?
Onde é que é triste, ó claro céu?
Eu quero sorrir-te, e não posso,
Ó céu azul, chamar-te meu...

E o escuro ruído da chuva
É constante em meu pensamento.
Meu ser é a invisível curva
Traçada pelo som do vento...

E eis que ante o sol e o azul do dia,
Como se a hora me estorvasse,
Eu sofro... E a luz e a sua alegria
Cai aos meus pés como um disfarce.

Ah, na minha alma sempre chove.
Há sempre escuro dentro em mim.
Se escuto, alguém dentro em mim ouve
A chuva, como a voz de um fim...

Quando é que eu serei da tua cor,
Do teu plácido e azul encanto,
Ó claro dia exterior,
Ó céu mais útil que o meu pranto?

Does it rain? No rain is falling…
Where, then, do I sense a day
with the sound of raindrops calling
to my idle, vain dismay?

Where is the rain, the rain I hear?
Where is the gloom, O sky so clear?
If only I could smile at you
and call you mine, O azure blue…

And the murky sound of rain
still is constant in my mind.
My being is the curve unseen
traced by the noise of gusting wind…

And so before the daylight clear,
as if the hour blocked my eyes,
I suffer… And the daylight's cheer
falls at my feet like a disguise.

Ah, in my soul it's always raining.
There's always darkness deep in me.
Someone deep down can hear, if straining,
the rainfall, like an ending's cry…

When will I shine as bright as you,
with your unclouded azure hue,
O outward day that charms and cheers,
O sky more useful than my tears?

Passos da cruz

VII

Fosse eu apenas, não sei onde ou como,
Uma coisa existente sem viver,
Noite de Vida sem amanhecer
Entre as sirtes do meu dourado assomo...

Fada maliciosa ou incerto gnomo
Fadado houvesse de não pertencer
Meu intuito gloríola com ter
A árvore do meu uso o único pomo...

Fosse eu uma metáfora somente
Escrita nalgum livro insubsistente
Dum poeta antigo, de alma em outras gamas,

Mas doente, e, num crepúsculo de espadas,
Morrendo entre bandeiras desfraldadas
Na última tarde de um império em chamas...

Stations of the Cross

VII

Would that I had, I know not when or how,
been but a lifeless, existential thing,
my Life benighted, and no daylight glow
among the shoals of golden glimmering...

Would I had been beguiled of faculty
by some shrewd fairy-sprite or fickle gnome,
charmed out of my vainglory at the tree
of my employ bearing its single pome...

Would that I were mere metaphoric words
into an insubstantial volume scrawled
by an old bard, his mind worlds off, who lay

and pined beneath a twilight gemmed with swords,
dying as round him banners flew unfurled
upon a smoldering empire's final day.

X

Aconteceu-me do alto do infinito
Esta vida. Através de nevoeiros,
Do meu próprio ermo ser fumos primeiros,
Vim ganhando, e através estranhos ritos

De sombra e luz ocasional, e gritos
Vagos ao longe, e assomos passageiros
De saudade incógnita, luzeiros
De divino, este ser fosco e proscrito...

Caiu chuva em passados que fui eu.
Houve planícies de céu baixo e neve
Nalguma coisa de alma do que é meu.

Narrei-me à sombra e não me achei sentido.
Hoje sei-me o deserto onde Deus teve
Outrora a sua capital de olvido...

X

From the height of the Infinite this life
befell me. Through dense fogs have I set out,
of my peculiar solitary self
early smoke-signs, to gain—as all about

shadow and flickering brightness held strange rites,
and low cries sounded from afar, and fast
shone gleams of unknown longing, twinkling lights
of the divine—this feeble self outcast…

I have been times when raindrops fell long since.
There have been plains of snow and heavy skies
in something of my own that seemed a soul.

I told the shade myself; the tale lacked sense.
Today I know I am the wilderness
where God once placed oblivion's capital…

XII

ELA IA, TRANQUILA PASTORINHA,
Pela estrada da minha imperfeição.
Seguia-a, como um gesto de perdão,
O seu rebanho, a saudade minha...

«Em longes terras hás-de ser rainha»
Um dia lhe disseram, mas em vão...
Seu vulto perde-se na escuridão...
Só sua sombra ante meus pés caminha...

Deus te dê lírios em vez desta hora,
E em terras longe do que eu hoje sinto
Serás, rainha não, mas só pastora —

Só sempre a mesma pastorinha a ir,
E eu serei teu regresso, esse indistinto
Abismo entre o meu sonho e o meu porvir...

XII

ALONG SHE WENT, A BLITHE YOUNG SHEPHERDESS,
upon the highway of my imperfection.
Behind her, like an act of pardoning grace,
followed her flock, my wistful recollection…

"In lands apart shall you be made a queen,"
she once was told, but such was not her fate…
Her figure in the darkness goes unseen…
Only her shadow walks before my feet…

God give you lilies in this hour's stead,
and lands apart from what I feel today,
you'll be no queen, but only shepherdess—

ever the same young shepherdess shall tread,
and I, between my dreams and future, be
your turning back, that indistinct abyss…

XIII

Emissário de um rei desconhecido,
Eu cumpro informes instruções de além,
E as bruscas frases que aos meus lábios vêm
Soam-me a um outro e anómalo sentido...

Inconscientemente me divido
Entre mim e a missão que o meu ser tem,
E a glória do meu Rei dá-me o desdém
Por este humano povo entre quem lido...

Não sei se existe o Rei que me mandou.
Minha missão será eu a esquecer,
Meu orgulho o deserto em que em mim estou...

Mas ah! eu sinto-me altas tradições
De antes de tempo e espaço e vida e ser...
Já viram Deus as minhas sensações...

XIII

AN EMISSARY FROM AN UNKNOWN KING,
I follow formless orders from beyond,
and from my lips what crude expressions spring,
to me another, rarer meaning sound…

Unconsciously I cleave myself between
me and the quest my being bears along,
and my king's glory lends me a disdain
for this same human race I toil among…

Whether my king exists, I do not know.
My quest shall be to unlearn my quest itself,
my pride the wastes where in myself I go…

But ah! I sense I am customs high and old,
older than time and space and life and self…
Already my sensations have seen God…

Súbita mão de algum fantasma oculto
Entre as dobras da noite e do meu sono
Sacode-me e eu acordo, e no abandono
Da noite não enxergo gesto ou vulto.

Mas um terror antigo, que insepulto
Trago no coração, como de um trono
Desce e se afirma meu senhor e dono
Sem ordem, sem meneio e sem insulto.

E eu sinto a minha vida de repente
Presa por uma corda de Inconsciente
A qualquer mão nocturna que me guia.

Sinto que sou ninguém salvo uma sombra
De um vulto que não vejo e que me assombra,
E em nada existo como a treva fria.

THE SUDDEN HAND OF SOME UNSEEN PHANTASM
between the folds of night and of my sleep
stirs me awake, and through the empty chasm
of night, I spy no motion and no shape.

But an unburied terror I had stored
of old within my heart, as from a throne
descends and claims itself my liege and lord,
with no behest, no flourish, no disdain.

And all at once I feel my life being led,
bound by a tether of the Unconscious Mind
to whosesoever darkling hand is there.

I sense that I am no one but a shade
of an uncanny shape I cannot find
and, like the chilly dark, exist nowhere.

Intervalo

Quem te disse ao ouvido esse segredo
Que raras deusas têm escutado —
Aquele amor cheio de crença e medo
Que é verdadeiro só se é segredado?...
Quem to disse tão cedo?

Não fui eu, que te não ousei dizê-lo.
Não foi um outro, porque o não sabia.
Mas quem roçou da testa teu cabelo
E te disse ao ouvido o que sentia?
Seria alguém, seria?

Ou foi só que o sonhaste e eu te o sonhei?
Foi só qualquer ciúme meu de ti
Que o supôs dito, porque o não direi,
Que o supôs feito, porque o só fingi
Em sonhos que nem sei?

Seja o que for, quem foi que levemente,
A teu ouvido vagamente atento,
Te falou desse amor em mim presente
Mas que não passa do meu pensamento
Que anseia e que não sente?

Foi um desejo que, sem corpo ou boca,
A teus ouvidos de eu sonhar-te disse
A frase eterna, imerecida e louca —

Entr'acte

Who told that secret in your ear
that goddesses have seldom heard—
that love so full of faith and fear
that's only true if mum's the word?…
Who had the speed, the gall?

I never told you—I'd not dare.
Nor someone else, for no one knew.
Who was it, then, brushed back your hair
and whispered what I felt to you?
Someone, would not it seem?

Or did I dream it your dreams' way?
Had I for you some jealousy
that guessed it said, since I won't say,
and done, since it was feigned by me
in some unwitting dream?

Yet who, whatever did unfold,
into your ear somewhat inclined
spoke softly of the love I hold
but keep within my yearning mind
that does not feel at all?

It was my wish, unmouthed, unclad,
that, as I dreamed you, told you this—
the timeless phrase, unearned and mad,

A que as deusas esperam da ledice
Com que o Olimpo se apouca.

which goddesses await with bliss
that makes Olympus small.

ONDE PUS A ESPERANÇA, AS ROSAS
Murcharam logo.
Na casa, onde fui habitar,
O jardim, que eu amei por ser
Ali o melhor lugar,
E por quem essa casa amei —
Deserto o achei,
E, quando o tive, sem razão pra o ter.

Onde pus a afeição, secou
A fonte logo.
Da floresta, que fui buscar
Por essa fonte ali tecer
Seu canto de rezar —
Quando na sombra penetrei,
Só o lugar achei
Da fonte seca, inútil de se ter.

Pra quê, pois, afeição, 'sperança,
Se perco, logo
Que as uso, a causa pra as usar,
Se tê-las sabe a não as ter?
Crer ou amar —
Até à raiz, do peito onde alberguei
Tais sonhos e os gozei,
O vento arranque e leve onde quiser
E eu os não possa achar!

WHERE I PLACED MY HOPE, THE ROSES
withered soon.
At the house to which I moved,
the garden I loved, for that
was the nicest place,
and the reason I loved the abode—
I found it bare,
no point in having it, once it was mine.

Where I placed my affection, the spring
dried up soon.
The forest, which I roved
to hear the spring there chant
with praying voice,
when I entered through its shade,
was empty where
the spring should flow, no use in having gone.

Why, then, keep affection, hope,
if they lose, as soon
as I use them, their grounds to be used,
if having them feels like not?
Love or faith—
out of my breast where I've stored
such dreams and held them dear,
let the wind uproot them, carry them where
I cannot find them again!

Natal

Nasce um deus. Outros morrem. A Verdade
Nem veio nem se foi: o Erro mudou.
Temos agora uma outra Eternidade,
E era sempre melhor o que passou.

Cega, a Ciência a inútil gleba lavra.
Louca, a Fé vive o sonho do seu culto.
Um novo deus é só uma palavra.
Não procures nem creias: tudo é oculto.

Christmas

A god is born. Other gods die. The Truth
has neither come nor gone: the Error has changed.
There is for us a new Eternity,
and what is past will always be preferred.

Blindly does Knowledge till her useless soil.
Madly does Faith live on, her followers' dream.
A new god is a word and nothing else.
Neither seek nor believe: all is concealed.

Canção

Silfos ou gnomos tocam?...
Roçam nos pinheirais
Sombras e bafos leves
De ritmos musicais.

Ondulam como em voltas
De estradas não sei onde,
Ou como alguém que entre árvores
Ora se mostra ou esconde.

Forma longínqua e incerta
Do que eu nunca terei...
Mal oiço, e quase choro,
Porque choro não sei.

Tão ténue melodia
Que mal sei se ela existe
Ou se é só o crepúsculo,
Os pinhais e eu estar triste.

Mas cessa, como uma brisa
Esquece a forma aos seus ais;
E agora não há mais música
Do que a dos pinheirais.

Song

Are sylphs or goblins playing?…
From across the pinewoods sigh
some rustling shadows and faint breaths
of rhythmic melody.

As if upon an unknown road
they come with bending strides,
like someone who among the trees
now shows himself, now hides.

A far, uncertain figure
of what I will never own…
I scarce have heard, and almost weep,
for weeping I know none.

So delicate the tune,
I hardly know if it is real,
or merely is the dusk, the pinewoods,
and the gloom I feel.

But off it ceases, as a breeze
forgets the strain it whines,
and now there is no music
but the music of the pines.

LEVE, BREVE, SUAVE,
Um canto de ave
Sobe no ar com que principia
O dia.
Escuto, e passou...
Parece que foi só porque escutei
Que parou.

Nunca, nunca, em nada,
Raie a madrugada,
Ou 'splenda o dia, ou doire no declive,
Tive
Prazer a durar
Mais do que o nada, a perda, antes de eu o ir
Gozar.

Soft, swift, sweet,
a bird's warbling tweet
soars through the air with the early ray
of day.
I listen, and it's passed…
It seems it was only because I listened
that it ceased.

Never, ever, not once,
in all my pale dawns,
or bright days, or gold lights sinking down,
have I known
enjoyment to last
beyond being nil, being gone before I
had a taste.

POBRE VELHA MÚSICA!
Não sei por que agrado,
Enche-se de lágrimas
Meu olhar parado.

Recordo outro ouvir-te.
Não sei se te ouvi
Nessa minha infância
Que me lembra em ti.

Com que ânsia tão raiva
Quero aquele outrora!
E eu era feliz? Não sei:
Fui-o outrora agora.

Poor old music-woman!
I know not how it cheers,
but as I stop to hear your tune,
my eyes well up with tears.

I recall another
who heard your music, too.
Perhaps it was my childhood self
I recollect in you.

With what furious yearning
I crave those days of yore!
And was I happy then? Who knows,
but now I was before.

Sol nulo dos dias vãos,
Cheios de lida e de calma,
Aquece ao menos as mãos
A quem não entras na alma!

Que ao menos a mão, roçando
A mão que por ela passe,
Com externo calor brando
O frio da alma disfarce!

Senhor, já que a dor é nossa
E a fraqueza que ela tem,
Dá-nos ao menos a força
De a não mostrar a ninguém!

Idle sun of useless days
filled with toil and calm,
do but warm the hands of those
whose souls you do not warm!

Do but let one passing hand,
over another rolled,
with its outward heat so bland
mask the spirit's cold!

Lord, since griefs to us belong
and frailty with them goes,
do but make your servants strong,
that none may see our woes!

TRILA NA NOITE UMA FLAUTA. É DE ALGUM
Pastor? Que importa? Perdida
Série de notas vagas e sem sentido nenhum,
Como a vida.

Sem nexo ou princípio ou fim ondeia
A ária alada.
Pobre ária fora de música e de voz, tão cheia
De não ser nada!

Não há nexo ou fio por que se lembre aquela
Ária, ao parar;
E já ao ouvi-la sofro a saudade dela
E o quando cessar.

A FLUTE TRILLS THROUGH THE NIGHT. A SHEPHERD'S WHINING
pipe? What does it matter? A lost air rife
with faint successive tones that have no meaning
at all, like life.

Without connection, start, or finish roll
the soaring notes.
Poor tune outside of song and voice, so full
of nothingness!

There is no thread or sense to reminisce it
when the air's done;
and even as I hearken now I miss it,
feeling it gone.

Manhã dos outros! Ó sol que dás confiança
    Só a quem já confia!
É só à dormente, e não à morta, 'sperança
    Que acorda o teu dia.

A quem sonha de dia e sonha de noite, sabendo
    Todo o sonho vão,
Mas sonha sempre, só para sentir-se vivendo
    E a ter coração.

A esses raias sem o dia que trazes, ou somente
    Como alguém que vem
Pela rua, invisível ao nosso olhar consciente,
    Por não ser-nos ninguém.

DAYBREAK FOR OTHERS! O SUN THAT TO THE BELIEVING
      alone gives faith!
Your day awakens only the hopes that are sleeping,
      not those in death.

To dreamers who dream both daytime and nighttime, knowing
      dreams have no worth,
but dreaming still, if only to feel themselves living
      and having a heart—

to them you shine without the day you come bringing,
      like someone who goes
on the street, invisible to our conscious looking,
      being no one to us.

DORME SOBRE O MEU SEIO,
Sonhando de sonhar...
No teu olhar eu leio
Um lúbrico vagar.
Dorme no sonho de existir
E na ilusão de amar...

Tudo é nada, e tudo
Um sonho finge ser.
O espaço negro é mudo.
Dorme, e, ao adormecer,
Saibas do coração sorrir
Sorrisos de esquecer.

Dorme sobre o meu seio,
Sem mágoa nem amor...
No teu olhar eu leio
O íntimo torpor
De quem conhece o nada-ser
De vida e gozo e dor.

Sleep against my bosom,
dreaming of a dream…
In your eyes I notice
an idle, wanton gleam.
Sleep in the dream of existence,
in a love that will so seem…

All that there is, is nothing,
but mimics a dream by guile.
The space is dark and silent.
Sleep, and all the while,
know that your heart is smiling
oblivion's tender smile.

Sleep against my bosom,
feeling no love, no grief…
In your eyes I notice
the intimate relief
of one who knows the nothingness
of pleasure and pain and life.

Ao longe, ao luar,
No rio uma vela,
Serena a passar,
Que é que me revela?

Não sei, mas meu ser
Tornou-se-me estranho,
E eu sonho sem ver
Os sonhos que tenho.

Que angústia me enlaça?
Que amor não se explica?
É a vela que passa
Na noite que fica.

OUT IN THE DISTANCE, UNDER THE MOONLIGHT,
there goes a sail,
tranquilly passing over the river:
what can it reveal?

I do not know, but my self has become
like a stranger to me,
and the dreams that I have, although I dream,
I cannot see.

What is the anguish that grips me? What love
is past explaining?
It is the sail that travels on
through the night remaining.

Ela canta, pobre ceifeira,
Julgando-se feliz talvez;
Canta, e ceifa, e a sua voz, cheia
De alegre e anónima viuvez,

Ondula como um canto de ave
No ar limpo como um limiar,
E há curvas no enredo suave
Do som que ela tem a cantar.

Ouvi-la alegra e entristece,
Na sua voz há o campo e a lida,
E canta como se tivesse
Mais razões pra cantar que a vida.

Ah, canta, canta sem razão!
O que em mim sente 'stá pensando.
Derrama no meu coração
A tua incerta voz ondeando!

Ah, poder ser tu, sendo eu!
Ter a tua alegre inconsciência,
E a consciência disso! Ó céu
Ó campo! ó canção! A ciência

Pesa tanto e a vida é tão breve!
Entrai por mim dentro! Tornai
Minha alma a vossa sombra leve!
Depois, levando-me, passai!

SHE SINGS, POOR REAPER-WOMAN,
and believes, perhaps, she is glad;
she sings as she reaps and, skimming
with blithe, nameless widowhood,

her voice like a birdsong sweeps
clean over the sill of the air,
and in the soft fabric are warps
of the sound her melodies bear.

A joy and a sorrow to hearken,
in her voice is the harvest strife
as she sings on, seeming certain
of more reasons for singing than life.

Ah, sing on, sing on without reason!
In me, my feeling part
keeps thinking. Pour your rising
and falling voice into my heart!

Oh to be you, and yet be me!
To be so unmindfully merry,
and mindful of it! O sky!
O field! O song! How heavy

is knowledge, how brief our lives!
Enter me! Make my soul anon
a faint shadow of yourselves!
Then, bearing me with you, begone!

O menino da sua mãe

No plaino abandonado
Que a morna brisa aquece,
De balas trespassado —
Duas, de lado a lado —,
Jaz morto, e arrefece.

Raia-lhe a farda o sangue.
De braços estendidos,
Alvo, louro, exangue,
Fita com olhar langue
E cego os céus perdidos.

Tão jovem! que jovem era!
(Agora que idade tem?)
Filho único, a mãe lhe dera
Um nome e o mantivera:
«O menino da sua mãe».

Caiu-lhe da algibeira
A cigarreira breve.
Dera-lhe a mãe. Está inteira
E boa a cigarreira,
Ele é que já não serve.

De outra algibeira, alada
Ponta a roçar o solo,
A brancura embainhada

Mother's Little Boy

Where temperate breezes warm
the empty battlefield,
with bullet-holes pierced through—
side by side, one, two—,
he lies dead and cold.

Blood streaks his uniform.
With sprawling arms uncrossed,
ashen-faced, fair-haired, drained,
his eyes stare dull and blind
at the heaven he has lost.

So young! How young he was!
(What is his age today?)
His mother's only child,
he had kept a name she called:
Mother's little boy.

A slender cigarette-case
his pocket held before,
from Mother, studs the ground.
The case is whole and sound,
but he will serve no more.

Its fine embroidered hem
grazing the dust with white,
from the other pocket peers

De um lenço... Deu-lho a criada
Velha que o trouxe ao colo.

Lá longe, em casa, há a prece:
«Que volte cedo, e bem!»
(Malhas que o Império tece!)
Jaz morto, e apodrece,
O menino da sua mãe.

a handkerchief… The old nurse
who held him gave him that.

Far off, a prayer: *Let him
soon be home safe, my joy!*
(The Empire's tightening knots!)
He lies dead and rots,
Mother's little boy.

Marinha

Ditosos a quem acena
Um lenço de despedida!
São felizes: têm pena...
Eu sofro sem pena a vida.

Doo-me até onde penso,
E a dor é já de pensar,
Órfão de um sonho suspenso
Pela maré a vazar...

E sobe até mim, já farto
De improfícuas agonias,
No cais de onde nunca parto,
A maresia dos dias.

Marine

Happy their lot the farewell kerchief
waves to until they are gone!
Happy are they, for they bear sorrow…
I bear my life with none.

As deeply as I think, I hurt;
in thought my pains reside;
I am the orphan of a dream
borne off on the ebbing tide…

And up to me, where I stand sick
of profitless dismays,
ascends by the dock I will never depart
the sea-swell of my days.

Qualquer música...

Qualquer música, ah, qualquer,
Logo que me tire da alma
Esta incerteza que quer
Qualquer impossível calma!

Qualquer música — guitarra,
Viola, harmónio, realejo...
Um canto que se desgarra...
Um sonho em que nada vejo...

Qualquer coisa que não vida!
Jota, fado, a confusão
Da última dança vivida...
Que eu não sinta o coração!

Some Music...

Some music! Oh, for any song
to sunder from my soul
this doubtfulness that vaguely longs
for peace impossible!

Any tune—strings, guitar,
harmonium, organ let it be...
A song that takes me far...
A dream with nothing there to see...

Anything else but life!
Jota, *fado*, whirling start
of the latest lively dance...
So I may not feel my heart!

Depois da feira

Vão vagos pela estrada,
Cantando sem razão
A última esp'rança dada
À última ilusão.
Não significam nada.
Mimos e bobos são.

Vão juntos e diversos
Sob um luar de ver,
Em que sonhos imersos
Nem saberão dizer,
E cantam aqueles versos
Que lembram sem querer.

Pajens de um morto mito,
Tão líricos!, tão sós!,
Não têm na voz um grito,
Mal têm a própria voz;
E ignora-os o infinito
Que nos ignora a nós.

After the Fair

Over the streets they wander,
singing out senselessly
the latest hopeful offering
to the latest fantasy.
They have no meaning—nothing
but clowns and fools are they.

A motley pack, they ramble
beneath a fine moonlight's pall,
and in what dreams they are carried
they cannot say at all,
but croon away the verses
they happen to recall.

Pages to some dead mythos,
so lyrical!, so lone!
There's barely a cry in their gullets,
their voices are scarce their own,
and the infinite ignores them,
as it does everyone.

NATAL. NA PROVÍNCIA NEVA.
Nos lares aconchegados,
Um sentimento conserva
Os sentimentos passados.

Coração oposto ao mundo,
Como a família é verdade!
Meu pensamento é profundo,
Estou só e sonho saudade.

E como é branca de graça
A paisagem que não sei,
Vista de trás da vidraça
Do lar que nunca terei!

CHRISTMAS. IT SNOWS IN THE COUNTRY.
In cozy cottage homes,
a warmth is felt, preserving
the warmth of older times.

Oh heart contrary to the world,
how true is family bliss!
Deep in my thoughts, I am lonely,
dreaming of people to miss.

And oh how white and winsome
the scene I have not known,
viewed from behind the window
of the place I will never call home!

TENHO DÓ DAS ESTRELAS
Luzindo há tanto tempo,
Há tanto tempo...
Tenho dó delas.

Não haverá um cansaço
Das coisas,
De todas as coisas,
Como das pernas ou de um braço?

Um cansaço de existir,
De ser,
Só de ser,
O ser triste brilhar ou sorrir...

Não haverá, enfim,
Para as coisas que são,
Não a morte, mas sim,
Uma outra espécie de fim,
Ou uma grande razão —
Qualquer coisa assim
Como um perdão?

I PITY THE STARS,
shining on for so long,
so long...
I pity them.

Must there not be a weariness
in things,
in all things,
like in an arm or a leg?

A weariness of existing,
of being,
of being at all,
being a mournful glow or a smile...

Must there not come, in the end,
to everything that is,
not death, but
another sort of end,
or some great reason—
something about
like forgiveness?

AQUI NA ORLA DA PRAIA, MUDO E CONTENTE DO MAR,
Sem nada já que me atraia, nem nada que desejar,
Farei um sonho, terei meu dia, fecharei a vida,
E nunca terei agonia, pois dormirei de seguida.

A vida é como uma sombra que passa por sobre um rio
Ou como um passo na alfombra de um quarto que jaz vazio;
O amor é um sono que chega para o pouco ser que se é;
A glória concede e nega; não tem verdades a fé.

Por isso na orla morena da praia calada e só,
Tenho a alma feita pequena, livre de mágoa e de dó;
Sonho sem quase já ser, perco sem nunca ter tido,
E comecei a morrer muito antes de ter vivido.

Dêem-me, onde aqui jazo, só uma brisa que passe,
Não quero nada do acaso, senão a brisa na face;
Dêem-me um vago amor de quanto nunca terei,
Não quero gozo nem dor, não quero vida nem lei.

Só, no silêncio cercado pelo som brusco do mar,
Quero dormir sossegado, sem nada que desejar,
Quero dormir na distância de um ser que nunca foi seu,
Tocado do ar sem fragrância da brisa de qualquer céu.

Here by the edge of the sea, lying silent and glad by the shore,
with nothing to occupy me and with nothing to want or desire,
I'll make a dream, I'll have my day, I'll shut out my life,
and I'll be off to sleep right away and will never feel anguish or grief.

For life is like a shadow drifting over a stream
or footsteps crossing the matted floor of an empty room;
love is a sleep that to our little selves is sufficient and soothes;
glory denies what it gives; in faith there are no truths.

And so on the tawny strand of the quiet, lonely shore,
my soul has become quite bland and small, free of pain and of care;
I dream now almost without being, I lose what I never did have,
and I have begun my dying long before I might live.

Here where I lie, give me nothing at all but a passing breeze;
from hazard and chance I want nothing but wind across my face;
give me an indistinct love for all that will never be mine;
I want neither life nor law; I want neither pleasure nor pain.

Alone in my silence encased all about by the ocean's roar,
I wish but to sleep in peace, with nothing to want or desire;
I wish but to sleep far, far from a self that was never my own,
touched by the odorless air of the breeze from a heaven unknown.

CONTEMPLO O LAGO MUDO
Que uma brisa estremece.
Não sei se penso em tudo
Ou se tudo me esquece.

O lago nada me diz.
Não sinto a brisa mexê-lo.
Não sei se sou feliz
Nem se desejo sê-lo.

Trémulos vincos risonhos
Na água adormecida.
Porque fiz eu dos sonhos
A minha única vida?

I LOOK AT THE SILENT LAKE
where rippling breezes fall.
I wonder if I'm thinking of everything
or if I've forgotten it all.

The lake, it gives no answer.
I can't feel the breezes stir.
I can't say for sure if I'm happy.
I can't say I wish that I were.

Quivering trails are smiling
there in the sleepy blue.
Why ever did I make dreaming
the only life I knew?

DÁ A SURPRESA DE SER.
É alta, de um louro escuro.
Faz bem só pensar em ver
Seu corpo meio maduro.

Seus seios altos parecem
(Se ela estivesse deitada)
Dois montinhos que amanhecem
Sem ter que haver madrugada.

E a mão do seu braço branco
Assenta em palmo espalhado
Sobre a saliência do flanco
Do seu relevo tapado.

Apetece como um barco.
Tem qualquer coisa de gomo.
Meu Deus, quando é que eu embarco?
Ó fome, quando é que eu como?

THE SHOCK SHE GIVES, JUST BEING.
She is sandy-haired, and tall.
It's nice even thinking of seeing
her ripening body at all.

Her two high bosoms look
(suppose she were lying down)
like little hills at daybreak,
although no day need dawn.

And at her pale arm's end
her fingers, spread out wide,
rest on the covered bend
of her protruding side.

She beckons like a barge,
or like some fleshy fruit.
Oh God, when do I go aboard?
Oh hunger, when do I eat?

Não: não digas nada!
Supor o que dirá
A tua boca velada
É ouvi-lo já.

É ouvi-lo melhor
Do que o dirias.
O que és não vem à flor
Das frases e dos dias.

És melhor do que tu.
Não digas nada: sê!
Graça do corpo nu
Que invisível se vê.

No, DON'T SAY A WORD!
For to guess ahead
what your sealed lips would tell me,
is to hear it unsaid—

and to hear it better
than what you would say.
Who you are doesn't shine through
by words or by day.

You're better than you.
Don't say a word: be!
The grace of your bare body
that, unseen, one can see.

O andaime

O tempo que eu hei sonhado
Quantos anos foi de vida!
Ah, quanto do meu passado
Foi só a vida mentida
De um futuro imaginado!

Aqui à beira do rio
Sossego sem ter razão.
Este seu correr vazio
Figura, anónimo e frio,
A vida vivida em vão.

A 'sp'rança que pouco alcança!
Que desejo vale o ensejo?
E uma bola de criança
Sobe mais que a minha 'sp'rança,
Rola mais que o meu desejo.

Ondas do rio, tão leves
Que não sois ondas sequer,
Horas, dias, anos, breves
Passam — verduras ou neves
Que o mesmo sol faz morrer.

Gastei tudo que não tinha.
Sou mais velho do que sou.
A ilusão, que me mantinha,

The Scaffold

Oh, the days I've spent dreaming!
Oh, the years I've let by!
How much time passed in scheming
of a future but seeming—
how much life but a lie!

By the riverside here
without reason I rest.
The blank flowing veneer,
cold and empty of cheer,
mocks a life lived in jest.

Highest hopes are too small!
Trifles, what one aspires!
And a child's bouncing ball
travels farther than all
of my hopes and desires.

Waves that in the stream flow
all as faintly as none,
hours, days, years, quickly go—
fields of green or of snow
withered by the same sun.

I have spent all I lacked.
I've aged more than my age,
by royal fantasies backed —

Só no palco era rainha:
Despiu-se, e o reino acabou.

Leve som das águas lentas,
Gulosas da margem ida,
Que lembranças sonolentas
De esperanças nevoentas!
Que sonhos o sonho e a vida!

Que fiz de mim? Encontrei-me
Quando estava já perdido.
Impaciente deixei-me
Como a um louco que teime
No que lhe foi desmentido.

Som morto das águas mansas
Que correm por ter que ser,
Leva não só as lembranças,
Mas as mortas esperanças —
Mortas, porque hão-de morrer.

Sou já o morto futuro.
Só um sonho me liga a mim —
O sonho atrasado e obscuro
Do que eu devera ser — muro
Do meu deserto jardim.

Ondas passadas, levai-me
Para o olvido do mar!
Ao que não serei legai-me,

but their reign was an act:
they were common offstage.

Muted waters that laze,
hungry for shores long gone,
how my mind is a daze
of old hopes dulled with haze!
Life and dreams but dreamed on!

What am I? When I found me
I was too lost to save.
I could not stay around me,
spouting lies. The unsound me,
I left there and let rave.

Floods that must flow, and do
mildly on with dead sound,
take remembrance with you,
and my lifeless hopes too—
dead, for they must be drowned.

I'm all I'll never be,
only bound to my burden
by a dim reverie—
of what should have been me—
walling my fruitless garden.

Out to sea on waves past
let my memories be spilt!
And my future erased

Que cerquei com um andaime
A casa por fabricar.

from the scaffold I placed
round a home never built.

Hoje que a tarde é calma e o céu tranquilo,
E a noite chega sem que eu saiba bem,
Quero considerar-me e ver aquilo
Que sou, e o que sou o que é que tem.

Olho por todo o meu passado e vejo
Que fui quem foi aquilo em torno meu,
Salvo o que o vago e incógnito desejo
De ser eu mesmo de meu ser me deu.

Como a páginas já relidas, vergo
Minha atenção sobre quem fui de mim,
E nada de verdade em mim albergo
Salvo uma ânsia sem princípio ou fim.

Como alguém distraído na viagem,
Segui por dois caminhos par a par.
Fui como o mundo, parte da paisagem;
Comigo fui, sem ver nem recordar.

Chegado aqui, onde hoje estou, conheço
Que sou diversos no que informe estou.
No meu próprio caminho me atravesso.
Não conheço quem fui no que hoje sou.

Serei eu, porque nada é impossível,
Vários trazidos de outros mundos, e
No mesmo ponto espacial sensível
Que sou eu, sendo eu por 'star aqui?

NOW THAT THE EVENING IS STILL AND THE SKIES ARE CALM
and, though I was hardly aware, the day's almost out,
I would like to consider myself and to see what I am,
and what being what I am has been about.

Looking throughout my past, my self, I find,
has always been whatever was around me,
save that with which my being's undefined
and unknown longing to be myself endowed me.

As if onto pages already reread, my attention,
to what self I have been as myself, I bend,
and note that in me no truth has found retention,
except for a longing that has no beginning or end.

Like someone who goes distracted on a journey,
two pathways have I followed, both together.
I have been like the world, a part of the scenery;
I have been on my own, have not seen or remembered.

Having arrived here, where I am today,
I find I am several in all that I formlessly am.
Myself I traverse along my very way.
I don't recognize who I have been in who I've become.

Could I be, for nothing is impossible,
many selves carried here from other worlds
to the point that is I in sensible space, and all
be me by being at this same point secured?

Serei eu, porque todo o pensamento
Podendo conceber, bem pode ser,
Um dilatado e múrmuro momento,
De tempos-seres de quem sou o viver?

Could I be, for anything that may be thought
and held as so, may as well be so, an instant
drawn out into a murmur—one begot
by time-selves, of which I am the life existent?

QUEM BATE À MINHA PORTA
Tão insistentemente
Saberá que está morta
A alma que em mim sente?

Saberá que eu a velo
Desde que a noite é entrada
Com o vácuo e vão desvelo
De quem não vela nada?

Saberá que estou surdo?
Porque o sabe ou não sabe,
E assim bate, ermo e absurdo,
Até que o mundo acabe?

WHO'S THAT KNOCKING ON MY DOOR
again and again and again?
Does he know the feeling soul
in me is dead and slain?

Does he know I keep watch for it
and have kept watch all the night
with the vain, vacant watchfulness
of one who watches naught?

Does he know that I am deaf?
For of that he is witless or sure,
and will he keep knocking, alone and absurd,
until the world's no more?

Na sombra do Monte Abiegno
Repousei de meditar.
Vi no alto o alto Castelo
Onde sonhei de chegar.
Mas repousei de pensar
Na sombra do Monte Abiegno.

Quanto fora amor ou vida,
Atrás de mim o deixei,
Quanto fora desejá-los,
Porque esqueci não lembrei.
À sombra do Monte Abiegno
Repousei porque abdiquei.

Talvez um dia, mais forte
Da força ou da abdicação,
Tentarei o alto caminho
Por onde ao Castelo vão.
Na sombra do Monte Abiegno
Por ora repouso, e não.

Quem pode sentir descanso
Com o Castelo a chamar?
Está no alto, sem caminho
Senão o que há por achar.
Na sombra do Monte Abiegno
Meu sonho é de o encontrar.

Mas por ora estou dormindo,
Porque é sono o não saber.

IN THE SHADOW OF MOUNT ABIEGNUS
I rested from meditation.
I saw at the height the high Castle,
my dreamed-of destination.
But in the shadow of Mount Abiegnus
I rested from contemplation.

All that was life or love—
all that, I left behind me.
Of all that was longing for either,
forgetting, I did not mind me.
Under the shadow of Mount Abiegnus
I rested, for there I resigned me.

Someday, perhaps, with more strength
of resignation or of brawn,
I shall attempt the high path
men go to the Castle upon.
For now in the shadow of Mount Abiegnus
I rest, and go not on.

Who, when the Castle beckons,
can enjoy his restful stay?
It stands at the height, with no path up,
but alone he must make out the way.
Here in the shadow of Mount Abiegnus,
my dream is to find out the way.

But until then I am sleeping,
for unknowledge is a sleep.

Olho o Castelo de longe,
Mas não olho o meu querer.
Da sombra do Monte Abiegno
Quem me virá desprender?

I view from afar the Castle,
but no view of desire do I keep.
Who, from the shadow of Mount Abiegnus,
will come and release me, asleep?

Autopsicografia

O poeta é um fingidor.
Finge tão completamente
Que chega a fingir que é dor
A dor que deveras sente.

E os que lêem o que escreve,
Na dor lida sentem bem,
Não as duas que ele teve,
Mas só a que eles não têm.

E assim nas calhas de roda
Gira, a entreter a razão,
Esse comboio de corda
Que se chama o coração.

Autopsychography

The poet is a feigner.
So fully does he feign
that even pain he truly feels,
he must pretend is pain.

And those who read his poems
feel, in the pain they've read,
not those same two the poet bore,
but one they never had.

And thus goes winding round its tracks,
diverting wits with art,
that clockwork locomotive engine
people call the heart.

Não sei se é sonho, se realidade,
Se uma mistura de sonho e vida,
Aquela terra de suavidade
Que na ilha extrema do sul se olvida.
É a que ansiamos. Ali, ali
A vida é jovem e o amor sorri.

Talvez palmares inexistentes,
Áleas longínquas sem poder ser,
Sombra ou sossego dêem aos crentes
De que essa terra se pode ter.
Felizes, nós? Ah, talvez, talvez,
Naquela terra, daquela vez.

Mas já sonhada se desvirtua,
Só de pensá-la cansou pensar,
Sob os palmares, à luz da lua,
Sente-se o frio de haver luar.
Ah, nessa terra também, também
O mal não cessa, não dura o bem.

Não é com ilhas do fim do mundo,
Nem com palmares de sonho ou não,
Que cura a alma seu mal profundo,
Que o bem nos entra no coração.
É em nós que é tudo. É ali, ali,
Que a vida é jovem e o amor sorri.

DREAM OR REALITY, I DO NOT KNOW,
or whether a blend of dream and truth,
that easeful country long ago
forgotten on the farthest island south:
the land of our yearning. For there, for there,
life is youthful, and love has a smile to wear.

Perhaps nonexistent palm-tree rows,
alleys far-flung and impossible
may offer comfort or shade to those
who believe such a land could be there at all.
Oh, might we be happy? Perchance, perchance,
in such a far country, by such happenstance.

But being dreamed of, the place becomes dreary;
even the thought makes our thoughts grow weary;
under the palm trees, by the moon's light,
one feels the chill of the moonlit night.
Oh, in this land, even here, even here,
there is no end of troubles, no lasting cheer.

It is not with isles at the end of the sea,
with fancied or actual rows of palm,
that the soul mends its malady,
that aching hearts let in their balm.
It all lies within us. For there, for there,
life is youthful, and love has a smile to wear.

Não sei que sonho me não descansa
E me faz mal...
Mas eia! o harmónio a guiar a dança
Nesse quintal.

E eu perco o fio ao que não existe
E oiço dançar,
Já não alheio, nem sequer triste,
Só de escutar.

Quanta alegria onde os outros são
E dançam bem!
Dei-lhes de graça meu coração
E o que ele tem.

Na noite calma o harmónio toca
Aquela dança,
E o que em mim sonha um momento evoca
Nova esperança.

Nova esperança, que há-de cessar
Quando, já dia,
O harmónio eterno que há-de acabar
Feche a alegria.

Ah, ser os outros! Se eu o pudesse
Sem outros ser!,
Enquanto o harmónio minha alma enchesse
De o não saber.

I KNOW NOT WHAT DREAM KEEPS ME RESTLESS FOR ANSWERS
troubled and tried...
But hey! the harmonium guiding the dancers
dancing outside.

And hearing the dance, I lose the thread
of the nonexistent,
no longer aloof, not even sad,
having but listened.

What joy where the others are, what joy
and how well they dance!
To them I have given my heart away
and what it contains.

Through the still night the harmonium keeps
the dance-tune up,
and where I dream from, for a brief lapse
there springs fresh hope.

Fresh hope that must cease, fresh hope that must fade
when, come the day,
the eternal harmonium stops being played
and ends the joy.

Oh, to be others! If only I could
and feel no difference,
while on and on the harmonium filled
my soul with ignorance.

Fernando Pessoa

FOI UM MOMENTO
O em que pousaste
Sobre o meu braço,
Num movimento
Mais de cansaço
Que pensamento,
A tua mão
E a retiraste.
Senti ou não?

Não sei. Mas lembro
E sinto ainda
Qualquer memória
Fixa e corpórea
Onde pousaste
A mão que teve
Qualquer sentido
Incompreendido,
Mas tão de leve!...

Tudo isto é nada,
Mas numa estrada
Como é a vida
Há muita coisa
Incompreendida...

Sei eu se quando
A tua mão
Senti pousando
Sobre meu braço,

THERE WAS A MOMENT
you came to rest your
hand on my arm,
in a soft gesture
more of tiredness
than of thought.
Then in a moment
you drew it away.
Did I feel it or not?

I cannot tell.
Yet I remember
and seem to sense
like a bodily member
the memory of where
you rested your hand
that held some meaning
I could not tell,
with such gentle care!...

This has no point,
but along a road
as long as life
are many points
not understood...

Could I tell, when
I felt it warm
laid down to rest
upon my arm,

E um pouco, um pouco,
No coração,
Não houve um ritmo
Novo no espaço?

Como se tu,
Sem o querer,
Em mim tocasses
Para dizer
Qualquer mistério,
Súbito e etéreo,
Que nem soubesses
Que tinha ser.

Assim a brisa
Nos ramos diz
Sem o saber
Uma imprecisa
Coisa feliz.

and a bit, a bit
deep in my chest,
if a new rhythm then
began to form?

Just as if you,
without meaning to,
were playing on me,
as if to tell
some mystery,
sudden and strange,
that you never knew
had its own being.

Just as the breeze
tells through the trees,
without quite knowing,
something uncertain
that's certain to please.

CESSA O TEU CANTO!
Cessa, que, enquanto
O ouvi, ouvia
Uma outra voz
Como que vindo
Nos interstícios
Do brando encanto
Com que o teu canto
Vinha até nós.

Ouvi-te e ouvi-a
No mesmo tempo
E diferentes
Juntas cantar.
E a melodia
Que não havia,
Se agora a lembro,
Faz-me chorar.

Foi tua voz
Encantamento
Que, sem querer,
Nesse momento,
Vago acordou
Um ser qualquer
Alheio a nós
Que nos falou?

Não sei. Não cantes!
Deixa-me ouvir

Stop your singing!
Stop, for, ringing
out through the fissures
in the mild magic
held in your voice,
I heard another
seeming to issue,
while your singing
came to us.

I heard you and heard it
both at once,
differently
singing together.
And the melody
the one that wasn't,
if I remember,
now makes me cry.

Was your voice
a spell you spoke
that, unwittingly,
just for the moment,
distantly woke
something or other,
other than us,
that to us spoke?

I do not know.
No, no singing!

Qual o silêncio
Que há a seguir
A tu cantares!

Ah, nada, nada!
Só os pesares
De ter ouvido,
De ter querido
Ouvir para além
Do que é o sentido
Que uma voz tem.

Que anjo, ao ergueres
A tua voz,
Sem o saberes
Veio baixar
Sobre esta terra
Onde a alma erra
E com as asas
Soprou as brasas
De ignoto lar?

Não cantes mais!
Quero o silêncio
Para dormir
Qualquer memória
Da voz ouvida,
Desentendida,
Que foi perdida
Por eu a ouvir...

Let me hear what silence
the next moment
afterward brings!

Ah, nothing, nothing!
But the chagrin
of having heard,
of having longed
to listen beyond
the meaning in
a voice that sings.

What angel flew,
unnoticed by you,
when you raised your voice,
down to this earth
where the soul wanders
and fluttered its wings,
fanning the cinders
of an unknown hearth?

No, no more singing!
Let me have silence
to put to rest
any memory
of the voice I heard,
without understanding,
that became lost
because I listened…

Neste mundo em que esquecemos
Somos sombras de quem somos,
E os gestos reais que temos
No outro em que, almas, vivemos,
São aqui esgares e assomos.

Tudo é nocturno e confuso
No que entre nós aqui há.
Projecções, fumo difuso
Do lume que brilha ocluso
Ao olhar que a vida dá.

Mas um ou outro, um momento,
Olhando bem, pode ver
Na sombra e seu movimento
Qual no outro mundo é o intento
Do gesto que o faz viver.

E então encontra o sentido
Do que aqui está a esgarar,
E volve ao seu corpo ido,
Imaginado e entendido,
A intuição de um olhar.

Sombra do corpo saudosa,
Mentira que sente o laço
Que a liga à maravilhosa
Verdade que a lança, ansiosa,
No chão do tempo e do espaço.

In this world where we forget,
we are but shadows of ourselves,
and our real actions in the next,
where as souls we live real lives,
here are hints and grimaces.

All is darkling and confused
in what here can be discovered—
dim projections, smoke diffused
from the fire that lightens covered
from the gaze our life here gives.

But one or other, for a moment,
looking closely, may detect
in the shadow and its movement
what is the other-worldly act
and intent whereby he lives.

And the meaning then he learns
of what here is only grimaced,
and to his gone body turns—
that far body, grasped, envisaged—
the intuition of his gaze.

Shadows yearning for our bodies,
though but lies, we sense the bond
that connects us to that wondrous
truth which casts us, as we long,
on the ground of time and space.

Montes, e a paz que há neles, pois são longe...
Paisagens, isto é, ninguém...
Tenho a alma feita para ser de um monge
Mas não me sinto bem.

Se eu fosse outro, fora outro. Assim
Aceito o que me dão,
Como quem espreita para um jardim
Onde os outros estão.

Que outros? Não sei. Há no sossego incerto
Uma paz que não há,
E eu fito sem o ler o livro aberto
Que nunca mo dirá...

HILLS, AND THE PEACE THEY CARRY, BEING FAR...
Landscapes—no one in sight...
A soul like mine would well beseem a friar,
but I do not feel right.

Were I another, I'd be different. Thus,
I take what I am given,
like someone who upon a garden spies
where others are living.

Who? I don't know. The doubtful stillness holds
a peace that is not there,
And where the book that will not say unfolds,
unreadingly I stare...

ONDA QUE, ENROLADA, TORNAS,
Pequena, ao mar que te trouxe
E ao recuar te transtornas
Como se o mar nada fosse,

Porque é que levas contigo
Só a tua cessação,
E, ao voltar ao mar antigo,
Não levas meu coração?

Há tanto tempo que o tenho
Que me pesa de o sentir.
Leva-o no som sem tamanho
Com que te oiço fugir!

WAVE RETURNING, CURLED AND SMALL,
to the sea that brought you in
as if to no place at all,
fading as you go again,

why is it you bear away
only your own fall-apart,
hying to the ancient sea
without bearing off my heart?

I have carried it so long
that it grieves me now to hold.
Take it in the boundless song
that I hear as you unfold!

O CÉU, AZUL DE LUZ QUIETA.
As ondas brandas a quebrar,
Na praia lúcida e completa —
Pontos de dedos a brincar.

No piano anónimo da praia
Tocam nenhuma melodia
De cujo ritmo por fim saia
Todo o sentido deste dia.

Que bom, se isto satisfizesse!
Que certo, se eu pudesse crer
Que esse mar e essas ondas e esse
Céu têm vida e têm ser.

THE SKY, BLUE WITH UNMOVING LIGHT.
Waves breaking placidly
against the seashore whole and bright—
fingertips at play.

On the blank piano of the beach
they tap no-melody;
its rhythm yields, at last complete,
the meaning of this day.

How well, were this to satisfy!
How right, could I believe
this sea, these waves, and this blue sky
had being and had life.

Dizem?
Esquecem.
Não dizem?
Disseram.

Fazem?
Fatal.
Não fazem?
Igual.

Porquê
Esperar?
— Tudo é
Sonhar.

Do they say so?
They'll forget it.
Never say so?
They have said it.

Do they do so?
It'll kill.
Never done so?
They'll die still.

Hope? What ever
to hope for?
All is but
a dream—no more.

Glosa

Quem me roubou a minha dor antiga,
E só a vida me deixou por dor?
Quem, entre o incêndio da alma em que o ser periga,
Me deixou só no fogo e no torpor?

Quem fez a fantasia minha amiga,
Negando o fruto e emurchecendo a flor?
Ninguém ou o Fado, e a fantasia siga
A seu infiel e irreal sabor...

Quem me dispôs para o que não pudesse?
Quem me fadou para o que não conheço
Na teia do real que ninguém tece?

Quem me arrancou ao sonho que me odiava
E me deu só a vida em que me esqueço,
«Onde a minha saudade a cor se trava?»

Gloss

Who took my former pain away from me,
and only left me life instead of pain?
Who, in the soul-fire that imperils the self,
left me in flames and numbness, all alone?

Who turned me to a friend of fantasy,
barring the fruit and letting wilt the flower?
No one, or Fate; let fantasy go on
with its unfaithful and unreal flavor…

Who swayed me to what I cannot realize?
Who doomed me to what I do not recognize
within the real-life web no weaver makes?

Who tore me out of my despising dream
and gave me this oblivious life to claim,
there where my heart keeps locked its fondest aches?

ASSIM, SEM NADA FEITO E O POR FAZER
Mal pensado, ou sonhado sem pensar,
Vejo os meus dias nulos decorrer,
E o cansaço de nada me aumentar.

Perdura, sim, como uma mocidade
Que a si mesma se sobrevive, a esperança,
Mas a mesma esperança o tédio invade,
E a mesma falsa mocidade cansa.

Ténue passar das horas sem proveito,
Leve correr dos dias sem acção,
Como a quem com saúde jaz no leito
Ou quem sempre se atrasa sem razão.

Vadio sem andar, meu ser inerte
Contempla-me, que esqueço de querer,
E a tarde exterior seu tédio verte
Sobre quem nada fez e nada quer.

Inútil vida, posta a um canto e ida
Sem que alguém nela fosse, nau sem mar,
Obra solenemente por ser lida,
Ah, deixem-me sonhar sem esperar!

With nothing done and what's to do
scarcely thought out, or dreamt unthinking,
I see my idle days pass lingering
and empty languor in me grow.

Like youthfulness that still endures
past days of youth, my hope prevails,
but that same hope tedium assails,
and that false youthfulness now tires.

Frail bootless hours that lightly skate,
actionless days with subtle stealth,
as though I were abed in health
or, for no reason, always late.

Unmoving tramp, my self inert
watches me disregard my will
and outward evening's tedium spill
on one who does and wishes naught.

Useless life, set aside and gone
unmanned, a ship without a sea,
writing unread so solemnly,
oh, let me hopelessly dream on!

da *Mensagem*

Ulisses

O mito é o nada que é tudo.
O mesmo sol que abre os céus
É um mito brilhante e mudo —
O corpo morto de Deus,
Vivo e desnudo.

Este, que aqui aportou,
Foi por não ser existindo.
Sem existir nos bastou.
Por não ter vindo foi vindo
E nos criou.

Assim a lenda se escorre
A entrar na realidade,
E a fecundá-la decorre.
Em baixo, a vida, metade
De nada, morre.

from *Message*

Ulysses

The myth's the nothing that is everything.
The very sun that opes the heavens wide
is a myth mute and shimmering—
the lifeless corpse of God,
living and naked.

This one, who docked here, by nonbeing got
existence. Inexistent as he was,
for us he was enough. In not
coming, he came of us,
whom he created.

Into reality
thus does the legend trickle out
and, rendering it fertile, come to be.
Below, life, half of naught,
is suffocated.

D. João, Infante de Portugal

Não fui alguém. Minha alma estava estreita
Entre tão grandes almas minhas pares,
Inutilmente eleita,
Virgemmente parada;

Porque é do português, pai de amplos mares,
Querer, poder só isto:
O inteiro mar, ou a orla vã desfeita —
O todo, ou o seu nada.

John, Prince of Portugal

I was not any. My soul was too confined
among such great souls equal with my own—
bootlessly named,
maidenly quit;

for to the Portuguese, sire of the wide main,
belongs but this in will, in might:
the ocean whole, or ravaged empty strand—
the all, or none of it.

D. Sebastião, Rei de Portugal

Louco, sim, louco, porque quis grandeza
Qual a Sorte a não dá.
Não coube em mim minha certeza;
Por isso onde o areal está
Ficou meu ser que houve, não o que há.

Minha loucura, outros que me a tomem
Com o que nela ia.
Sem a loucura o que é o homem
Mais que a besta sadia,
Cadáver adiado que procria?

Sebastian, King of Portugal

Mad, aye, mad was I, for I wished for grandeur
such as Fate not gives,
too widely strove my candor;
wherefore upon the sand there
remained my self which was, not that which lives.

For my madness, let others take it on
with what it encased;
without his madness, what is man
but a clean beast,
a corpse deferred that breeds until deceased?

O Infante D. Henrique

Em seu trono entre o brilho das esferas,
Com seu manto de noite e solidão,
Tem aos pés o mar novo e as mortas eras —
O único imperador que tem, deveras,
O globo mundo em sua mão.

Prince Henry

Throned amid the brilliance of the spheres
in his nocturnal, solitary robe,
at his feet the new sea and perished years,
sits the one emperor who truly bears
within his grasp the globe.

O mostrengo

O mostrengo que está no fim do mar
Na noite de breu ergueu-se a voar;
À roda da nau voou três vezes
Voou três vezes a chiar,
E disse, «Quem é que ousou entrar
Nas minhas cavernas que não desvendo,
Meus tectos negros do fim do mundo?»
E o homem do leme disse, tremendo,
«El-Rei D. João Segundo!»

«De quem são as velas onde me roço?
De quem as quilhas que vejo e ouço?»
Disse o mostrengo, e rodou três vezes,
Três vezes rodou imundo e grosso,
«Quem vem poder o que só eu posso,
Que moro onde nunca ninguém me visse
E escorro os medos do mar sem fundo?»
E o homem do leme tremeu, e disse,
«El-Rei D. João Segundo!»

Três vezes do leme as mãos ergueu,
Três vezes ao leme as repreendeu,
E disse no fim de tremer três vezes,
«Aqui ao leme sou mais do que eu:
Sou um Povo que quer o mar que é teu;
E mais que o mostrengo, que me a alma teme
E roda nas trevas do fim do mundo,

The Monster

The monster that haunts the sea's end, one night,
rose up through the pitch-black darkness in flight;
about the ship it flew thrice round,
thrice round it flew as it screeched,
saying: *Who is the one so bold that has breached*
my cavern of shadows whereon none must look?
Who comes to the world's end unbeckoned?
Answered the helmsman, who trembled and shook:
King John the Second!

—*Whose are the sails I brush so near?*
Whose these keels I do see and hear?
demanded the monster, and whirled thrice round,
thrice round full foulsome it whirled as it cried:
Who enters where I alone may bide,
and, seen to none, every fright forth pour
that in all the all-deep may be reckoned?
Answered the trembling helmsman once more:
King John the Second!

Thrice from the helm his hands he raised,
thrice to the helm again replaced,
and said after trembling thrice up and down:
More than a helmsman am I at the helm:
a nation am I, that would have thy sea my realm;
and more than thee, monster, though swirling thou goest
in the dark at world's end, my soul dreads most

Manda a vontade, que me ata ao leme,
De El-Rei D. João Segundo!»

his will by whom I come beckoned:
the will, which holds me to my post,
of King John the Second!

Noite

A nau de um deles tinha-se perdido
No mar indefinido.
O segundo pediu licença ao Rei
De, na fé e na lei
Da descoberta ir em procura
Do irmão no mar sem fim e a névoa escura.

Tempo foi. Nem primeiro nem segundo
Volveu do fim profundo
Do mar ignoto à pátria por quem dera
O enigma que fizera.
Então o terceiro a El-Rei rogou
Licença de os buscar, e El-Rei negou.

*

Como a um cativo, o ouvem a passar
Os servos do solar.
E, quando o vêem, vêem a figura
Da febre e da amargura,
Com fixos olhos rasos de ânsia
Fitando a proibida azul distância.

*

Senhor, os dois irmãos do nosso Nome —
O Poder e o Renome —

Night

One of them drifted long, his ship and he
lost on the boundless sea.
The second got leave of the King
to go forth in faith, by his domain
over the sea, to discover his brother
upon the vast and dim and misty main.

Time went by. Not the first nor the other
back from the deep uncharted bourne
to that country made return
for whose sake he had yielded the riddle so posed.
Anon the third begged leave of the King
to seek them, and the King refused.

*

Like one held captive, bondmen of his hall
still hear his footsteps fall,
and when they see him, they behold a vision
of fever and of gall,
his staring eyeballs glazed with yearning fond,
gazing toward the forbidden blue beyond.

*

Lord, these two brothers of our name—
Power and Fame—

Ambos se foram pelo mar da idade
À tua eternidade;
E com eles de nós se foi
O que faz a alma poder ser de herói,
Queremos ir buscá-los, desta vil
Nossa prisão servil:
É a busca de quem somos, na distância
De nós; e, em febre de ânsia,
A Deus as mãos alçamos.

Mas Deus não dá licença que partamos.

both are gone out across the ancient sea
to thy eternity;
and with them is gone that part of us
that lets the soul a hero's spirit be.
We would go seek them, leaving this our villainous
and servile prison:
to find out who we are, at the farthest offing
from ourselves, we yearn; and in a fever-throe
we lift our hands to God.

But God will not give leave for us to go.

Gomes Leal

Sagra, sinistro, a alguns o astro baço.
Seus três anéis irreversíveis são
A desgraça, a tristeza, a solidão.
Oito luas fatais fitam no espaço.

Este, poeta, Apolo em seu regaço
A Saturno entregou. A plúmbea mão
Lhe ergueu ao alto o aflito coração,
E, erguido, o apertou, sangrando lasso.

Inúteis oito luas da loucura
Quando a cintura tríplice denota
Solidão, e desgraça, e amargura!

Mas da noite sem fim um rastro brota,
Vestígio de maligna formosura:
É a lua, além de Deus, álgida e ignota.

Gomes Leal

Some doth the dim star hallow to his gloom.
His triple rings, which nothing can reverse,
misfortune, woe, and solitude foredoom.
Beyond, eight fatal moons look on through space.

This one, a bard, Apollo's cradling arm
gave o'er to Saturn, who with hand of lead
lifted aloft that heart to sorrows born
and clenched it fast as languidly it bled.

Eight moons of madness all to no avail
when in their round the treble girdle-bands
betoken of misery, woe, and solitude!

Yet from the endless night breaks forth a trail,
the vestige of a baleful elegance:
unmapped and cold, the farthest moon from God.

O último sortilégio

«Já repeti o antigo encantamento,
E a grande Deusa aos olhos se negou.
Já repeti, nas pausas do amplo vento,
As orações cuja alma é um ser fecundo.
Nada me o abismo deu ou o céu mostrou.
Só o vento volta onde estou toda e só,
E tudo dorme no confuso mundo.

«Outrora meu condão fadava as sarças
E a minha evocação do solo erguia
Presenças concentradas das que esparsas
Dormem nas formas naturais das coisas.
Outrora a minha voz acontecia.
Fadas e elfos, se eu chamasse, via,
E as folhas da floresta eram lustrosas.

«Minha varinha, com que da vontade
Falava às existências essenciais,
Já não conhece a minha realidade.
Já, se o círculo traço, não há nada.
Murmura o vento alheio extintos ais,
E ao luar que sobe além dos matagais
Não sou mais do que os bosques ou a estrada.

«Já me falece o dom com que me amavam.
Já me não torno a forma e o fim da vida
A quantos que, buscando-os, me buscavam.

Her Last Enchantment

Once more have I intoned the ancient spell,
and the great goddess has refused my sight;
once more repeated in the wide wind's lulls
those prayers whose spirit is a fecund being.
The depths have yielded nothing, heaven nothing shown.
Only the wind returns where I stand whole, alone,
and all is sleeping in the puzzled world.

There was a time my magic charmed the briars,
and at my beckon, from the ground arose
such concentrated presences as sleep
dispersed within the natural forms of things.
There was a time my voice was an event revered.
Fairies and elves, if summoned by my call, appeared,
and the leaves of the forest came aglow.

My wand, wherewith so often of my will
I spoke to the primitive existences,
no longer knows of my reality.
Now when I trace my circle, nothing comes.
The wind, unheeding, murmurs at a lifeless hush,
and in the moonlight rising now above the brush
I am no greater than the wood or road.

My gift, which I was loved for, now I lack.
Now do I not become life's form and end
to those who, seeking for them, sought me of old.

Já, praia, o mar dos braços não me inunda.
Nem já me vejo ao sol saudado erguida,
Ou, em êxtase mágico perdida,
Ao luar, à boca da caverna funda.

«Já as sacras potências infernais,
Que, dormentes sem deuses nem destino,
À substância das coisas são iguais,
Não ouvem minha voz ou os nomes seus,
A música partiu-se do meu hino.
Já meu furor astral não é divino
Nem meu corpo pensado é já um deus.

«E as longínquas deidades do atro poço,
Que tantas vezes, pálida, evoquei
Com a raiva de amar em alvoroço,
Inevocadas hoje ante mim estão.
Como, sem que as amasse, eu as chamei,
Agora, que não amo, as tenho, e sei
Que meu vendido ser consumirão.

«Tu, porém, Sol, cujo ouro me foi presa,
Tu, Lua, cuja prata converti,
Se já não podeis dar-me essa beleza
Que tantas vezes tive por querer,
Ao menos meu ser findo dividi —
Meu ser essencial se perca em si,
Só meu corpo sem mim fique alma e ser!

A beach, the ocean's arms now whelm me not.
Myself no longer with the greeted sun I see
risen, nor raptured in a magic reverie
by moonlight, at the mouth of the deep cave.

No more do the infernal sacred powers,
which, dormant without gods or destinies,
are equal to the substances of things,
hearken my voice, nor answer their own names.
The music is departed from this hymn of mine.
My astral vehemence no longer is divine,
my body no more fancied as a God.

And the far deities of the black well
whom I full often, blanching, have evoked
with all the rage of a tumultuous love,
unbidden now before me stand about.
As then I called them forth, but did not love them, so
now that I do not love, I have them, and I know
that they are to consume my bargained self.

But thou, O Sun, whose gold has been my spoil,
thou, Moon, whose silver I have alchemized,
if ye no more can lend that beauteousness
which I so often had as I desired,
do ye at least but rend apart my finished self—
let my essential being be lost within itself;
my body abide without me, self and soul!

«Converta-me a minha última magia
Numa estátua de mim em corpo vivo!
Morra quem sou, mas quem me fiz e havia,
Anónima presença que se beija,
Carne do meu abstracto amor cativo,
Seja a morte de mim em que revivo;
E tal qual fui, não sendo nada, eu seja!»

Let the last of my magic render me
into a living statue of myself!
Die who I am, but who I did become,
who was, a nameless presence to be kissed,
the flesh of that abstract and captive love I lived,
be the death of me wherein I am to life revived,
and as I was, being nothing, let me be!

Iniciação

Não dormes sob os ciprestes,
Pois não há sono no mundo.
. . . .
O corpo é a sombra das vestes
Que encobrem teu ser profundo.

Vem a noite, que é a morte,
E a sombra acabou sem ser.
Vais na noite só recorte,
Igual a ti sem querer.

Mas na estalagem do Assombro
Tiram-te os Anjos a capa.
Segues sem capa no ombro,
Com o pouco que te tapa.

Então Arcanjos da Estrada
Despem-te e deixam-te nu.
Não tens vestes, não tens nada:
Tens só teu corpo, que és tu.

Por fim, na funda caverna,
Os Deuses despem-te mais.
Teu corpo cessa, alma externa,
Mas vês que são teus iguais.

. . . .

Initiation

You do not sleep 'neath the cypresses,
for there is no sleep in this world.
. . . .
Your body is the shadow of garments
that around your deep self are furled.

The night arrives, the night that is death,
and the shadow, selfless, expire.
You go through the night but a figure,
like you, but without desire.

But in the guesthouse of Wonder
the Angels take off your robe.
You go on with no robe on your shoulder,
with what little covering you have.

Then on the Highway Archangels
unclothe you and leave you bare.
You have no more garments, you have nothing:
your body is all that you are.

Last of all, in the deep cavern,
the Gods undress you too.
Your body is gone, the outward soul,
but you see that they are like you.

. . . .

A sombra das tuas vestes
Ficou entre nós na Sorte,
Não 'stás morto entre ciprestes.
. . . .
Neófito, não há morte.

The shadow of your garments
to us does Fate bequeath.
You are not dead 'mongst the cypresses.
. . . .
Neophyte, there is no death.

No túmulo de Christian Rosenkreutz

Não tínhamos ainda visto o cadáver de nosso Pai prudente e sábio. Por isso afastámos para um lado o altar. Então pudemos levantar uma chapa forte de metal amarelo, e ali estava um belo corpo célebre, inteiro e incorrupto..., e tinha na mão um pequeno livro em pergaminho, escrito a ouro, intitulado T., que é, depois da Bíblia, o nosso mais alto tesouro nem deve ser facilmente submetido à censura do mundo.

FAMA FRATERNITATIS ROSEÆ CRUCIS

I

QUANDO, DESPERTOS DESTE SONO, A VIDA,
Soubermos o que somos, e o que foi
Essa queda até Corpo, essa descida
Até à Noite que nos a Alma obstrui,

Conheceremos pois toda a escondida
Verdade do que é tudo que há ou flui?
Não: nem na Alma livre é conhecida...
Nem Deus, que nos criou, em Si a inclui.

Deus é o Homem de outro Deus maior:
Adão Supremo, também teve Queda;
Também, como foi nosso Criador,

Foi criado, e a Verdade lhe morreu...
De além o Abismo, 'Sp'rito Seu, Lha veda;
Aquém não a há no Mundo, Corpo Seu.

On the Tomb of Christian Rosenkreutz

We had not yet seen the corpse of our wise and sage Father. Therefore we drew the altar to one side. Then we were able to lift a strong sheet of yellow metal, and there lay a beautiful famous body, sound and uncorrupted... and in his hand was a little book in parchment, written in gold, entitled T., which is, after the Bible, our highest treasure and must not be easily submitted to the judgment of the world.

FAMA FRATERNITATIS ROSEÆ CRUCIS

I

WHEN WE AWAKEN FROM THIS SLEEP, OUR LIVES,
and learn of what we are, and of what was
that fall to Body, what was that descent
into the Night that bars from us the Soul,

will we then come to learn the hidden Truth
of what all things that flow or happen are?
No: not to Souls in freedom is it known...
Not God, who made us, holds it in Himself.

God is the Man to yet a greater God:
Adam Supreme, He also had his Fall;
and, just as He was our Creator, so

was he created, and to Him Truth died...
the Abyss, His Spirit, keeps it barred beyond;
it dwells not in the World, His Body, here.

II

MAS ANTES ERA O VERBO, AQUI PERDIDO
Quando a Infinita Luz, já apagada,
Do Caos, chão do Ser, foi levantada
Em Sombra, e o Verbo ausente escurecido.

Mas se a Alma sente a sua forma errada,
Em si, que é Sombra, vê enfim luzido
O Verbo deste Mundo, humano e ungido,
Rosa Perfeita, em Deus crucificada.

Então, senhores do limiar dos Céus,
Podemos ir buscar além de Deus
O Segredo do Mestre e o Bem profundo;

Não só de aqui, mas já de nós, despertos,
No sangue actual de Cristo enfim libertos
Do a Deus que morre a geração do Mundo.

II

But first there was the Word, here vanished when
the Light Unending, which has now gone out,
from Chaos, ground of Being, was upraised
in Shadow, and the absent Word bedimmed.

Yet if the Soul perceives its erring form,
then in itself, though Shadow, it sees gleam
the Word—anointed, human—of this World,
a Rose Unblemished, crucified in God.

Thereafter, lords upon the sill of Heaven,
may we seek farther, past the brink of God,
the Master's Secret and the deeper Good;

not only from the World, but from ourselves
awoken, freed in actual blood of Christ
from God, who dies the World's incipience.

III

Ah, mas aqui, onde irreais erramos,
Dormimos o que somos, e a verdade,
Inda que enfim em sonhos a vejamos,
Vemo-la, porque em sonho, em falsidade.

Sombras buscando corpos, se os achamos
Como sentir a sua realidade?
Com mãos de sombra, Sombras, que tocamos?
Nosso toque é ausência e vacuidade.

Quem desta Alma fechada nos liberta?
Sem ver, ouvimos para além da sala
De ser: mas como, aqui, a porta aberta?

....

Calmo na falsa morte a nós exposto,
O Livro ocluso contra o peito posto,
Nosso Pai Roseacruz conhece e cala.

III

AH, BUT IN THIS WORLD WHERE, UNREAL, WE ERR,
our being is a slumber, and the truth,
though yet in dreams we glimpse it by and by,
we see but with the falsehood of a dream.

Shadows in search of bodies, how, if once
we find them, will we sense that they are real?
With hands of shadow, what may Shadows touch?
Our touch is absence and vacuity.

Who from this Soul confined will make us free?
Though sightless, yet we hearken past the hall
of being: but how, here, to ope the door?

....

Calm in his seeming death before our view,
the Book sealed up and placed against his heart,
Our Father Rose-Cross knows and does not tell.

Liberdade

Ai que prazer
Não cumprir um dever,
Ter um livro para ler
E não o fazer!
Ler é maçada,
Estudar é nada.
O sol doira
Sem literatura.
O rio corre, bem ou mal,
Sem edição original.
E a brisa, essa,
De tão naturalmente matinal
Como tem tempo não tem pressa...

Livros são papéis pintados com tinta.
Estudar é uma coisa em que está indistinta
A distinção entre nada e coisa nenhuma.

Quanto é melhor, quando há bruma,
Esperar por D. Sebastião,
Quer venha ou não!

Grande é a poesia, a bondade e as danças...
Mas o melhor do mundo são as crianças,
Flores, música, o luar, e o sol, que peca
Só quando, em vez de criar, seca.

Liberty

What pleasure indeed
not to do what is needed,
to have a book to read
and not read it!
Reading's a bore,
study's a chore.
The sun still glitters,
unlearned in letters.
The river runs on, bettered or worsened,
without a first-edition version.
And the breeze, that faint flurry,
so naturally early,
has plenty of time and is in no hurry...

Books are bits of paper inked.
Study is something that makes indistinct
the distinction that lies between nothing and naught.

Much better, if in a fog you're caught,
to wait for King Sebastian,
whether he shows up or not!

Poetry, kindness, and dances are great...
but of all things children are better yet,
flowers, music, moonlight, and sunshine, which only goes wrong
when it makes things dry instead of strong.

O mais do que isto
É Jesus Cristo,
Que não sabia nada de finanças
Nem consta que tivesse biblioteca...

And the best of the best
is Jesus Christ,
who knew nothing of matters monetary
and as far as is known never kept a library…

TRANSLATIONS

by Fernando Pessoa

Edgar Allan Poe

O corvo

(Tradução de Fernando Pessoa, ritmicamente conforme com o original)

Numa meia-noite agreste, quando eu lia, lento e triste,
Vagos, curiosos tomos de ciências ancestrais,
E já quase adormecia, ouvi o que parecia
O som de alguém que batia levemente a meus umbrais.
«Uma visita», eu me disse, «está batendo a meus umbrais.
      É só isto, e nada mais».

Ah, que bem disso me lembro! Era no frio Dezembro,
E o fogo, morrendo negro, urdia sombras desiguais.
Como eu qu'ria a madrugada, toda a noite aos livros dada
Pra esquecer (em vão!) a amada, hoje entre hostes celestiais —
Essa cujo nome sabem as hostes celestiais,
      Mas sem nome aqui jamais!

Como, a tremer frio e frouxo, cada reposteiro roxo
Me incutia, urdia estranhos terrores nunca antes tais!
Mas, a mim mesmo infundindo força, eu ia repetindo,
«É uma visita pedindo entrada aqui em meus umbrais;
Uma visita tardia pede entrada em meus umbrais.
      É só isto, e nada mais».

E, mais forte num instante, já nem tardo ou hesitante,
«Senhor» eu disse, «ou senhora, decerto me desculpais;

Mas eu ia adormecendo, quando viestes batendo,
Tão levemente batendo, batendo por meus umbrais,
Que mal ouvi…» E abri largos, franqueando-os, meus umbrais.
     Noite, noite e nada mais.

A treva enorme fitando, fiquei perdido, receando,
Dúbio e tais sonhos sonhando que os ninguém sonhou iguais.
Mas a noite era infinita, a paz profunda e maldita,
E a única palavra dita foi um nome cheio de ais —
Eu o disse, o nome *dela*, e o eco disse os meus ais.
     Isto só e nada mais.

Para dentro então volvendo, toda a alma em mim ardendo,
Não tardou que ouvisse novo som batendo mais e mais.
«Por certo», disse eu, «aquela bulha é na minha janela.
Vamos ver o que está nela, e o que são estes sinais.
Meu coração se distraía pesquisando estes sinais.
     É o vento, e nada mais».

Abri então a vidraça, e eis que, com muita negaça,
Entrou grave e nobre um corvo dos bons tempos ancestrais.
Não fez nenhum cumprimento, não parou nem um momento,
Mas com ar solene e lento pousou sobre os meus umbrais,
Num alvo busto de Atena que há por sobre meus umbrais.
     Foi, pousou, e nada mais.

E esta ave estranha e escura fez sorrir minha amargura
Com o solene decoro de seus ares rituais.
«Tens o aspecto tosquiado», disse eu, «mas de nobre e ousado,
Ó velho corvo emigrado lá das trevas infernais!

Diz-me qual o teu nome lá nas trevas infernais».
    Disse o corvo, «Nunca mais».

Pasmei de ouvir este raro pássaro falar tão claro,
Inda que pouco sentido tivessem palavras tais.
Mas deve ser concedido que ninguém terá havido
Que uma ave tenha tido pousada nos seus umbrais,
Ave ou bicho sobre o busto que há por sobre seus umbrais,
    Com o nome «Nunca mais».

Mas o corvo, sobre o busto, nada mais dissera, augusto,
Que essa frase, qual se nela a alma lhe ficasse em ais.
Nem mais voz nem movimento fez, e eu, em meu pensamento
Perdido, murmurei lento, «Amigos, sonhos — mortais
Todos — todos já se foram. Amanhã também te vais».
    Disse o corvo, «Nunca mais».

A alma súbito movida por frase tão bem cabida,
«Por certo», disse eu, «são estas suas vozes usuais.
Aprendeu-as de algum dono, que a desgraça e o abandono
Seguiram até que o entono da alma se quebrou em ais,
E o bordão de desesp'rança de seu canto cheio de ais
    Era este «Nunca mais».

Mas, fazendo inda a ave escura sorrir a minha amargura,
Sentei-me defronte dela, do alvo busto e meus umbrais,
E, enterrado na cadeira, pensei de muita maneira
Que qu'ria esta ave agoureira dos maus tempos ancestrais,
Esta ave negra e agoureira dos maus tempos ancestrais,
    Com aquele «Nunca mais».

Comigo isto discorrendo, mas nem sílaba dizendo
À ave que na minha alma cravava os olhos fatais,
Isto e mais ia cismando, a cabeça reclinando
No veludo onde a luz punha vagas sombras desiguais,
Naquele veludo onde *ela*, entre as sombras desiguais,
      Reclinar-se-á nunca mais!

Fez-se então o ar mais denso, como cheio dum incenso
Que anjos dessem, cujos leves passos soam musicais.
«Maldito!» a mim disse, «deu-te Deus, por anjos concedeu-te
O esquecimento; valeu-te. Toma-o, esquece, com teus ais,
O nome da que não esqueces, e que faz esses teus ais!»
      Disse o corvo, «Nunca mais».

«Profeta», disse eu, «profeta — ou demónio ou ave preta! —,
Fosse diabo ou tempestade quem te trouxe a meus umbrais,
A este luto e este degredo, a esta noite e este segredo,
A esta casa de ânsia e medo, diz a esta alma a quem atrais
Se há um bálsamo longínquo para esta alma a quem atrais!»
      Disse o corvo, «Nunca mais».

«Profeta», disse eu, «profeta — ou demónio ou ave preta! —,
Pelo Deus ante quem ambos somos fracos e mortais,
Diz a esta alma entristecida se no Éden de outra vida
Verá essa hoje perdida entre hostes celestiais,
Essa cujo nome sabem as hostes celestiais!»
      Disse o corvo, «Nunca mais».

«Que esse grito nos aparte, ave ou diabo!», eu disse. «Parte!
Torna à noite e à tempestade! Torna às trevas infernais!
Não deixes pena que ateste a mentira que disseste!

Minha solidão me reste! Tira-te de meus umbrais!
Tira o vulto de meu peito e a sombra de meus umbrais!»
    Disse o corvo, «Nunca mais».

E o corvo, na noite infinda, está ainda, está ainda
No alvo busto de Atena que há por sobre os meus umbrais.
Seu olhar tem a medonha dor de um demónio que sonha,
E a luz lança-lhe a tristonha sombra no chão mais e mais.
E a minh'alma dessa sombra que no chão há mais e mais,
    Libertar-se-á... nunca mais!

Os poemas finais de Edgar Poe

(Tradução de Fernando Pessoa, ritmicamente conforme com o original)

Annabel Lee

Foi há muitos e muitos anos já,
    Num reino de ao pé do mar.
Como sabeis todos, vivia lá
    Aquela que eu soube amar;
E vivia sem outro pensamento
    Que amar-me e eu a adorar.

Eu era criança e ela era criança,
    Neste reino ao pé do mar;
Mas o nosso amor era mais que amor —
    O meu e o dela a amar;
Um amor que os anjos do céu vieram
    A ambos nós invejar.

E foi esta a razão por que, há muitos anos,
    Neste reino ao pé do mar,
Um vento saiu duma nuvem, gelando
    A linda que eu soube amar;
E o seu parente fidalgo veio
    De longe a me a tirar,
Para a fechar num sepulcro
    Neste reino ao pé do mar.

E os anjos, menos felizes no céu,
    Ainda a nos invejar…

Sim, foi essa a razão (como sabem todos,
    Neste reino ao pé do mar)
Que o vento saiu da nuvem de noite
    Gelando e matando a que eu soube amar.

Mas o nosso amor era mais do que o amor
    De muitos mais velhos a amar,
    De muitos de mais meditar,
E nem os anjos do céu lá em cima,
    Nem demónios debaixo do mar
Poderão separar a minha alma da alma
    Da linda que eu soube amar.

Porque os luares tristonhos só me trazem sonhos
    Da linda que eu soube amar;
E as estrelas nos ares só me lembram olhares
    Da linda que eu soube amar;
E assim 'stou deitado toda a noite ao lado
Do meu anjo, meu anjo, meu sonho e meu fado.
    No sepulcro ao pé do mar,
    Ao pé do murmúrio do mar.

Ulalume

O céu era lívido e frio,
      As folhas de um louro mortal,
      As folhas de um seco mortal;
Era noite no Outubro vazio
      No fim do meu ano fatal;
Era ao pé desse lago sombrio
      Na média região 'spectral —
Era perto do pego sombrio
      Na fria floresta 'spectral.

Aqui, por uma álea titânica,
      Ciprestea, errei com minha alma —
      Ciprestea, com Psiche, minha alma.
Eram dias de mente vulcânica
      Como o rio que quente se espalma —
      Como a lava que em rio se espalma,
Em fúria sulfúrea e vesânica
      Nas últimas terras sem calma —
Que geme com mágoa vesânica
      Nas terras extremas sem calma.

Cada um no falar fora frio,
      Mas na alma dum gelo mortal —
      Na alma dum dolo mortal,
Pois não demos plo Outubro vazio
      Nem pla noite do ano fatal —
      (Ah noite entre todas fatal!),

Nem notámos o lago sombrio
    (Que outrora já víramos tal),
Nem lembrámos o pego sombrio
    Nem a fria floresta 'spectral.

Mas a noite era já senescente
    E os astros sonhavam com dia —
    E os astros mostravam o dia,
Quando um baço luzir liquescente
    Ao fim do caminho surgia,
E da luz se formou um crescente
    Que com pontas distintas luzia —
O de Astarte subido crescente
    Com as pontas agudas luzia.

E eu disse, «Ela é lua em Verão,
    Num éter de amor a boiar;
    Vai num éter de ardor a boiar.
Viu que as lágrimas não poderão
    Nestas faces comidas secar,
E as estrelas passou do Leão
    O caminho do céu a mostrar —
    A paz que há nos céus a mostrar;
Veio aqui apesar do Leão
    Nos trazer o amor no olhar —
Através da caverna do Leão
    Com amor no seu lúcido olhar».

Mas Psiche, erguendo seu dedo,
    Disse, «Nada a esta estrela me dou —
    A seu pálido ser me não dou.

Não tardeis! Não tardeis! Vinde cedo
    Para longe, onde a alma está só».
Falou pálida e triste, e com medo
    Suas asas caíram no pó —
Soluçou angustiada, e com medo
    Suas plumas roçaram no pó,
    Tristemente roçaram no pó.

Respondi, «Isto é sonho somente.
    Que nos guie esta trémula luz!
    Que nos banhe esta nítida luz!
Seu sibílio 'splendor é fulgente
    De beleza e 'speranças a flux —
    Ah, no ar e na noite 'stá a flux!
Confiemos em sua luzente
    Visão que nos certos conduz!
Poderemos confiar na luzente
    Visão que nos certos conduz,
    Que na noite e no ar 'stá a flux.»

E a Psiche eu afago e a beijo,
    E a tiro da dor que a consume —
    Da dúvida e da dor que a consume,
E no fim do caminho nos vejo
    Que um sepulcro com porta resume...
    Um sepulcro lendário resume.
Perguntei, «Que legenda é que vejo
    Que esta lúgubre porta resume?»
E ela disse, «Ulalume! Ulalume!
    'Stá aqui tua amada Ulalume!»

E o meu ser ficou lívido e frio
  Como as folhas dum louro mortal —
  Como as folhas dum seco mortal,
E exclamei, «Era o Outubro vazio,
  E *esta* noite do ano fatal,
  Que aqui vim, aqui vim afinal,
Que aqui trouxe esse fardo final!
  Nesta noite de todas fatal
  Que demónio me trouxe afinal?
Ah, conheço este lago sombrio,
  Esta média região 'spectral!
Bem conheço este pego sombrio
  E esta fria floresta 'spectral!»

Aleister Crowley

Hino a Pã

Vibra do cio subtil da luz,
Meu homem e afã!
Vem turbulento da noite a flux
De Pã! Iô Pã!
Iô Pã! Iô Pã! Do mar de além
Vem da Sicília e da Arcádia vem!
Vem como Baco, com fauno e fera
E ninfa e sátiro à tua beira,
Num asno lácteo, do mar sem fim,
A mim, a mim!
Vem com Apolo, nupcial na brisa
(Pegureira e pitonisa),
Vem com Ártemis, leve e estranha,
E a coxa branca, Deus lindo, banha
Ao luar do bosque, em marmóreo monte,
Manhã malhada da âmbrea fonte!
Mergulha o roxo da prece ardente
No ádito rubro, no laço quente,
A alma que aterra em olhos de azul
O ver errar teu capricho exul
No bosque enredo, nos nós que espalma
A árvore viva que é espírito e alma
E corpo e mente — do mar sem fim
(Iô Pã! Iô Pã!),
Diabo ou deus, vem a mim, a mim!

Meu homem e afã!
Vem com trombeta estridente e fina
Pela colina!
Vem com tambor a rufar à beira
Da primavera!
Com frautas e avenas vem sem conto!
Não estou eu pronto?
Eu, que espero e me estorço e luto
Com ar sem ramos onde não nutro
Meu corpo, lasso do abraço em vão,
Áspide aguda, forte leão —
Vem, está vazia
Minha carne, fria
Do cio sozinho da demonia.
À espada corta o que ata e dói,
Ó Tudo-Cria, Tudo-Destrói!
Dá-me o sinal do Olho Aberto,
E da coxa áspera o toque erecto,
E a palavra do Louco e do Secreto,
Ó Pã! Iô Pã!
Iô Pã! Iô Pã Pã! Pã Pã! Pã,
Sou homem e afã:
Faz o teu querer sem vontade vã,
Deus grande! Meu Pã!
Iô Pã! Iô Pã! Despertei na dobra
Do aperto da cobra.
A águia rasga com garra e fauce;
Os deuses vão-se;
As feras vêm. Iô Pã! A matado,
Vou no corno levado
Do Unicornado.

Sou Pã! Iô Pã! Iô Pã Pã! Pã!
Sou teu, teu homem e teu afã,
Cabra das tuas, ouro, deus, clara
Carne em teu osso, flor na tua vara.
Com patas de aço os rochedos roço
De solstício severo a equinócio.
E raivo, e rasgo, e roussando fremo,
Sempiterno, mundo sem termo,
Homem, homúnculo, ménade, afã,
Na força de Pã.
Iô Pã! Iô Pã Pã! Pã! Iô Pã!

ALBERTO CAEIRO

de «O Guardador de Rebanhos»

V

HÁ METAFÍSICA BASTANTE EM NÃO PENSAR EM NADA.

O que penso eu do mundo?
Sei lá o que penso do mundo!
Se eu adoecesse pensaria nisso.

Que ideia tenho eu das coisas?
Que opinião tenho sobre as causas e os efeitos?
Que tenho eu meditado sobre Deus e a alma
E sobre a criação do mundo?
Não sei. Para mim pensar nisso é fechar os olhos
E não pensar. É correr as cortinas
Da minha janela (mas ela não tem cortinas).

O mistério das coisas? Sei lá o que é mistério!
O único mistério é haver quem pense no mistério.
Quem está ao sol e fecha os olhos,
Começa a não saber o que é o sol,
E a pensar muitas coisas cheias de calor.
Mas abre os olhos e vê o sol,
E já não pode pensar em nada,
Porque a luz do sol vale mais que os pensamentos
De todos os filósofos e de todos os poetas.
A luz do sol não sabe o que faz
E por isso não erra e é comum e boa.

from "The Keeper of Flocks"

V

There's plenty of metaphysics in not thinking about anything.

What do I think of the world?
How should I know what I think of the world?!
If I got sick I'd think about that.

What insight do I have about things?
What opinion do I have on causes and effects?
What are my reflections on God and the soul
and the creation of the world?
I don't know. For me, thinking about any of that would be closing my eyes
and not thinking. It'd be drawing the curtains
over my window (but my window doesn't have curtains).

The mystery of things? What do I know about any mystery?!
The only mystery is that anybody thinks about mystery.
Somebody out in the sunshine, who closes his eyes,
starts not knowing what the sun is,
and thinking a lot of warm thoughts.
But when he opens his eyes and see the sun,
then he can't think about anything anymore,
because the sun's light is more brilliant than the thoughts
of all the philosophers and all the poets.
Sunlight doesn't know what it's doing,
and so it doesn't make mistakes and it's ordinary and good.

Metafísica? Que metafísica têm aquelas árvores?
A de serem verdes e copadas e de terem ramos
E a de dar fruto na sua hora, o que não nos faz pensar,
A nós, que não sabemos dar por elas.
Mas que melhor metafísica que a delas,
Que é a de não saber para que vivem
Nem saber que o não sabem?

«Constituição íntima das coisas»...
«Sentido íntimo do universo»...
Tudo isto é falso, tudo isto não quer dizer nada.
É incrível que se possa pensar em coisas dessas.
É como pensar em razões e fins
Quando o começo da manhã está raiando, e pelos lados das árvores
Um vago ouro lustroso vai perdendo a escuridão.

Pensar no sentido íntimo das coisas
É acrescentado, como pensar na saúde
Ou levar um copo à água das fontes.

O único sentido íntimo das coisas
É elas não terem sentido íntimo nenhum.

Não acredito em Deus porque nunca o vi.
Se ele quisesse que eu acreditasse nele,
Sem dúvida que viria falar comigo
E entraria pela minha porta dentro
Dizendo-me, *Aqui estou!*

Metaphysics? What metaphysics do those trees have?
The metaphysics of being green and leafy and having branches
and of yielding fruit in their season, which doesn't make us think,
in fact, we don't even notice them.
But what better metaphysics than their metaphysics,
of not knowing what they're alive for,
or even knowing that they don't know?

"Inner constitution of things…"
"Inner meaning of the universe…"
That's all fake, that's all gibberish.
It's amazing that anyone can think about that kind of thing.
That's be like thinking about reasons and purposes
when the first morning light is just breaking, and all around the trees
a soft sheeny gold is brightening the darkness away.

Thinking about the inner meaning of things
is pointless, like thinking about your health
or taking a cup of water to the spring.

The only inner meaning of things
is that they have no inner meaning at all.

I don't believe in God because I've never seen him.
If he wanted me to believe in him,
I'm sure he'd come on over to talk to me
and waltz right through my door
telling me, *Here I am*!

(Isto é talvez ridículo aos ouvidos
De quem, por não saber o que é olhar para as coisas,
Não compreende quem fala delas
Com o modo de falar que reparar para elas ensina).

Mas se Deus é as flores e as árvores
E os montes e sol e o luar,
Então acredito nele,
Então acredito nele a toda a hora,
E a minha vida é toda uma oração e uma missa,
E uma comunhão com os olhos e pelos ouvidos.

Mas se Deus é as árvores e as flores
E os montes e o luar e o sol,
Para que lhe chamo eu Deus?
Chamo-lhe flores e árvores e montes e sol e luar;
Porque, se ele se fez, para eu o ver,
Sol e luar e flores e árvores e montes,
Se ele me aparece como sendo árvores e montes
E luar e sol e flores,
É que ele quer que eu o conheça
Como árvores e montes e flores e luar e sol.

E por isso eu obedeço-lhe,
(Que mais sei eu de Deus que Deus de si próprio?),
Obedeço-lhe a viver, espontaneamente,
Como quem abre os olhos e vê,
E chamo-lhe luar e sol e flores e árvores e montes,
E amo-o sem pensar nele,

(This might sound ridiculous
to somebody who, because he doesn't know what it's like to look at things,
can't understand a person talking about them
with the way of speaking you learn from noticing them.)

But if God is the flowers and the trees
and the hills and the moonlight and the sunshine,
then I believe in him,
then I believe in him all the time,
and my whole life is a prayer and a mass,
and a communion taken with my eyes and my ears.

But if God is the trees and the flowers
and the hills and the moonlight and the sunshine,
why should I call him God?
I call him flowers and trees and hills and sunshine and moonlight;
because, if in order for me to see him he made himself
be sunshine and moonlight and flowers and trees and hills,
if he appears to me as trees and hills
and moonlight and sunshine and flowers,
he must want me to know him
as trees and hills and flowers and moonlight and sunshine.

And so I obey him,
(what more do I know about God than God does?),
I obey him by living, spontaneously,
as someone who opens his eyes and sees,
and I call him moonlight and sunshine and flowers and trees and hills,
and I love him without thinking about him,

E penso-o vendo e ouvindo,
E ando com ele a toda a hora.

and I think of him by seeing and hearing,
and I walk with him all the time.

VIII

Num meio-dia de fim de primavera
Tive um sonho como uma fotografia.
Vi Jesus Cristo descer à terra.

Veio pela encosta de um monte
Tornado outra vez menino,
A correr e a rolar-se pela erva
E a arrancar flores para as deitar fora
E a rir de modo a ouvir-se de longe.

Tinha fugido do céu.
Era nosso de mais para fingir
De segunda pessoa da trindade.
No céu era tudo falso, tudo em desacordo
Com flores e árvores e pedras.
No céu tinha que estar sempre sério
E de vez em quando de se tornar outra vez homem
E subir para a cruz, e estar sempre a morrer
Com uma coroa toda à roda de espinhos
E os pés espetados por um prego com cabeça,
E até com um trapo à roda da cintura
Como os pretos nas ilustrações.
Nem sequer o deixavam ter pai e mãe
Como as outras crianças.
O seu pai era duas pessoas —
Um velho chamado José, que era carpinteiro,
E que não era pai dele;
E o outro pai era uma pomba estúpida,

VIII

ONE MIDDAY IN LATE SPRING
I had a dream like a photograph.
I saw Jesus Christ descend to the earth.

He came down the side of a hill
as a little boy again,
running and rolling around in the grass
and pulling up flowers to toss them back down
and laughing so you could hear from a long way off.

He had run away from heaven.
He was too much one of us to play along as
the second person in the trinity.
Everything in heaven was fake, all out of keeping
with flowers and trees and rocks.
Back in heaven he had to be always serious
and turn back into a man every so often
and ascend to the cross, and keep dying all over again
with a crown of thorns around his head
and nails stuck through his feet
and even a rag around his waist
like the black men in pictures.
They didn't even let him have a father and a mother
like other children.
His father was two people—
an old man called Joseph, who was a carpenter,
and wasn't actually his father;
and the other father was a fool dove,

A única pomba feia do mundo
Porque não era do mundo nem era pomba.
E a sua mãe não tinha amado antes de o ter.
Não era mulher: era uma mala
Em que ele tinha vindo do céu.
E queriam que ele, que só nascera da mãe,
E nunca tivera pai para amar com respeito,
Pregasse a bondade e a justiça!

Um dia que Deus estava a dormir
E o Espírito Santo andava a voar,
Ele foi à caixa dos milagres e roubou três.
Com o primeiro fez que ninguém soubesse que ele tinha fugido.
Com o segundo criou-se eternamente humano e menino.
Com o terceiro criou um Cristo eternamente na cruz
E deixou-o pregado na cruz que há no céu
E serve de modelo às outras.
Depois fugiu para o sol
E desceu pelo primeiro raio que apanhou.

Hoje vive na minha aldeia comigo.
É uma criança bonita de riso e natural.
Limpa o nariz ao braço direito,
Chapinha nas poças de água,
Colhe as flores e gosta delas e esquece-as.
Atira pedras aos burros,
Rouba a fruta dos pomares
E foge a chorar e a gritar dos cães.
E, porque sabe que elas não gostam
E que toda a gente acha graça,

the world's only ugly dove,
because it wasn't of the world and it wasn't a dove.
And his mother hadn't lain with a man before she had him.
She wasn't a woman: she was a travel bag
he had come from heaven in.
And they wanted him, who was only born from his mother
and had never had a father to love and respect,
to preach kindness and justice!

One day when God was asleep
and the Holy Spirit was out flying around,
he went to the miracle box and stole three miracles.
With the first one he made it so nobody would know he had run
away.
With the second one he made himself eternally human and childlike.
With the third he created a Christ eternally on the cross
and left him nailed up on the cross in heaven
that's used as a model for other crosses.
Then he escaped to the sun
and caught the first sunbeam down to earth.

Now he lives in my village with me.
He's a handsome child, goofy, natural.
He wipes his nose on his right arm,
splashes around in puddles,
picks flowers and likes them and forgets about them.
He throws rocks at the donkeys,
he steals fruit from the orchards,
and runs away crying and screaming from dogs.
And, because he knows they don't like it,

Corre atrás das raparigas
Que vão em rancho pelas estradas
Com as bilhas às cabeças
E levanta-lhes as saias.

A mim ensinou-me tudo.
Ensinou-me a olhar para as coisas.
Aponta-me todas as coisas que há nas flores.
Mostra-me como as pedras são engraçadas
Quando a gente as tem na mão
E olha devagar para elas.

Diz-me muito mal de Deus.
Diz que ele é um velho estúpido e doente,
Sempre a escarrar no chão
E a dizer indecências.
A Virgem Maria leva as tardes da eternidade a fazer meia.
E o Espírito Santo coça-se com o bico
E empoleira-se nas cadeiras e suja-as.
Tudo no céu é estúpido como a Igreja Católica.
Diz-me que Deus não percebe nada
Das coisas que criou —
«Se é que ele as criou, do que duvido» —.
«Ele diz, por exemplo, que os seres cantam a sua glória,
Mas os seres não cantam nada.
Se cantassem seriam cantores.
Os seres existem e mais nada,
E por isso se chamam seres».

he chases after the girls
that troop down the road together
with their buckets on their heads
and lifts up their skirts.

He's taught me everything I know.
He taught me how to look at things.
He points out all the things that are in flowers to me.
He shows me how nice rocks are
to hold in your hand
and look at slowly.

He speaks ill of God to me a lot.
He says he's a sick old fool,
always spitting on the ground
and saying nasty things.
The Virgin Mary spends the afternoons of eternity knitting socks.
And the Holy Spirit preens itself with its beak
and perches up on the chairs and gets them filthy.
Everybody in heaven is foolish like the Catholic Church.
He tells me God doesn't get
the things he created at all—
"If he even did create them, which I doubt."—
"Like he says that beings sing his praise,
but beings don't sing anything.
If they did they'd be singers.
Beings are just there and that's it,
that's why they're called beings."

E depois, cansado de dizer mal de Deus,
O Menino Jesus adormece nos meus braços
E eu levo-o ao colo para casa.

. . . .

Ele mora comigo na minha casa a meio do outeiro.
Ele é a Eterna Criança, o deus que faltava,
Ele é o humano que é natural,
Ele é o divino que sorri e que brinca.
E por isso é que eu sei com toda a certeza
Que ele é o Menino Jesus verdadeiro.

E a criança tão humana que é divina
É esta minha quotidiana vida de poeta,
E é porque ele anda sempre comigo que eu sou poeta sempre,
E que o meu mínimo olhar
Me enche de sensação,
E o mais pequeno som, seja do que for,
Parece falar comigo.

A Criança Nova que habita onde vivo
Dá-me uma mão a mim
E a outra a tudo que existe
E assim vamos os três pelo caminho que houver,
Saltando e cantando e rindo
E gozando o nosso segredo comum
Que é o de saber por toda a parte
Que não há mistério no mundo
E que tudo vale a pena.

And after he gets tired of ranting on about God,
the Boy Jesus falls asleep in my arms
and I carry him home.

. . . .

He lives with me in my house halfway up the hill.
He's the Eternal Child, the god who was missing,
He's the human who is natural,
He's the divine that smiles and plays.
And that's how I know beyond any doubt
that he's the real Boy Jesus.

And this child that is human he's divine
is my everyday poet's life,
and it's because he's always with me that I'm a poet always,
and that my tiniest glance
fills me with feeling,
and and the slightest sound, whatever it is,
seems to speak to me.

This New Child who resides where I live
holds out one hand to me
and the other to everything that exists,
and so the three of us go skipping and singing and laughing
along whatever our path may be,
enjoying our shared secret,
which is knowing that wherever we are
there is no mystery in the world
and everything is worthwhile.

A Criança Eterna acompanha-me sempre.
A direcção do meu olhar é o seu dedo apontando.
O meu ouvido atento alegremente a todos os sons
São as cócegas que ele me faz, brincando, nas orelhas.

Damo-nos tão bem um com o outro
Na companhia de tudo
Que nunca pensamos um no outro,
Mas vivemos juntos e dois
Com um acordo íntimo
Como a mão direita e a esquerda.

Ao anoitecer brincamos as cinco pedrinhas
No degrau da porta de casa,
Graves como convém a um deus e a um poeta,
E como se cada pedra
Fosse todo um universo
E fosse por isso um grande perigo para ela
Deixá-la cair no chão.

Depois eu conto-lhe histórias das coisas só dos homens
E ele sorri, porque tudo é incrível.
Ri dos reis e dos que não são reis,
E tem pena de ouvir falar das guerras,
E dos comércios, e dos navios
Que ficam fumo no ar dos altos mares.
Porque ele sabe que tudo isso falta àquela verdade
Que uma flor tem ao florescer
E que anda com a luz do sol

The Eternal Child is always with me.
The direction my eyes look is his finger pointing.
My ear listening gladly to every sound
is the way he tickles me playfully on the ears.

We get along so well with one another
in the company of everything
that we never even think about each other,
just live together as two
with an internal bond
like right hand and left.

After sundown we play jacks
out on the doorstep at home,
solemnly, as befits a god and a poet,
as if each jackstone
was a whole universe
and so it would be very dangerous
to drop it on the ground.

Afterwards I tell him stories about people stuff
and he smiles, because it's all amazing.
He laughs at kings and people who aren't kings,
and feels sorry when he hears about wars,
and trade, and ships
that vanish into smoke over the high seas.
Because he knows that all that lacks the truth
that a flower has when it blooms
and that travels with the sunlight

A variar os montes e os vales
E a fazer doer aos olhos os muros caiados.

Depois ele adormece e eu deito-o.
Levo-o ao colo para dentro de casa
E deito-o, despindo-o lentamente
E como seguindo um ritual muito limpo
E todo materno até ele estar nu.

Ele dorme dentro da minha alma
E às vezes acorda de noite
E brinca com os meus sonhos.
Vira uns de pernas para o ar,
Põe uns em cima dos outros
E bate as palmas sozinho
Sorrindo para o meu sono.

. . . .

Quando eu morrer, filhinho,
Seja eu a criança, o mais pequeno.
Pega-me tu ao colo
E leva-me para dentro da tua casa.
Despe o meu ser cansado e humano
E deita-me na tua cama.
E conta-me histórias, caso eu acorde,
Para eu tornar a adormecer.
E dá-me sonhos teus para eu brincar
Até que nasça qualquer dia
Que tu sabes qual é.

changing the hills and the valleys
and making it hurt your eyes to look at whitewashed walls.

Then he falls asleep, and I put him to bed.
I carry him inside
and lay him down, undressing him slowly,
like I'm following a very tidy,
maternal ritual, until he's bare.

He sleeps inside my soul
and sometimes he'll wake in the night
and play with my dreams.
He flips some of them upside down,
stands some on top of the others,
and claps his hands all to himself
while he smiles at my sleep.

. . . .

When I die, boy,
let me be the child, the little one.
You pick me up
and carry me inside your house.
Take off my tired human self
and lay me down on your bed.
And tell me stories, if I wake up,
to put me back to sleep.
And let me have your dreams to play with
until some day comes,
you'll know which one.

. . . .

Esta é a história do meu Menino Jesus.
Por que razão que se perceba
Não há-de ser ela mais verdadeira
Que tudo quanto os filósofos pensam
E tudo quanto as religiões ensinam?

. . . .

This is the story of my little Boy Jesus.
For what discernible reason
shouldn't it be more true
than anything the philosophers think
and all that the religions teach?

IX

SOU UM GUARDADOR DE REBANHOS.
O rebanho é os meus pensamentos
E os meus pensamentos são todos sensações.
Penso com os olhos e com os ouvidos
E com as mãos e os pés
E com o nariz e a boca.

Pensar uma flor é vê-la e cheirá-la
E comer um fruto é saber-lhe o sentido.

Por isso quando num dia de calor
Me sinto triste de gozá-lo tanto,
E me deito ao comprido na erva,
E fecho os olhos quentes,
Sinto todo o meu corpo deitado na realidade,
Sei a verdade e sou feliz.

IX

I AM A KEEPER OF FLOCKS.
My flock is my thoughts,
and my thoughts are all sensations.
I think with my eyes and my ears
and with my hands and feet
and my nose and my mouth.

Thinking about a flower is seeing it and smelling it,
and eating a fruit is knowing what it means.

So on a warm day
when I feel sad from enjoying the day so much,
and I lie out on the grass,
and close my warm eyes,
I feel my whole body laid out on reality,
I know the truth, and I am happy.

X

«OLÁ, GUARDADOR DE REBANHOS,
Aí à beira da estrada,
Que te diz o vento que passa?»

«Que é vento, e que passa,
E que já passou antes,
E que passará depois.
E a ti o que te diz?»

«Muita coisa mais do que isso.
Fala-me de muitas outras coisas.
De memórias e de saudades
E de coisas que nunca foram.»

«Nunca ouviste passar o vento.
O vento só fala do vento.
O que lhe ouviste foi mentira,
E a mentira está em ti.»

X

"Hello there, keeper of flocks,
over by the side of the road,
what does the wind blowing by say to you?"

"That it's wind, and that it's blowing by,
and that it's blown by before,
and that it'll blow by again.
What does it say to you?"

"Plenty else more than that.
It tells me about lots of things.
About memories and heartaches
and things that never were."

"You've never heard the wind blow.
The wind only tells about the wind.
What you heard was a lie,
and the lie is in you."

XX

O TEJO É MAIS BELO QUE O RIO QUE CORRE PELA MINHA ALDEIA,
Mas o Tejo não é mais belo que o rio que corre pela minha aldeia
Porque o Tejo não é o rio que corre pela minha aldeia.

O Tejo tem grandes navios
E navega nele ainda,
Para aqueles que vêem em tudo o que lá não está,
A memória das naus.

O Tejo desce de Espanha
E o Tejo entra no mar em Portugal.
Toda a gente sabe disso.
Mas poucos sabem qual é o rio da minha aldeia
E para onde ele vai
E donde ele vem.
E por isso, porque pertence a menos gente,
É mais livre e maior o rio da minha aldeia.

Pelo Tejo vai-se para o mundo.
Para além do Tejo há a América
E a fortuna daqueles que a encontram.
Ninguém nunca pensou no que há para além
Do rio da minha aldeia.

O rio da minha aldeia não faz pensar em nada.
Quem está ao pé dele está só ao pé dele.

XX

THE TAGUS IS PRETTIER THAN THE RIVER THAT RUNS THROUGH MY VILLAGE,
but the Tagus is not prettier than the river that runs through my village,
because the Tagus is not the river that runs through my village.

The Tagus has big ships on it,
and also sailing on it,
for those who see in everything what isn't there,
are the memories of ships.

The Tagus flows down from Spain,
and the Tagus enters the sea in Portugal.
Everybody knows that.
But not many people know the river in my village
and where it goes
and where it comes from.
And so, because it belongs to fewer people,
the river in my village it is freer and bigger.

The Tagus takes you out into the world.
Past the end of the Tagus is America
and fortune for those who can find it.
Nobody's ever thought about what's past the end
of the river in my village.

The river in my village doesn't make you think about anything.
When you stand beside it you just stand beside it.

XXVIII

Li hoje quase duas páginas
Do livro dum poeta místico,
E ri como quem tem chorado muito.

Os poetas místicos são filósofos doentes,
E os filósofos são homens doidos.

Porque os poetas místicos dizem que as flores sentem
E dizem que as pedras têm alma
E que os rios têm êxtases ao luar.

Mas as flores, se sentissem, não eram flores,
Eram gente;
E se as pedras tivessem alma, eram coisas vivas, não eram pedras;
E se os rios tivessem êxtases ao luar,
Os rios seriam homens doentes.

É preciso não saber o que são flores e pedras e rios
Para falar dos sentimentos deles.
Falar da alma das pedras, das flores, dos rios,
É falar de si próprio e dos seus falsos pensamentos.
Graças a Deus que as pedras são só pedras,
E que os rios não são senão rios,
E que as flores são apenas flores.

Por mim, escrevo a prosa dos meus versos
E fico contente,

XXVIII

TODAY I READ ALMOST TWO PAGES
of a book by a mystic poet,
and I laughed like I'd been crying a long time.

The mystic poets are sick philosophers,
and philosophers are deranged men.

Because the mystic poets say that flowers have feelings,
and they say rocks have souls
and that rivers have moonlight raptures.

But if flowers had feelings, they wouldn't be flowers,
they'd be people;
and if rocks had souls, they would be living things, not rocks;
and if rivers went into raptures in the moonlight,
the rivers would be unhealthy people.

You'd have to not know what flowers and rocks and rivers are
to talk about their feelings.
Talking about the souls of rocks, of flowers, of rivers,
is just talking about yourself and your own made-up thoughts.
Thank God rocks are only rocks,
and rivers are nothing but rivers,
and flowers are just flowers.

Me, I write out the prose of my verses
and I'm content,

Porque sei que compreendo a Natureza por fora;
E não a compreendo por dentro
Porque a Natureza não tem dentro;
Senão não era a Natureza.

because I know that I understand Nature on the outside;
and I don't understand Nature on the inside
because Nature doesn't have an inside;
otherwise it wouldn't be Nature.

XXXII

Ontem à tarde um homem das cidades
Falava à porta da estalagem.
Falava comigo também.
Falava da justiça e da luta para haver justiça
E dos operários que sofrem,
E do trabalho constante, e dos que têm fome,
E dos ricos, que só têm costas para isso.

E, olhando para mim, viu-me lágrimas nos olhos
E sorriu com agrado, julgando que eu sentia
O ódio que ele sentia, e a compaixão
Que ele dizia que sentia.

(Mas eu mal o estava ouvindo.
Que me importam a mim os homens
E o que sofrem ou supõem que sofrem?
Sejam como eu — não sofrerão.
Todo o mal do mundo vem de nos importarmos uns com os outros,
Quer para fazer bem, quer para fazer mal.
A nossa alma e o céu e a terra bastam-nos.
Querer mais é perder isto, e ser infeliz.)

Eu no que estava pensando
Quando o amigo de gente falava
(E isso me comoveu até às lágrimas),
Era em como o murmúrio longínquo dos chocalhos
A esse entardecer
Não parecia os sinos duma capela pequenina

XXXII

Yesterday afternoon a city man
was talking outside the inn.
He was talking to me, too.
He talked about justice and the fight for justice
and the suffering workers,
and the constant toil, and the people going hungry,
and the rich, who keep their backs turned to all that.

And as he looked at me he saw tears in my eyes
and he smiled a satisfied smile, believing that I felt
the hatred he felt, and the compassion
that he said he felt.

(But I was barely listening.
What do I care about people
and what they suffer or suppose they suffer?
Let them be like me—they won't suffer.
All the evil in the world comes from folks caring about one another,
whether to do each other good or do wrong.
Our souls and the sky and the earth are all we need.
Wanting more means losing that, and being unhappy.)

What I was thinking about
when that friend of people was talking
(and what moved me to tears)
was how the faraway tinkling of the sheep-bells
that evening
did not sound like the worship-bells of a little chapel

A que fossem à missa as flores e os regatos
E as almas simples como a minha.

(Louvado seja Deus que não sou bom,
E tenho o egoísmo natural das flores
E dos rios que seguem o seu caminho
Preocupados sem o saber
Só com o florir e ir correndo.
É essa a única missão no mundo,
Essa — existir claramente,
E saber fazê-lo sem pensar nisso.)

E o homem calara-se, olhando o poente.
Mas que tem com o poente quem odeia e ama?

where flowers and streams
and simple souls like mine went in to mass.

(Praise be to God that I'm not good,
and have the natural selfishness of the flowers
and the rivers that run on along,
concerned, and not even knowing it,
with nothing but blooming and running on.
That is ours only mission in the world—
to exist plainly,
and be able to do so without thinking about it.)

And the man got quiet as he watched the sun set.
But what's in a sunset for someone who hates and loves?

XXXIX

O mistério das coisas, onde está ele?
Onde está ele que não aparece
Pelo menos a mostrar-nos que é mistério?

Que sabe o rio disso e que sabe a árvore?
E eu, que não sou mais do que eles, que sei disso?
Sempre que olho para as coisas e penso no que os homens pensam delas,
Rio como um regato que soa fresco numa pedra.

Porque o único sentido oculto das coisas
É elas não terem sentido oculto nenhum.
É mais estranho do que todas as estranhezas
E do que os sonhos de todos os poetas
E os pensamentos de todos os filósofos,
Que as coisas sejam realmente o que parecem ser
E não haja nada que compreender.

Sim, eis o que os meus sentidos aprenderam sozinhos: —
As coisas não têm significação: têm existência.
As coisas são o único sentido oculto das coisas.

XXXIX

THE MYSTERY OF THINGS, WHERE IS IT?
Where is it, never showing itself
even to let us see that it's a mystery?

What does the river know about that, or the tree?
And me, as I'm no more than they are, what do I know about it?
Every time I look at things and think about what folks think of them,
I laugh like a cool stream babbling over a rock.

Because the only hidden meaning of things
is that they have no hidden meaning at all.
This is more strange than any wonder,
stranger than the dreams of all the poets
and the thoughts of all the philosophers,
that things should really be what they appear
and there be nothing to understand.

Yes, this is what my senses have learned on their own:—
things don't have meaning: they have existence.
Things are the only hidden meaning of things.

XLVI

Deste modo ou daquele modo,
Conforme calha ou não calha,
Podendo às vezes dizer o que penso,
E outras vezes dizendo-o mal e com misturas,
Vou escrevendo os meus versos sem querer,
Como se escrever não fosse uma coisa feita de gestos,
Como se escrever fosse uma coisa que me acontecesse
Como dar-me o sol de fora.

Procuro dizer o que sinto
Sem pensar em que o sinto.
Procuro encostar as palavras à ideia
E não precisar dum corredor
Do pensamento para as palavras.

Nem sempre consigo sentir o que sei que devo sentir.
O meu pensamento só muito devagar atravessa o rio a nado
Porque lhe pesa o fato que os homens o fizeram usar.

Procuro despir-me do que aprendi,
Procuro esquecer-me do modo de lembrar que me ensinaram,
E raspar a tinta com que me pintaram os sentidos,
Desencaixotar as minhas emoções verdadeiras,
Desembrulhar-me e ser eu, não Alberto Caeiro,
Mas um animal humano que a Natureza produziu.

E assim escrevo, querendo sentir a Natureza, nem sequer como um homem,
Mas como quem sente a Natureza, e mais nada.

XLVI

THIS WAY OR THAT WAY,
as it happens or as it doesn't,
sometimes able to say what I'm thinking,
other times saying it wrong and jumbled,
I write out my verses involuntarily,
as if writing were not something done with gestures,
as if it were something happening to me
like the sunlight hitting me from outside.

I try to say what I feel
without thinking about feeling it,
try to lean the words up on the idea
and not need a corridor
from the thought to the words.

I don't always manage to feel what I know I ought to feel.
My thought has to swim very slowly to get across the river
because the suit people have put it in sits heavy on it.

I try to strip off what I've learned,
try to forget the way of recalling that I was taught,
and scrape away the paint they colored my senses with,
unpack my true emotions,
unwrap myself and be me, not Alberto Caeiro,
but a human animal that Nature created.

And that's how I write, trying to feel Nature, not even as a man,
but as someone who feels Nature, and nothing else.

E assim escrevo, ora bem, ora mal,
Ora acertando com o que quero dizer, ora errando,
Caindo aqui, levantando-me acolá,
Mas indo sempre no meu caminho como um cego teimoso.

Ainda assim, sou alguém.
Sou o Descobridor da Natureza.
Sou o Argonauta das sensações verdadeiras.
Trago ao Universo um novo Universo
Porque trago ao Universo ele próprio.

Isto sinto e isto escrevo
Perfeitamente sabedor e sem que não veja
Que são cinco horas do amanhecer
E que o sol, que ainda não mostrou a cabeça
Por cima do muro do horizonte,
Ainda assim já se lhe vêem as pontas dos dedos
Agarrando o cimo do muro
Do horizonte cheio de montes baixos.

And that's how I write, sometimes well, sometimes badly,
sometimes getting at what I want to say, other times missing,
stumbling here, picking myself back up over there,
but always making my way along like a stubborn blind man.

Nevertheless, I'm somebody.
I'm the Discoverer of Nature.
I'm the Argonaut of true sensations.
I bring a new Universe to the Universe,
because I bring the Universe to itself.

I feel this and I write this
knowing perfectly well and not without seeing
that it's five o'clock in the morning
and that the sun, although it hasn't reared it's head yet
over the wall of the horizon,
is already showing its fingertips
holding on to the top of the wall
of the horizon curved with rolling hills.

XLVIII

Da mais alta janela da minha casa
Com um lenço branco digo adeus
Aos meus versos que partem para a humanidade.

E não estou alegre nem triste.
Esse é o destino dos versos.
Escrevi-os e devo mostrá-los a todos
Porque não posso fazer o contrário
Como a flor não pode esconder a cor,
Nem o rio esconder que corre,
Nem a árvore esconder que dá fruto.

Ei-los que vão já longe como que na diligência
E eu sem querer sinto pena
Como uma dor no corpo.

Quem sabe quem os lerá?
Quem sabe a que mãos irão?

Flor, colheu-me o meu destino para os olhos.
Árvore, arrancaram-me os frutos para as bocas.
Rio, o destino da minha água era não ficar em mim.
Submeto-me e sinto-me quase alegre,
Quase alegre como quem se cansa de estar triste.

Ide, ide de mim!
Passa a árvore e fica dispersa pela Natureza.

XLVIII

FROM THE HIGHEST WINDOW IN MY HOUSE
with a white handkerchief I bid farewell
to my verses as they go off to humanity.

And I'm not happy or sad.
This is my verses' fate.
I wrote them, and I must show them to everyone
because I can't do otherwise,
just like the flower can't hide its color,
or the river hide its running,
or the tree hide that it bears fruit.

Off they go now, already far, like they're traveling by stagecoach,
and I can't help feeling sorry about it,
like a pain in my body.

Who knows who will read them?
Who knows what hands they'll wind up in?

A flower, I was plucked by my fate for eyes.
A tree, my fruits were picked for mouths.
A river, my water was destined to leave me.
I submit and feel almost happy,
almost happy like someone tired of being sad.

Go on, go on away from me!
The tree dies and is scattered by Nature.

Murcha a flor e o seu pó dura sempre.
Corre o rio e entra no mar e a sua água é sempre a que foi sua.

Passo e fico, como o Universo.

The flower withers and the dust of it lasts forever.
The river flows into the sea and its water is it own.

I pass on and I remain, like the Universe.

XLIX

Meto-me para dentro, e fecho a janela.
Trazem o candeeiro e dão as boas noites,
E a minha voz contente dá as boas-noites.
Oxalá a minha vida seja sempre isto:
O dia cheio de sol, ou suave de chuva,
Ou tempestuoso como se acabasse o mundo,
A tarde suave e os ranchos que passam
Fitados com interesse da janela,
O último olhar amigo dado ao sossego das árvores,
E depois, fechada a janela, o candeeiro aceso,
Sem ler nada, nem pensar em nada, nem dormir,
Sentir a vida correr por mim como um rio por seu leito,
E lá fora um grande silêncio como um deus que dorme.

XLIX

I COME INSIDE AND SHUT THE WINDOW.
I'm brought my lamp and told good night,
and my contented voice says good night.
May my life be always this:
the day filled with sunshine, or soft with rain,
or stormy like the world is ending,
the gentle evening and the groups of people passing by
looking curiously in my window,
the one last friendly glance at the quiet in the trees,
and then, the window closed, the lamp lighted,
not reading anything, not thinking about anything, not sleeping,
feeling the life run through me like a river through its bed,
and outside a great silence like a sleeping god.

O penúltimo poema

Também sei fazer conjecturas.
Há em cada coisa aquilo que ela é que a anima.
Na planta está por fora e é uma ninfa pequena.
No animal é um ser interior longínquo.
No homem é a alma que vive com ele e é já ele.
Nos deuses tem o mesmo tamanho
E o mesmo espaço que o corpo
E é a mesma coisa que o corpo.
Por isso se diz que os deuses nunca morrem.
Por isso os deuses não têm corpo e alma
Mas só corpo e são perfeitos.
O corpo é que lhes é alma
E têm a consciência na própria carne divina.

The Penultimate Poem

I can make conjectures, too.
There is in each thing what that thing is, what gives it life.
In a plant it's situated on the outside as a little nymph.
In an animal it's a distant inward self.
In a man it's his soul that lives with him and is him.
In gods it's the same size
and occupies the same space as their bodies,
and is the same thing as their bodies.
That's why people say the gods never die.
That's why the gods don't have body and soul
but just a body and they're perfect.
For them, their body is their soul,
and their consciousness is in their godly flesh.

dos «Poemas Inconjuntos»

DIZES-ME: TU ÉS MAIS ALGUMA COISA
Que uma pedra ou uma planta.
Dizes-me: sentes, pensas e sabes
Que pensas e sentes.
Então as pedras escrevem versos?
Então as plantas têm ideias sobre o mundo?

Sim: há diferença.
Mas não é a diferença que encontras;
Porque o ter consciência não me obriga a ter teorias sobre as coisas:
Só me obriga a ser consciente.

Se sou mais que uma pedra ou uma planta? Não sei.
Sou diferente. Não sei o que é mais ou menos.

Ter consciência é mais que ter cor?
Pode ser e pode não ser.
Sei que é diferente apenas.
Ninguém pode provar que é mais que só diferente.

Sei que a pedra é a real, e que a planta existe.
Sei isto porque elas existem.
Sei isto porque os meus sentidos mo mostram.
Sei que sou real também.
Sei isto porque os meus sentidos mo mostram,

from "Unconnected Poems"

You say to me: you're something more
than a rock or a plant.
You say to me: you feel, you think, and you're aware
that you feel and think.
I mean, do rocks write poetry?
Do plants have thoughts about the world?

Yes, there's a difference.
But it's not the difference you think;
because having a consciousness doesn't mean I must have theories
about things;
it only means I must be conscious.

Am I more than a rock or a plant? I don't know.
I'm different. I don't know what's more or less.

Is having a consciousness more than having a color?
Maybe it is and maybe it isn't.
I just know it's different.
Nobody can prove that it's more than just different.

I know that a rock is real, and that a plant exists.
I know it because they exist.
I know it because my senses show it to me.
I know that I'm real, too.
I know it because my senses show it to me,

Embora com menos clareza que me mostram a pedra e a planta.
Não sei mais nada.

Sim, escrevo versos, e a pedra não escreve versos.
Sim, faço ideias sobre o mundo, e a planta nenhumas.
Mas é que as pedras não são poetas, são pedras;
E as plantas são plantas só, e não pensadores.
Tanto posso dizer que sou superior a elas por isto,
Como que sou inferior.
Mas não digo isso: digo da pedra, «é uma pedra»,
Digo da planta, «é uma planta»,
Digo de mim, «sou eu».
E não digo mais nada. Que mais há a dizer?

although not as clearly as they show me the rock and the plant.
I don't know any more than that.

Yes, I do write poetry, and the rock doesn't.
Yes, I do have thoughts about the world, and the plant doesn't have any.
But that's because rocks aren't poets, they're rocks;
and plants are only plants, not thinkers.
I could just as well say I'm greater than them on that account,
or that I'm lesser.
But I don't say either one; I say about the rock, "it's a rock,"
I say about the plant, "it's a plant,"
I say about myself, "I'm myself."
And that's all I say. What more is there to say?

A ESPANTOSA REALIDADE DAS COISAS
É a minha descoberta de todos os dias.
Cada coisa é o que é,
E é difícil explicar a alguém quanto isso me alegra,
E quanto isso me basta.

Basta existir para se ser completo.

Tenho escrito bastantes poemas.
Hei-de escrever muitos mais, naturalmente.
Cada poema meu diz isto,
E todos os meus poemas são diferentes,
Porque cada coisa que há é uma maneira de dizer isto.

Às vezes ponho-me a olhar para uma pedra.
Não me ponho a pensar se ela sente.
Não me perco a chamar-lhe minha irmã.
Mas gosto dela por ela ser uma pedra,
Gosto dela porque ela não sente nada,
Gosto dela porque ela não tem parentesco nenhum comigo.

Outras vezes oiço passar o vento,
E acho que só para ouvir passar o vento vale a pena ter nascido.

Eu não sei o que é que os outros pensarão lendo isto;
Mas acho que isto deve estar bem porque o penso sem esforço,
Nem ideia de outras pessoas a ouvir-me pensar;
Porque o penso sem pensamentos,
Porque o digo como as minhas palavras o dizem.

THE ASTONISHING REALITY OF THINGS
is what I discover every day.
Each thing is what it is,
and it's hard to explain to someone how happy that makes me,
and how it's everything I need.

Existing is all it takes to be complete.

I've written a number of poems.
I'll surely write many more.
Each of my poems says this,
and all of my poems are different,
because each thing that is is a different way of saying it.

Sometimes I'll be looking at a rock.
I won't start wondering whether it can feel.
I won't get carried away calling it my sibling.
But I like it for being a rock,
I like it for not feeling a thing,
I like it for being no kin to me at all.

Other times I'll hear the wind blow by,
and I'll reckon it was worth being born just to hear the wind blow.

I don't know what others will think when they read this;
but I reckon it must be okay, because I think of it without any effort
or thoughts about other people hearing me think;
because I think of it without thoughts,
because I say it the way my words tell it.

Uma vez chamaram-me poeta materialista,
E eu admirei-me, porque não julgava
Que se me pudesse chamar qualquer coisa.
Eu nem sequer sou poeta: vejo.
Se o que escrevo tem valor, não sou eu que o tenho:
O valor está ali, nos meus versos.
Tudo isso é absolutamente independente da minha vontade.

Once I was called a materialist poet,
and I was surprised, because I didn't believe
I could be called something at all.
I'm not even a poet: I see.
If what I write has any worth, it doesn't belong to me:
the worth is in there in my verses.
It's all completely independent of my will.

Se eu morrer novo,
Sem poder publicar livro nenhum,
Sem ver a cara que têm os meus versos em letra impressa,
Peço que, se se quiserem ralar por minha causa,
Que não se ralem.
Se assim aconteceu, assim está certo.

Mesmo que os meus versos nunca sejam impressos,
Eles lá terão a sua beleza, se forem belos.
Mas eles não podem ser belos e ficar por imprimir,
Porque as raízes podem estar debaixo da terra
Mas as flores florescem ao ar livre e à vista.
Tem que ser assim por força. Nada o pode impedir.

Se eu morrer muito novo, oiçam isto:
Nunca fui senão uma criança que brincava.
Fui gentio como o sol e a água,
De uma religião universal que só os homens não têm.
Fui feliz porque não pedi coisa nenhuma,
Nem procurei achar nada,
Nem achei que houvesse mais explicação
Que a palavra explicação não ter sentido nenhum.

Não desejei senão estar ao sol ou à chuva —
Ao sol quando havia sol
E à chuva quando estava chovendo
(E nunca a outra coisa),
Sentir calor e frio e vento.
E não ir mais longe.

IF I DIE YOUNG,
before I'm able to get a book published,
before I ever see how my verses look in print,
I ask, if you feel like getting upset over me,
that you don't get upset.
If it's the way it happened, it's the way it ought to be.

Even if my verses are never printed,
they'll still have their beauty, if they're beautiful.
But they can't be beautiful and stay unprinted,
because the roots may be underground
but the flowers bloom in the open air and in plain view.
That's the way it has to be. No one can stop it.

If I die quite young, hear this:
I was only ever a child at play.
I was heathen like the sun and the water,
following a universal religion only humans lack.
I was happy because I never asked for anything,
never tried to find anything,
never reckoned there was any further explanation
than the word explanation being meaningless.

All I ever wished for was to be out in the sun or the rain—
in the sunshine when it was sunny
and in the rain when it was raining
(and never the other one),
feeling the warmth and the cool and the wind.
And not to go any further than that.

Uma vez amei, julguei que me amariam,
Mas não fui amado.
Não fui amado pela única grande razão —
Porque não tinha que ser.

Consolei-me voltando ao sol e à chuva,
E sentando-me outra vez à porta de casa.
Os campos, afinal, não são tão verdes para os que são amados
Como para os que o não são.
Sentir é estar distraído.

I loved once, believed I'd be loved back,
but I was unloved.
I was unloved for the one great reason—
because it wasn't meant to be.

I consoled myself by going back to the sunshine and the rain,
and sitting back down outside the door to my house.
The fields, after all, aren't as green to those who are loved
as to those who are not.
Feeling is being distracted.

Se, depois de eu morrer, quiserem escrever a minha biografia,
Não há nada mais simples.
Tem só duas datas — a da minha nascença e a da minha morte.
Entre uma e outra coisa todos os dias são meus.

Sou fácil de definir.
Vi como um danado.
Amei as coisas sem sentimentalidade nenhuma.
Nunca tive um desejo que não pudesse realizar, porque nunca ceguei.
Mesmo ouvir nunca foi para mim senão um acompanhamento de
ver.
Compreendi que as coisas são reais e todas diferentes umas das
outras;
Compreendi isto com os olhos, nunca com o pensamento.
Compreender isto com o pensamento seria achá-las todas iguais.

Um dia deu-me o sono como a qualquer criança.
Fechei os olhos e dormi.
Além disso, fui o único poeta da Natureza.

IF, AFTER I DIE, YOU WANT TO WRITE MY BIOGRAPHY
nothing could be simpler.
It only has two dates—my birth and my death.
Every day between those two belongs to me.

I'm easy to define.
I saw like hell.
I loved things unsentimentally.
I never had a wish I couldn't fulfill, because I never went blind.
Even hearing for me was always just an accompaniment to seeing.
I understood that things are real and are all different from each other;
I understood this with my eyes, never with my mind.
Understanding it with my mind would have been reckoning they
                                                    were all the same.

One day I got sleepy like any child does.
I closed my eyes and went to sleep.
Other than that, I was the only Nature poet.

RICARDO
REIS

Odes
LIVRO PRIMEIRO

I

SEGURO ASSENTO NA COLUNA FIRME
  Dos versos em que fico,
Nem temo o influxo inúmero futuro
  Dos tempos e do olvido;
Que a mente, quando, fixa, em si contempla
  Os reflexos do mundo,
Deles se plasma torna, e à arte o mundo
  Cria, que não a mente.
Assim na placa o externo instante grava
  Seu ser, durando nela.

Odes

THE FIRST BOOK

I

Secure I sit upon the sturdy column
  of verses where I bide,
nor fear the future numberless influx
  of time's oblivion;
for when the steady mind within itself
  beholds the world's reflections,
their plasma it becomes; and art, the world—
  and not the mind—creates.
Thus on the slab the outward instant carves
  its self, to last thereon.

II

As rosas amo dos jardins de Adónis,
Essas vólucres amo, Lídia, rosas,
    Que em o dia em que nascem,
    Em esse dia morrem.
A luz para elas é eterna, porque
Nascem nascido já o sol, e acabam
    Antes que Apolo deixe
    O seu curso visível.
Assim façamos nossa vida *um dia*,
Inscientes, Lídia, voluntariamente
    Que há noite antes e após
    O pouco que duramos.

II

I LOVE THE ROSES OF ADONIS' GARDEN,
those brief-lived roses, Lydia, I love,
  that on the day they are born,
  upon that same day die.
Light is to them eternal, for they rise
when once the sun is risen, and fade away
  before Apollo leaves
  his observable course.
So let us make our life a single day,
unwitting, Lydia, full willingly,
  that night goes 'fore and after
  the little we endure.

VII

PONHO NA ALTIVA MENTE O FIXO ESFORÇO
    Da altura, e à sorte deixo,
    E a suas leis, o verso;
Que, quando é alto e régio o pensamento,
    Súbdita a frase o busca
    E o 'scravo ritmo o serve.

VII

SETTING FAST IN MY LOFTY MIND THE LABOR
      of heaven, I leave to chance,
      and to her laws, the verse;
for when the thought is high and sovereign,
      the sentence, subject, seeks it
      and the slave rhythm serves it.

VIII

Quão breve tempo é a mais longa vida
E a juventude nela! Ah Cloe, Cloe,
    Se não amo, nem bebo,
    Nem sem querer não penso,
Pesa-me a lei inimplorável, dói-me
A hora invita, o tempo que não cessa,
    E aos ouvidos me sobe
    Dos juncos o ruído
Na oculta margem onde os lírios frios
Da ínfera leiva crescem, e a corrente
    Não sabe onde é o dia,
    Sussurro gemebundo.

VIII

How brief a time is even the longest life
and the youth too therein! Ah, Chloe, Chloe,
     if I love not, drink not,
     nor think but purposely,
to me the law unswayable is heavy,
painful the unwished hour, the ceaseless time,
     and rises to my ears
     the swishing of the reeds
upon the hidden shore where lilies cold
grow from the nether furrow, and the current
     knows not where it is day,
     a murmuring whispered moan.

IX

Coroai-me de rosas,
Coroai-me em verdade
        De rosas —
Rosas que se apagam
Em fronte a apagar-se
        Tão cedo!
Coroai-me de rosas
E de folhas breves.
        E basta.

IX

CROWN YE ME WITH ROSES,
crown ye me in truth
  with roses—
roses that shall wither
on a brow that withers
  so soon!
Crown ye me with roses
and with fading leaves,
  alone!

X

MELHOR DESTINO QUE O DE CONHECER-SE
Não frui quem mente frui. Antes, sabendo
    Ser nada, que ignorando:
    Nada dentro de nada.
Se não houver em mim poder que vença
As parcas três e as moles do futuro,
    Já me dêem os deuses
    O poder de sabê-lo;
E a beleza, incriável por meu sestro,
Eu goze externa e dada, repetida
    Em meus passivos olhos,
    Lagos que a morte seca.

X

A BETTER DESTINY THAN MAN'S SELF-KNOWLEDGE
no man enjoys that does a mind enjoy.
>> Better know he is nothing
>> than not know: naught in naught.
If in me lives no power to subdue
the three Fates and the masses of the future,
>> let the gods grant me now
>> the power so to know;
and beauty, which my skill cannot create,
may I enjoy, an outward gift, remade
>> upon my passive eyes,
>> these lakes that death shall dry.

XII

A FLOR QUE ÉS, NÃO A QUE DÁS, EU QUERO.
Porque me negas o que te não peço?
  Tempo há para negares
  Depois de teres dado.
Flor, sê-me flor! Se te colher avaro
A mão da infausta 'sfinge, tu perene
  Sombra errarás absurda,
  Buscando o que não deste.

XII

THE FLOWER THOU ART, NOT THAT THOU GIVEST, I WANT.
For thou deniest me what I ask not.
>   There will be time enough
>   to deny when 'tis given.
Flower, be my flower! If, miserly, thou art plucked
by the hand of the ill-starred sphinx, a shade eternal
>   shalt thou wander absurd,
>   seeking that thou gavest not.

XIX

PRAZER, MAS DEVAGAR,
Lídia, que a sorte àqueles não é grata
    Que lhe das mãos arrancam.
Furtivos retiremos do horto mundo
    Os depredandos pomos.
Não despertemos, onde dorme, a Erínis
    Que cada gozo trava.
Como um regato, mudos passageiros,
    Gozemos escondidos.
A sorte inveja, Lídia. Emudeçamos.

XIX

Pleasure, but not too fast,
Lydia; fate ungrateful is to those
    that snatch it from her hand.
Let us draw stealthy from the garden world
    the pomes that we would plunder,
lest we awake Erinys where she sleeps,
    who every pleasure hoards.
Like a brook may we, soundless travelers,
    hidden enjoy ourselves.
Fate envies, Lídia. Let us silent be.

Outras Odes

NÃO SÓ VINHO, MAS NELE O OLVIDO, DEITO
Na taça: serei ledo, porque a dita
    É ignara. Quem, lembrando
    Ou prevendo, sorrira?
Dos brutos, não a vida, senão a alma,
Consigamos, pensando; recolhidos
    No impalpável destino
    Que não 'spera nem lembra.
Com mão mortal elevo à mortal boca
Em frágil taça o passageiro vinho,
    Baços os olhos feitos
    Para deixar de ver.

Other Odes

NOT WINE ALONE, BUT THEREIN DO I POUR
oblivion in my glass: I shall be merry,
        for fate's unsure. Who, minding
        or foretelling, hath smiled?
Of brutes let us attain, never the life,
but, with our thoughts, the soul; withdrawn unto
        fortune impalpable,
        that neither hopes nor minds.
With mortal hand to mortal lips I raise
in a glass frail the transitory wine,
        my eyes made dull and dim,
        that they may cease to see.

Quanta tristeza e amargura afoga
Em confusão a 'streita vida! Quanto
    Infortúnio mesquinho
    Nos oprime supremo!
Feliz ou o bruto que nos verdes campos
Pasce, para si mesmo anónimo, e entra
    Na morte como em casa;
    Ou o sábio que, perdido
Na ciência, a fútil vida austera eleva
Além da nossa, como o fumo que ergue
    Braços que se desfazem
    A um céu inexistente.

How great a sorrow and a bitterness
drowns our small lives in turmoil! With what might
    does mean adversity
    oppress us thoroughly!
Happy the brute that in green fields doth graze,
nameless unto itself, and enters death
    as into its own home;
    or the wise man who, lost
in knowledge, hoists his austere, futile life
above our own, as 'twere the smoke which raises
    arms that efface themselves
    to inexistent heaven.

A NADA IMPLORAM TUAS MÃOS JÁ COISAS,
Nem convencem teus lábios já parados,
  No abafo subterrâneo
  Da húmida imposta terra.
Só talvez o sorriso com que amavas
Te embalsama remota, e nas memórias
  Te ergue qual eras, hoje
  Cortiço apodrecido.
E o nome inútil que teu corpo morto
Usou, vivo, na terra, como uma alma,
  Não lembra. A ode grava,
  Anónimo, um sorriso.

NOTHING NOW DO THY HANDS, MERE THINGS, ENTREAT;
nothing persuade thy lips now silenced
    with subterranean cloak
    of dampening earth laid on.
Only perhaps the smile thou worest in love
embalms thee, distant, and in memories
    raises thee as thou wert,
    today a moldering hive.
And the name, useless, your dead body used
alive, on earth, is as a soul forgotten.
    So let this ode record,
    anonymous, a smile.

O RASTRO BREVE QUE DAS ERVAS MOLES
Ergue o pé findo, o eco que oco coa,
    A sombra que se adumbra,
    O branco que a nau larga —
Nem maior nem melhor deixa a alma às almas,
O ido aos indos. A lembrança esquece.
    Mortos, inda morremos.
    Lídia, somos só nossos.

THE FLEETING PRINT THAT FROM THE GRASSES SOFT
lifts finished foot; the hollow seeping echo,
>   the shadow darkening,
>   the white wake left of ships—
no more, no better, leaves the soul that's gone
to souls still going. Memory fades from memory.
>   Dead, we die on. Lydia,
>   we are none but our own.

Já SOBRE A FRONTE VÃ SE ME ACINZENTA
O cabelo do jovem que perdi.
     Meus olhos brilham menos.
Já não tem jus a beijos minha boca.
Se me ainda amas, por amor não ames:
     Traíras-me comigo.

NOW OVER MY VAIN BROW ALREADY GRAYS
the hair of the young man whom I have lost.
My eyes shine not so bright.
Now are my lips unworthy to be kissed.
If thou still love me, for love's sake love not:
thou wouldst have strayed with me.

Quando, Lídia, vier o nosso Outono
Com o Inverno que há nele, reservemos
Um pensamento, não para a futura
      Primavera, que é de outrem,
Nem para o Estio, de quem somos mortos,
Senão para o que fica do que passa —
O amarelo actual que as folhas vivem
      E as torna diferentes.

WHEN, LYDIA, OUR AUTUMN SEASON COMES
and winter therewithal, let us reserve
a thought, not for the springtime yet to be,
  which to others belongs,
nor for the summer, of whose dead we are,
but for what still remains of what is passing—
the present yellow living in the leaves
  that makes them different.

Ténue, como se de Éolo a esquecessem,
A brisa da manhã titila o campo,
　　E há começo do sol.
Não desejemos, Lídia, nesta hora
Mais sol do que ela, nem mais alta brisa
　　Que a que é pequena e existe.

FAINTLY, AS IF BY AEOLUS FORGOTTEN,
the breeze of morning titillates the field,
        and the first sunlight starts.
Lydia, let us not desire this hour
more sun than this, nor any stronger breeze
        than the light one that is.

PARA SER GRANDE, SÊ INTEIRO: NADA
    Teu exagera ou exclui.
Sê todo em cada coisa. Põe quanto és
    No mínimo que fazes.
Assim em cada lago a lua toda
    Brilha, porque alta vive.

To be great, be entire: not a whit
  done over or left out.
Be total in each thing. Put all you are
  into the least you do.
So onto every lake the moon shines whole,
  because it lives on high.

ÁLVARO DE CAMPOS

Dois excertos de odes
(Fins de duas odes, naturalmente)

I

VEM, NOITE ANTIQUÍSSIMA E IDÊNTICA,
Noite Rainha nascida destronada,
Noite igual por dentro ao silêncio, Noite
Com as estrelas lantejoulas rápidas
No teu vestido franjado de Infinito.

Vem, vagamente,
Vem, levemente,
Vem sozinha, solene, com as mãos caídas
Ao teu lado, vem
E traz os montes longínquos para ao pé das árvores próximas,
Funde num campo teu todos os campos que vejo,
Faz da montanha um bloco só do teu corpo,
Apaga-lhe todas as diferenças que de longe vejo,
Todas as estradas que a sobem,
Todas as várias árvores que a fazem verde-escuro ao longe,
Todas as casas brancas e com fumo entre as árvores,
E deixa só uma luz e outra luz e mais outra,
Na distância imprecisa e vagamente perturbadora,
Na distância subitamente impossível de percorrer.

Nossa Senhora
Das coisas impossíveis que procuramos em vão,
Dos sonhos que vêm ter connosco ao crepúsculo, à janela,

Excerpts of Two Odes

(Evidently the endings of two odes)

I

Come, most ancient selfsame Night,
thou Queen Night born dethroned,
thou Night inwardly like the silence, Night
with the stars flashing sequins
on thy gown edged with the Infinite.

Come thou, faintly,
come thou, softly,
come thou alone, solemn, with thy hands down
by thy sides, come
and bring the far hills up close to the nearby trees,
fuse every field I see into a field of thy own,
make the mountain one sole mass of thy body,
snuff out all the differences I see in it from afar,
all the roads that climb it,
all the many trees making it dark green off ahead,
all the white houses smoking through the trees,
and leave only a light and another light and another,
off in the dim and faintly unsettling distance,
the distance suddenly untraversable.

Our Lady
of the impossible things we seek in vain,
of the dreams which meet us in twilight at our windows,

Dos propósitos que nos acariciam
Nos grandes terraços dos hotéis cosmopolitas
Ao som europeu das músicas e das vozes longe e perto,
E que doem por sabermos que nunca os realizaremos...
Vem, e embala-nos,
Vem e afaga-nos,
Beija-nos silenciosamente na fronte,
Tão levemente na fronte que não saibamos que nos beijam
Senão por uma diferença na alma
E um vago soluço partindo melodiosamente
Do antiquíssimo de nós
Onde têm raiz todas essas árvores de maravilha
Cujos frutos são os sonhos que afagamos e amamos
Porque os sabemos fora de relação com o que há na vida.

Vem soleníssima,
Soleníssima e cheia
De uma oculta vontade de soluçar,
Talvez porque a alma é grande e a vida pequena,
E todos os gestos não saem do nosso corpo
E só alcançamos onde o nosso braço chega,
E só vemos até onde chega o nosso olhar.

Vem, dolorosa,
Mater-Dolorosa das Angústias dos Tímidos,
Turris-Eburnea das Tristezas dos Desprezados,
Mão fresca sobre a testa em febre dos humildes,
Sabor de água sobre os lábios secos dos Cansados.
Vem, lá do fundo

of the intentions which caress us
on the grand terraces of cosmopolitan hotels
to the European tune of music and voices far and near,
and pain us because we know we shall never achieve them...
Come, and cradle us,
come and cherish us,
kiss us silently on the forehead,
so softly on the forehead that we cannot tell we have been kissed
but for a difference in our souls
and a faint whimper breaking melodiously
from the ancientest part of us,
at the root of all those trees of wonder
whose fruits are the dreams we cherish and love
because we know they lack relation to the stuff of life.

Come thou most solemn,
most solemn and filled
with a secret urge to weep,
perhaps because our souls are great and our lives small,
and none of our gestures ever leave of our bodies,
and we can only reach as far as our arms will go,
and only look as far as our eyes can see.

Come thou in sorrow,
Mater Dolorosa of the Anguish of the Timid,
Turris Eburnea of the Grief of the Despised,
cool hand upon the fevered brow of the humble,
savor of water upon the dry lips of the Weary.
Come thou, out of the depths

Do horizonte lívido,
Vem e arranca-me
Do solo de angústia e de inutilidade
Onde vicejo.
Apanha-me do meu solo, malmequer esquecido,
Folha a folha lê em mim não sei que sina
E desfolha-me para teu agrado,
Para teu agrado silencioso e fresco.
Uma folha de mim lança para o Norte,
Onde estão as cidades de Hoje que eu tanto amei;
Outra folha de mim lança para o Sul,
Onde estão os mares que os Navegadores abriram;
Outra folha minha atira ao Ocidente,
Onde arde ao rubro tudo o que talvez seja o Futuro,
Que eu sem conhecer adoro;
E a outra, as outras, o resto de mim
Atira ao Oriente,
Ao Oriente donde vem tudo, o dia e a fé,
Ao Oriente pomposo e fanático e quente,
Ao Oriente excessivo que eu nunca verei,
Ao Oriente budista, bramânico, sintoísta,
Ao Oriente que tudo o que nós não temos,
Que tudo o que nós não somos,
Ao Oriente onde — quem sabe? — Cristo talvez ainda hoje viva,
Onde Deus talvez exista realmente e mandando tudo...

Vem sobre os mares,
Sobre os mares maiores,
Sobre os mares sem horizontes precisos,

of the pale horizon,
come and uproot me
from the soil of anguish and futility
where I thrive.
Pull me up from my soil, a forgotten daisy,
read some fortune in me petal by petal,
and pluck off my petals to suit thy pleasure,
to suit thy cool and silent pleasure.
One of my petals cast thou to the North,
where stand the cities of Today which I have so loved;
another of my petals cast thou to the South,
where lie the seas the Navigators opened wide;
another petal of mine throw to the West,
where all that the Future may be burns red,
which, though unknown to me, I adore;
and the other, the others, the rest of me
throw thou to the East,
to the East whence all things come, our days and our faith,
the East of pomp and zealotry and heat,
the East of excesses I shall never see,
the East of Buddhism, Brahmanism, Shintoism,
the East that is all that we have not,
all that we are not,
the East where—who knows? Christ may still be living today,
where God may really exist commanding over all…

Come thou across the seas,
across the widest seas,
the seas with no distinct horizons,

Vem e passa a mão pelo dorso de fera,
E acalma-o misteriosamente,
Ó domadora hipnótica das coisas que se agitam muito!

Vem, cuidadosa,
Vem, maternal,
Pé ante pé enfermeira antiquíssima, que te sentaste
À cabeceira dos deuses das fés já perdidas,
E que viste nascer Jeová e Júpiter,
E sorriste porque tudo te é falso e inútil.

Vem, Noite silenciosa e extática,
Vem envolver na noite manto branco
O meu coração...
Serenamente como uma brisa na tarde leve,
Tranquilamente como um gesto materno afagando,
Com as estrelas luzindo nas tuas mãos
E a lua máscara misteriosa sobre a tua face.
Todos os sons soam de outra maneira
Quando tu vens.
Quando tu entras baixam todas as vozes,
Ninguém te vê entrar.
Ninguém sabe quando entraste,
Senão de repente, vendo que tudo se recolhe,
Que tudo perde as arestas e as cores,
E que no alto céu ainda claramente azul
Já crescente nítido, ou círculo branco, ou mera luz nova que vem,
A lua começa a ser real.

come and stroke the beast's back,
and calm it mysteriously,
O hypnotic tamer of wild, rough things!

Come, caringly,
come, motherly,
most ancient tiptoeing nurse, who sat
by the bedside of the gods of long-lost faiths,
who was by at the birth of Jehovah and of Jupiter,
and smiled because all to thee is false and avails not.

Come, thou silent, rapturous Night,
come fold thy pale night-mantle
round my heart…
Calmly as a breeze in the mild afternoon,
gently as a mother's cherishing touch,
with the stars glittering in thy hands
and the moon a mysterious mask across thy face.
All sounds sound differently
when thou comest.
When thou enterest every voice falls low,
no one sees thee enter.
No one can tell when thou hast entered,
except all at once, seeing everything drawing away,
losing its edges and its colors,
and up in the sky still faintly blue,
now a sharp crescent, or a white circle, or a new light just coming in,
the moon beginning to be real.

II

Ah o crepúsculo, o cair da noite, o acender das luzes nas
                                                        grandes cidades,
E a mão de mistério que abafa o bulício,
E o cansaço de tudo em nós que nos corrompe
Para uma sensação exacta e precisa e activa da Vida!
Cada rua é um canal de uma Veneza de tédios
E que misterioso o fundo unânime das ruas,
Das ruas ao cair da noite, ó Cesário Verde, ó Mestre,
Ó do «Sentimento de um Ocidental»!

Que inquietação profunda, que desejo de outras coisas,
Que nem são países, nem momentos, nem vidas,
Que desejo talvez de outros modos de estados de alma
Humedece interiormente o instante lento e longínquo!

Um horror sonâmbulo entre luzes que se acendem,
Um pavor terno e líquido, encostado às esquinas
Como um mendigo de sensações impossíveis
Que não sabe quem lhas possa dar...

Quando eu morrer,
Quando me for, ignobilmente, como toda a gente,
Por aquele caminho cuja ideia se não pode encarar de frente,
Por aquela porta a que, se pudéssemos assomar, não assomaríamos
Para aquele porto que o capitão do Navio não conhece,
Seja por esta hora condigna dos tédios que tive,
Por esta hora mística e espiritual e antiquíssima,

II

AH THE DUSK HOUR, THE FALL OF NIGHT, THE LIGHTING OF THE LIGHTS
                              ALL ACROSS THE GREAT CITIES,
and the hand of mystery that muffles the din,
and the fatigue of everything in us that spoils us
from an accurate, precise and active sensation of Life!
Each street is a canal in a Venice of tediums
and how uncanny the unanimous ends of the streets,
of the streets at nightfall, O Cesário Verde, O Master,
O you of the "Feeling of a Westerner"!

What a profound unrest, what a longing for other things,
not for countries, nor moments, nor lives,
a longing perhaps for other modes of moods,
internally clammies the distant, creeping moment!

A horror sleepwalking past the lighted lights,
a pitiful ooze of dread leaning up at street-corners
like a beggar for impossible sensations,
wondering who can give him any…

When I die,
when I go, ignobly, as we all do,
out on that road the idea of which cannot be faced head-on,
through the doorway which we would not peer through if we could,
towards the harbor with which the captain of the Ship is unaquainted,
let it be at this hour, well worthy of the tediums I have known,
this mystical, spiritual, ancient hour,

Por esta hora em que talvez, há muito mais tempo do que parece,
Platão sonhando viu a ideia de Deus
Esculpir corpo e existência nitidamente plausível
Dentro do seu pensamento exteriorizado como um campo.

Seja por esta hora que me leveis a enterrar,
Por esta hora que eu não sei como viver,
Em que não sei que sensações ter ou fingir que tenho,
Por esta hora cuja misericórdia é torturada e excessiva,
Cujas sombras vêm de qualquer outra coisa que não as coisas,
Cuja passagem não roça vestes no chão da Vida Sensível
Nem deixa perfume nos caminhos do Olhar.

Cruza as mãos sobre o joelho, ó companheira que eu não tenho nem
quero ter,
Cruza as mãos sobre o joelho e olha-me em silêncio
A esta hora em que eu não posso ver que tu me olhas,
Olha-me em silêncio e em segredo e pergunta a ti própria
— Tu que me conheces — quem eu sou...

this hour when, far longer ago than it seems,
a dreaming Plato may have glimpsed the idea of God
sculpting body and clearly plausible existence
within his thoughts externalized as a field.

Let it be at this hour that I am taken to be buried,
this hour that I do not know how to experience,
when I do not know what sensations to have or feign that I have,
this hour whose mercy is tortured and excessive,
whose shadows come from some other thing than from things,
whose passage trails no garments over the floor of Sensible Life
and leaves no scent along the pathways of our View.

Fold your hands across your knee, O companion I neither have nor
wish I had,
fold your hands across your knee and view me in silence
at this hour when I cannot see you viewing me,
view me in silence and in secret and wonder to yourself,
You who know me… who am I…

Soneto já antigo

Olha, Daisy: quando eu morrer tu hás-de
Dizer aos meus amigos aí de Londres,
Embora não o sintas, que tu escondes
A grande dor da minha morte. Irás de

Londres pra York, onde nasceste (dizes...
Que eu nada que tu digas acredito),
Contar àquele pobre rapazito
Que me deu tantas horas tão felizes,

Embora não o saibas, que morri...
Mesmo ele, a quem eu tanto julguei amar,
Nada se importará... Depois vai dar

A notícia a essa estranha Cecily
Que acreditava que eu seria grande...
Raios partam a vida e quem lá ande!

A Sonnet, Old Now

Look, Daisy, when I die, all that I'm asking
is that you say to my old mates in London,
even though you'll feel nothing, that you're masking
the great grief of my death. You'll go from London

back up to York, where you were born (you say…
though half the things you say are wind and piss)
to tell that poor young chap who, by the way,
has given me full many an hour of bliss,

even though you knew nothing, that I'm dead…
Much as I thought I loved him, even he
won't care a jot… Next, find a way to spin it

to that odd bird who got it in her head
that I'd be great one day, that Cecily…
Well, damn this life and everybody in it!

Lisbon revisited
(1923)

Não: não quero nada.
Já disse que não quero nada.

Não me venham com conclusões!
A única conclusão é morrer.

Não me tragam estéticas!
Não me falem em moral!
Tirem-me daqui a metafísica!
Não me apregoem sistemas completos, não me enfileirem conquistas
Das ciências (das ciências, Deus meu, das ciências!) —
Das ciências, das artes, da civilização moderna!

Que mal fiz eu aos deuses todos?

Se têm a verdade, guardem-na!

Sou um técnico, mas tenho técnica só dentro da técnica,
Fora disso sou doido, com todo o direito a sê-lo.
Com todo o direito a sê-lo, ouviram?

Não me macem, por amor de Deus!

Queriam-me casado, fútil, quotidiano e tributável?
Queriam-me o contrário disto, o contrário de qualquer coisa?
Se eu fosse outra pessoa, fazia-lhes, a todos, a vontade.

Lisbon revisited

(1923)

No: I want none of it.
I've already said I want none of it.

Don't come to me with conclusions!
The only conclusion is death.

Bring me no aesthetics!
Do not speak to me of morals!
Get metaphysics away from me!
Tout me no comprehensive systems, showcase me no achievements
in the sciences (the sciences, good Lord, the sciences!)—
in the sciences, in the arts, in modern civilization!

What have I done to offend all the gods?

If you have the truth, then keep it!

I am a technician, but my technique is purely within the technical,
outside of that I'm loony, and have every right to be so.
And have every right to be so, do you hear?

Don't bother me, for God's sake!

Would you have me married, feckless, ordinary and taxable?
Would you have me the opposite of that, the opposite of anything?
If I were someone else, I would oblige you all.

Assim, como sou, tenham paciência!
Vão para o diabo sem mim,
Ou deixem-me ir sozinho para o diabo!
Para que havermos de ir juntos?

Não me peguem no braço!
Não gosto que me peguem no braço. Quero ser sozinho.
Já disse que sou só sozinho!
Ah, que maçada quererem que eu seja de companhia!

Ó céu azul — o mesmo da minha infância —,
Eterna verdade vazia e perfeita!
Ó macio Tejo ancestral e mudo,
Pequena verdade onde o céu se reflecte!
Ó mágoa revisitada, Lisboa de outrora de hoje!
Nada me dais, nada me tirais, nada sois que eu me sinta.

Deixem-me em paz! Não tardo, que eu nunca tardo...
E enquanto tarda o Abismo e o Silêncio quero estar sozinho!

Such as I am, let me be!
Go on to hell without me,
or let me go to hell on my own!
Why must we go together?

Don't grab my arm!
I don't like having my arm grabbed. I want to be alone.
I've already said I am only to be alone!
What a blasted nuisance to be wanted for company!

O blue sky—the same as in my childhood—,
perfect, empty, ageless truth!
O gentle Tagus, ancient and unspeaking,
little truth where the sky is reflected!
O heartache revisited, Lisbon of yesteryear today!
Ye give me nothing, ye take from me nothing, ye are nothing I feel as
myself.

Leave me alone! I shan't be long, I'm never long…
And as long the Abyss and the Silence keep off I want to be alone!

Lisbon revisited

(1926)

Nada me prende a nada.
Quero cinquenta coisas ao mesmo tempo.
Anseio com uma angústia de fome de carne
O que não sei que seja —
Definidamente pelo indefinido...
Durmo irrequieto, e vivo num sonhar irrequieto
De quem dorme irrequieto, metade a sonhar.

Fecharam-me todas as portas abstractas e necessárias.
Correram cortinas de todas as hipóteses que eu poderia ver da rua.
Não há na travessa achada o número da porta que me deram.

Acordei para a mesma vida para que tinha adormecido.
Até os meus exércitos sonhados sofreram derrota.
Até os meus sonhos se sentiram falsos ao serem sonhados.
Até a vida só desejada me farta — até essa vida...

Compreendo a intervalos desconexos;
Escrevo por lapsos de cansaço;
E um tédio que é até do tédio arroja-me à praia.

Não sei que destino ou futuro compete à minha angústia sem leme;
Não sei que ilhas do Sul impossível aguardam-me náufrago;
Ou que palmares de literatura me darão ao menos um verso.

Não, não sei isto, nem outra coisa, nem coisa nenhuma...
E, no fundo do meu espírito, onde sonho o que sonhei,

Lisbon revisited
(1926)

Nothing holds me to any of it.
I want fifty things all at once.
With a meat-hungry angst I crave
I don't know quite what—
definitely something indefinite…
I sleep restlessly, and live out the restless dream-state
of a restless sleeper, half dreaming.

The abstract doors I needed have all shut me out.
Curtains are drawn over every possibility I might see from outside.
Having found the lane I find the address I was given is not there.

I have awoken to the same life I fell asleep to.
Even the armies I dreamt of suffered defeat.
Even my dreams felt false as I dreamt them.
Even the life I merely wish for leaves me cold—even that life…

I make sense of things at disjointed intervals;
I write through lapses in fatigue;
and boredom with my very boredom washes me ashore.

I do not know what destiny or future appertains to my rudderless angst;
I do not know what impossible southerly isles await me as a castaway;
or what palm-groves of literature will yield me even one verse.

No, I don't know that, or anything else, or anything at all…
And deep in my spirit, where I dream what I have dreamt,

Nos campos últimos da alma, onde memoro sem causa
(E o passado é uma névoa natural de lágrimas falsas),
Nas estradas e atalhos das florestas longínquas
Onde supus o meu ser,
Fogem desmantelados, últimos restos
Da ilusão final,
Os meus exércitos sonhados, derrotados sem ter sido,
As minhas coortes por existir, esfaceladas em Deus.

Outra vez te revejo,
Cidade da minha infância pavorosamente perdida...
Cidade triste e alegre, outra vez sonho aqui...
Eu? Mas sou eu o mesmo que aqui vivi, e aqui voltei,
E aqui tornei a voltar, e a voltar.
E aqui de novo tornei a voltar?
Ou somos todos os Eu que estive aqui ou estiveram,
Uma série de contas-entes ligada por um fio-memória,
Uma série de sonhos de mim de alguém de fora de mim?

Outra vez te revejo,
Com o coração mais longínquo, a alma menos minha.

Outra vez te revejo — Lisboa e Tejo e tudo —,
Transeunte inútil de ti e de mim,
Estrangeiro aqui como em toda a parte,
Casual na vida como na alma,
Fantasma a errar em salas de recordações,
Ao ruído dos ratos e das tábuas que rangem
No castelo maldito de ter que viver...

across my soul's farthest reaches, where I remember without cause,
(and the past is a natural haze of false tears),
over the roads and tracks through distant forests
where I have supposed my self should be,
scatter and fly—last remnants
of the ultimate illusion—
my dream-armies, defeated having never been,
my non-existing cohorts, riven apart into God.

Once more I see thee,
city of my dreadfully lost childhood...
City both sad and happy, here once more I dream...
I? But am I the same one who lived here, and returned here,
and returned here again, and again,
and have I once again returned here?
Or are we all the I's that I was here, or were here,
so many being-beads strung together by a memory-thread,
so many dreams of myself dreamt by someone outside of me?

Once more I see thee,
with a heart more distant, a soul not as much my own.

Once more I see thee—Lisbon and Tagus and all—,
a pointless traverser of thee and of myself,
a stranger here as everywhere,
desultory in life as in my soul,
a phantom drifting through rooms of mementos
amid the noise of the mice and the creaking floorboards
in the cursed castle of having to live...

Outra vez te revejo,
Sombra que passa através de sombras, e brilha
Um momento a uma luz fúnebre desconhecida,
E entra na noite como um rastro de barco se perde,
Na água que deixa de se ouvir...

Outra vez te revejo,
Mas, ai, a mim não me revejo!
Partiu-se o espelho mágico em que me revia idêntico,
E em cada fragmento fatídico vejo só um bocado de mim —
Um bocado de ti e de mim!...

Once more I see thee,
a shadow passing through shadows, that shines
a moment in a strange ghastly glow,
and fades into the night like the wake of a barge receding
into the water that quietens to a hush...

Once more I see thee,
but alas, I see none of myself!
Cracked is the magic mirror where I recognized my same self,
and in each fateful fragment I see only a sliver of me—
a sliver of thee and of me!...

Tabacaria

Não sou nada.
Nunca serei nada.
Não posso querer ser nada.
À parte isso, tenho em mim todos os sonhos do mundo.

Janelas do meu quarto,
Do meu quarto de um dos milhões do mundo que ninguém sabe quem é
(E se soubessem quem é, o que saberiam?),
Dais para o mistério de uma rua cruzada constantemente por gente,
Para uma rua inacessível a todos os pensamentos,
Real, impossivelmente real, certa, desconhecidamente certa,
Com o mistério das coisas por baixo das pedras e dos seres,
Com a morte a pôr humidade nas paredes e cabelos brancos nos homens,
Com o Destino a conduzir a carroça de tudo pela estrada de nada.

Estou hoje vencido, como se soubesse a verdade.
Estou hoje lúcido, como se estivesse para morrer,
E não tivesse mais irmandade com as coisas
Senão uma despedida, tornando-se esta casa e este lado da rua
A fileira de carruagens de um comboio, e uma partida apitada
De dentro da minha cabeça,
E uma sacudidela dos meus nervos e um ranger de ossos na ida.

Estou hoje perplexo, como quem pensou e achou e esqueceu.
Estou hoje dividido entre a lealdade que devo

Tobacco Shop

I am nothing.
I shall always be nothing.
I can only wish to be nothing.
That aside, I have in me all the dreams in the world.

My bedroom windows,
from the bedroom of one of the millions in the world whom no one
                                                         knows about
(and if they knew about him, what would they know?),
you face the mystery of a street crossed constantly by people,
a street not reachable by any thought,
real, impossibly real, certain, unknowably certain,
with the mystery of things beneath the stones and selves,
with death putting damp on the walls and white hairs on the men,
with Destiny driving the cartload of everything over the road of nothing.

I feel defeated today, as if I had found out the truth.
I feel lucid today, as if I were going to die,
and had no other kinship with things
but to bid them farewell, with this house and this house-row becoming
a line of locomotive cars, and a whistle sounding for departure
from inside my head,
and jolt to my nerves and a creaking of bones as we're off.

I feel bewildered today, like one who has thought and figured and
                                                              forgotten.
I feel torn today between the loyalty I owe

À Tabacaria do outro lado da rua, como coisa real por fora,
E à sensação de que tudo é sonho, como coisa real por dentro.

Falhei em tudo.
Como não fiz propósito nenhum, talvez tudo fosse nada.
A aprendizagem que me deram,
Desci'dela pela janela das traseiras da casa.
Fui até ao campo com grandes propósitos.
Mas lá encontrei só ervas e árvores,
E quando havia gente era igual à outra.

Saio da janela, sento-me numa cadeira. Em que hei-de pensar?

Que sei eu do que serei, eu que não sei o que sou?
Ser o que penso? Mas penso ser tanta coisa!
E há tantos que pensam ser a mesma coisa que não pode haver tantos!
Génio? Neste momento
Cem mil cérebros se concebem em sonho génios como eu,
E a história não marcará, quem sabe?, nem um,
Nem haverá senão estrume de tantas conquistas futuras.
Não, não creio em mim.
Em todos os manicómios há doidos malucos com tantas certezas!
Eu, que não tenho nenhuma certeza, sou mais certo ou menos certo?
Não, nem em mim...
Em quantas mansardas e não-mansardas do mundo
Não estão nesta hora génios-para-si-mesmos sonhando?
Quantas aspirações altas e nobres e lúcidas —
Sim, verdadeiramente altas e nobres e lúcidas —,

to the Tobacco Shop across the street, as something real without,
and to the sense that all is but a dream, as something real within.

I have failed in everything.
As I never made any intentions, perhaps it was nothing all along.
What learning I got,
I have climbed out of through the window at the back of the house.
Out to the country I have gone with a great purpose.
But all I found there was grass and trees,
and where there were people they were like the rest.

I leave the window, seat myself in a chair. What shall I think about?

How can I know what I shall be, when I do not know what I am?
Could I be what I think? But I think I could be so many things!
And there are so many more who think the same than there can

possibly be!
A genius? At this instant
a hundred thousand dreaming minds surmise themselves geniuses as I do,
and history may not mark even one,
nor so many conquests-yet-to-be come but to muck.
No, I do not believe in myself.
In every asylum are raving lunatics so full of certainties!
Am I, having no certainties whatsoever, more certain or less?
No, not in myself…
In how many of the world's mansard roofs and non-mansard roofs
are self-reckoned geniuses now dreaming?
How many high and noble and bright aspirations—
indeed, truly high and noble and bright—,

E quem sabe se realizáveis,
Nunca verão a luz do sol real nem acharão ouvidos de gente?
O mundo é para quem nasce para o conquistar
E não para quem sonha que pode conquistá-lo, ainda que tenha razão.
Tenho sonhado mais que o que Napoleão fez.
Tenho apertado ao peito hipotético mais humanidades do que Cristo.
Tenho feito filosofias em segredo que nenhum Kant escreveu.
Mas sou, e talvez serei sempre, o da mansarda,
Ainda que não more nela;
Serei sempre o que *não nasceu para isso*;
Serei sempre só o que *tinha qualidades*;
Serei sempre o que esperou que lhe abrissem a porta ao pé de uma
                                                    parede sem porta,
E cantou a cantiga do Infinito numa capoeira,
E ouviu a voz de Deus num poço tapado.
Crer em mim? Não, nem em nada.
Derrame-me a Natureza sobre a cabeça ardente
O seu sol, a sua chuva, o vento que me acha o cabelo,
E o resto que venha se vier, ou tiver que vir, ou não venha.
Escravos cardíacos das estrelas,
Conquistámos todo o mundo antes de nos levantar da cama;
Mas acordámos e ele é opaco,
Levantámo-nos e ele é alheio,
Saímos de casa e ele é a terra inteira,
Mais o sistema solar e a Via Láctea e o Indefinido.

(Come chocolates, pequena;
Come chocolates!
Olha que não há mais metafísica no mundo senão chocolates.

and for all one knows achievable,
will never see the real light of day or reach the ears of people?
The world is for those who are born to conquer it
and not for those who, even rightly, dream they could.
I have dreamt more than Napoleon ever accomplished.
I have held in my hypothetical embrace more of humanity than Christ.
I have privately worked out philosophies no Kant ever wrote.
But I am, and may always be, the man in the mansard,
even if I don't live in one;
I shall always be the one who *wasn't born for it*;
I shall only ever be the one who *had the makings*;
I shall forever be the one who waited to have the door opened for him
                                        by a wall with no door,
and sang the song of the Infinite in a chicken-coop,
and heard the voice of God in a covered well.
Believe in myself? No, not in anything.
Let Nature pour upon my burning head
her sun, her rain, her wind that catches my hair,
and whatever else will come as it may, or must, or mustn't.
Cardiac slaves to the stars,
we have conquered the world before rising from bed;
but we have awoken to find it opaque,
roused ourselves to find it alien,
left the house to find it was all the earth,
plus the solar system and the Milky Way and the Undefined.

(Eat your chocolates, little one;
eat your chocolates!
There's no other metaphysics in the world but chocolates, mind you.

Olha que as religiões todas não ensinam mais que a confeitaria.
Come, pequena suja, come!
Pudesse eu comer chocolates com a mesma verdade com que comes!
Mas eu penso e, ao tirar o papel de prata, que é de folha de estanho,
Deito tudo para o chão, como tenho deitado a vida.)

Mas ao menos fica da amargura do que nunca serei
A caligrafia rápida destes versos,
Pórtico partido para o Impossível.
Mas ao menos consagro a mim mesmo um desprezo sem lágrimas,
Nobre ao menos no gesto largo com que atiro
A roupa suja que sou, sem rol, pra o decurso das coisas,
E fico em casa sem camisa.

(Tu, que consolas, que não existes e por isso consolas,
Ou deusa grega, concebida como estátua que fosse viva,
Ou patrícia romana, impossivelmente nobre e nefasta,
Ou princesa de trovadores, gentilíssima e colorida,
Ou marquesa do século dezoito, decotada e longínqua,
Ou cocote célebre do tempo dos nossos pais,
Ou não sei quê moderno — não concebo bem o quê —,
Tudo isso, seja o que for, que sejas, se pode inspirar que inspire!
Meu coração é um balde despejado.
Como os que invocam espíritos invocam espíritos invoco
A mim mesmo e não encontro nada.
Chego à janela e vejo a rua com uma nitidez absoluta.
Vejo as lojas, vejo os passeios, vejo os carros que passam,
Vejo os entes vivos vestidos que se cruzam,
Vejo os cães que também existem,

No religion will teach you any more than the sweetshop, mind you.
Eat up, filthy girl, eat up!
I wish I could eat chocolates as truthfully as you do!
But I think it over and, once I've taken off the silver tinfoil wrapper,
I throw mine all to the ground, as I have thrown away my life.)

Yet at least there abides of the sorrow of what I shall not be
the quick typing of these lines,
a fractured gateway to the Impossible.
At the least I reserve for myself an unweeping disdain,
noble at least in the sweeping gesture with which I toss
the dirty washing I am, without a laundry list, into the course of things,
and sit at home shirtless.

(You, who console, who do not exist and therefore console,
whether a Greek goddess, conceived as a statue come to life,
or a patrician lady of Rome, impossibly noble and nefarious,
or a princess of troubadours, most gentle and colorful,
or an eighteenth-century marchioness, décolletée and distant,
or a famous cocotte from our parents' time,
or a modern something-or-other—I can't quite picture what—,
whatever-all it is that you are, if it can inspire let it inspire!
My heart is an emptied pail.
As summoners of spirits summon spirits I summon
myself and find nothing.
I shift towards the window and view the street with an absolute clarity.
I see the shops, see the pavements, see the cars going by,
I see the living beings in clothes passing one another,
I see the dogs that are there as well,

E tudo isto me pesa como uma condenação ao degredo,
E tudo isto é estrangeiro, como tudo.)

Vivi, estudei, amei, e até cri,
E hoje não há mendigo que eu não inveje só por não ser eu.
Olho a cada um os andrajos e as chagas e a mentira,
E penso: talvez nunca vivesses nem estudasses nem amasses nem cresses
(Porque é possível fazer a realidade de tudo isso sem fazer nada disso);
Talvez tenhas existido apenas, como um lagarto a quem cortam o rabo
E que é rabo para aquém do lagarto remexidamente.

Fiz de mim o que não soube,
E o que podia fazer de mim não o fiz.
O dominó que vesti era errado.
Conheceram-me logo por quem não era e não desmenti, e perdi-me.
Quando quis tirar a máscara,
Estava pegada à cara.
Quando a tirei e me vi ao espelho,
Já tinha envelhecido.
Estava bêbado, já não sabia vestir o dominó que não tinha tirado.
Deitei fora a máscara e dormi no vestiário
Como um cão tolerado pela gerência
Por ser inofensivo
E vou escrever esta história para provar que sou sublime.

Essência musical dos meus versos inúteis,
Quem me dera encontrar-te como coisa que eu fizesse,
E não ficasse sempre defronte da Tabacaria de defronte,

and it all weighs on me like an exile sentence,
and it all feels alien, like everything does.)

I have lived, learned, loved, and even believed,
and today there is not a beggar I do not envy simply for not being me.
I look over each one's rags and sores and made-up tale,
and I think: you may never have lived or learned or loved or believed
(for one can achieve the reality of all that without doing any of it);
you may have simply existed, like a lizard with its tail cut off
that's one tail wrigglingly short of a lizard.

I have made of myself what I could not,
and what I could have made of myself I did not.
The domino I put on wasn't right.
They knew me straight away for who I wasn't and I didn't say
                                          otherwise, and I was lost.
When I tried to remove the mask,
it was stuck to my face.
By the time I got it off and saw myself in the mirror,
I had grown old.
I was too drunk by then to know how to wear the domino I hadn't
                                          taken off.
I threw out the mask and slept in the cloakroom
like a dog the management puts up with
because it's harmless,
and I shall write this story down to prove that I am sublime.

Musical essence of my pointless poetry,
if only I could find you to be something I accomplished,
instead of always facing the Tobacco Shop across the way,

Calcando aos pés a consciência de estar existindo,
Como um tapete em que um bêbado tropeça
Ou um capacho que os ciganos roubaram e não valia nada.

Mas o Dono da Tabacaria chegou à porta e ficou à porta.
Olho-o com o desconforto da cabeça mal voltada
E com o desconforto da alma mal-entendendo.
Ele morrerá e eu morrerei.
Ele deixará a tabuleta, e eu deixarei versos.
A certa altura morrerá a tabuleta também, e os versos também.
Depois de certa altura morrerá a rua onde esteve a tabuleta,
E a língua em que foram escritos os versos.
Morrerá depois o planeta girante em que tudo isto se deu.
Em outros satélites de outros sistemas qualquer coisa como gente
Continuará fazendo coisas como versos e vivendo por baixo de
                                        coisas como tabuletas,
Sempre uma coisa defronte da outra,
Sempre uma coisa tão inútil como a outra,
Sempre o impossível tão estúpido como o real,
Sempre o mistério do fundo tão certo como o sono de mistério da
                                        superfície,
Sempre isto ou sempre outra coisa ou nem uma coisa nem outra.

Mas um homem entrou na Tabacaria (para comprar tabaco?),
E a realidade plausível cai de repente em cima de mim
Semiergo-me enérgico, convencido, humano,
E vou tencionar escrever estes versos em que digo o contrário.

trampling underfoot the awareness that I am existing,
like a rug that trips up a drunkard
or a doormat the gypsies stole that was worthless anyway.

But the Owner of the Tobacco Shop has come to the door and stood
in the doorway.
I look at him through the discomfort in my mis-cocked head
and the discomfort in my misunderstanding soul.
He will die, and I shall die.
He will leave his signboard, and I my poetry.
At a certain point the signboard will die as well, and the poetry too.
After a certain point the street where the signboard hung will die,
and the language the poetry was written in.
Eventually the whirling planet where all this took place will die.
On other satellites of other solar systems something like people
will go on making things like poetry and and living under things like
signboards,
still just across from one another,
still just as pointless as one another,
the impossible still as stupid as the real,
the underlying mystery still as certain as the slumber of mystery at
the surface,
still one thing or still another or neither the one or the other.

But a man has gone into the Tobacco Shop (to purchase tobacco?),
and plausible reality hits me all at once.
I sit up with energy, with assurance, human,
and will endeavor to write these lines in which I say the opposite.

Acendo um cigarro ao pensar em escrevê-los
E saboreio no cigarro a libertação de todos os pensamentos.
Sigo o fumo como a uma rota própria,
E gozo, num momento sensitivo e competente,
A libertação de todas as especulações
E a consciência de que a metafísica é uma consequência de estar mal
                                                                    disposto.

Depois deito-me para trás na cadeira
E continuo fumando.
Enquanto o Destino mo conceder, continuarei fumando.

(Se eu casasse com a filha da minha lavadeira
Talvez fosse feliz.)
Visto isto, levanto-me da cadeira. Vou à janela.

O homem saiu da Tabacaria (metendo troco na algibeira das calças?).
Ah, conheço-o: é o Esteves sem metafísica.
(O Dono da Tabacaria chegou à porta.)
Como por um instinto divino o Esteves voltou-se e viu-me.
Acenou-me adeus, gritei-lhe *Adeus ó Esteves!*, e o universo
Reconstruiu-se-me sem ideal nem esperança, e o Dono da Tabacaria
                                                                    sorriu.

I light a cigarette as I think about writing them
and savor in it my deliverance from all thought.
I follow the smoke like a path of my own,
and enjoy for a fitting, sensitive moment
the deliverance from all speculation
and the awareness that metaphysics is a consequence of being unwell.

Then I lie back in my chair
and go on smoking.
As long as Destiny allows me, I shall go on smoking.

(Perhaps if I married my washerwoman's daughter
I might be happy.)
In view of this, I get up from my chair. I go to the window.

The man has left the Tobacco Shop (slipping change in his
                                                    trousers-pocket?).
Oh, I know him: it's Esteves with no metaphysics.
(The Tobacco Shop Owner has come to the door).
As by some divine instinct Esteves has turned round and seen me.
He's waved cheerio, I've called out Cheerio, Esteves!, and the universe
has reconstructed itself before me without ideals or hopes, and the
                                    Tobacco Shop Owner has smiled.

Escrito num livro abandonado em viagem

Venho dos lados de Beja.
Vou para o meio de Lisboa.
Não trago nada e não acharei nada.
Tenho o cansaço antecipado do que não acharei,
E a saudade que sinto não é nem no passado nem do futuro.
Deixo escrita neste livro a imagem do meu desígnio morto:
Fui, como ervas, e não me arrancaram.

Written in a book left behind mid-journey

I have come from outside Beja.
I am bound for the heart of Lisbon.
I am bringing nothing and I shall find nothing.
I hold an expectant weariness of what I shall not find,
and the yearning I feel is neither from the past nor for the future.
I will leave written in this book the image of my failed purpose:
I was here, like a weed, and no one pulled me out.

Apostila

Aproveitar o tempo!
Mas o que é o tempo, para que eu o aproveite?
Aproveitar o tempo!
Nenhum dia sem linha...
O trabalho honesto e superior...
O trabalho à Virgílio, à Milton...
Mas é tão difícil ser honesto ou ser superior!
É tão pouco provável ser Milton ou ser Virgílio!

Aproveitar o tempo!
Tirar da alma os bocados precisos — nem mais nem menos —
Para com eles juntar os cubos ajustados
Que fazem gravuras certas na história
(E estão certas também do lado de baixo, que se não vê)...
Pôr as sensações em castelo de cartas, pobre China dos serões,
E os pensamentos em dominó, igual contra igual,
E a vontade em carambola difícil...
Imagens de jogos ou de paciências ou de passatempos —
Imagens da vida, imagens das vidas, Imagem da Vida...

Verbalismo...
Sim, verbalismo...
Aproveitar o tempo!
Não ter um minuto que o exame de consciência desconheça...
Não ter um acto indefinido nem factício...
Não ter um movimento desconforme com propósitos...
Boas maneiras da alma...
Elegância de persistir...

Sidenote

To make much of time!
And what is time, that I should make much of it?
To make much of time!
Not a day without a line...
Honest, superior workmanship...
Workmanship à la Virgil, à la Milton...
But being honest or superior is so hard!
Being Virgil or being Milton is so unlikely!

To make much of time!
To take out the proper bits of the soul—no more, no less—
adding to them the fitted blocks
that make precise imprints in history
(precise underneath, as well, on the side we can't see)...
To place the sensations in a card-tower, a poor after-supper China,
and the thoughts in dominoes, like against like,
and the will in a tricky carom...
Images of games or solitaires or pastimes—
images of a life, images of lives, Image of Life...

Verbalism...
Yes, verbalism...
To make much of time!
No minute overlooked in the mind's examination...
No action indefinite or contrived...
No movement at odds with its intent...
Good manners of the soul...
The grace to persist...

Aproveitar o tempo!
Meu coração está cansado como mendigo verdadeiro.
Meu cérebro está pronto como um fardo posto ao canto.
Meu canto (verbalismo!) está tal como está e é triste.
Aproveitar o tempo!
Desde que comecei a escrever passaram cinco minutos.
Aproveitei-os ou não?
Se não sei se os aproveitei, que saberei de outros minutos?

(Passageira que viajavas tantas vezes no mesmo compartimento comigo
No comboio suburbano,
Chegaste a interessar-te por mim?
Aproveitei o tempo olhando para ti?
Qual foi o ritmo do nosso sossego no comboio andante?
Qual foi o entendimento que não chegámos a ter?
Qual foi a vida que houve nisto? Que foi isto à vida?)

Aproveitar o tempo!...
Ah, deixem-me não aproveitar nada!
Nem tempo, nem ser, nem memórias de tempo ou de ser!...
Deixem-me ser uma folha de árvore, titilada por brisas,
A poeira de uma estrada, involuntária e sozinha,
O regato casual das chuvas que vão acabando,
O vinco deixado na estrada pelas rodas enquanto não vêm outras,
O pião do garoto, que vai a parar,
E oscila, no mesmo movimento que o da terra,
E estremece, no mesmo movimento que o da alma,
E cai, como caem os deuses, no chão do Destino.

To make much of time!
My heart is weary like a genuine beggar.
My brain is ready like a bundle laid in the corner.
My song (verbalism!) is as it is, and it's a sad one.
To make much of time!
Since I started writing five minutes have passed.
Have I made much of them or not?
If I don't if I have, how shall I know about other minutes?

(Passenger who rode so often in the same car as me
on the suburban train,
did you ever take an interest in me?
Did I make much of the time by glancing over at you?
What was the rhythm of our tranquility in the moving train?
What was the understanding we never got to reach?
What was the life in it? What was it to life?)

To make much of time!…
Oh, let me not make much of anything!
Not time, not being, not memories of time or of being!…
Let me be a breeze-tickled leaf on a tree,
the dust on a road, unwillful and alone,
The uneven stream flowing from the ending rains,
the ruts that wheels leave in the road until more wheels come along,
the boy's spinning top that slows to a stop,
and oscillates, with the same motion as the earth,
and quivers with the same motion as the soul,
and falls, as the gods do, onto the ground of Destiny.

Adiamento

Depois de amanhã, sim, só depois de amanhã...
Levarei amanhã a pensar em depois de amanhã,
E assim será possível; mas hoje não...
Não, hoje nada; hoje não posso.
A persistência confusa da minha subjectividade objectiva,
O sono da minha vida real, intercalado,
O cansaço antecipado e infinito,
Um cansaço de mundos para apanhar um eléctrico...
Esta espécie de alma...
      Só depois de amanhã...
Hoje quero preparar-me,
Quero preparar-me para pensar amanhã no dia seguinte...
Ele é que é decisivo.
Tenho já o plano traçado; mas não, hoje não traço planos...
Amanhã é o dia dos planos.
Amanhã sentar-me-ei à secretária para conquistar o mundo;
Mas só conquistarei o mundo depois de amanhã...
Tenho vontade de chorar,
Tenho vontade de chorar muito de repente, de dentro...
Não, não queiram saber mais nada, é segredo, não digo.
Só depois de amanhã...
Quando era criança o circo de domingo divertia-me toda a semana.
Hoje só me diverte o circo de domingo de toda a semana da minha
             infância...
Depois de amanhã serei outro,
A minha vida triunfar-se-á,
Todas as minhas qualidades reais de inteligente, lido e prático

Deferral

The day after tomorrow, yes, not until the day after tomorrow...
I shall spend tomorrow thinking ahead to the next day,
and then that day will do; but not today...
No, none of it today; I can't today.
The addled persistence of my objective subjectivity,
the intercalated sleep of my real life,
the infinite expectant weariness,
worlds of weariness over catching a streetcar...
This sort of soul...
                              Not until the day after tomorrow...
Today I'd like to prepare,
I'd like to prepare for thinking ahead tomorrow to the next day...
That's the one that counts.
I've got it all planned out; but no, no plans today...
Tomorrow is the day for planning.
Tomorrow I shall sit down at my desk to conquer the world;
but I won't conquer the world until the day after...
I feel like crying,
I feel like crying all of a sudden, from within...
No, no more prying, it's a secret, I won't tell.
Not until the day after tomorrow...
When I was a child the Sunday circus used to amuse me all week.
Now all that amuses me is the Sunday circus from every week of my
                                                                        childhood.
The day after tomorrow I'll be someone else,
triumphant over my life,
and all my real qualities as an intelligent, well-read, practical person

Serão convocadas por um edital...
Mas por um edital de amanhã...
Hoje quero dormir, redigirei amanhã...
Por hoje, qual é o espectáculo que me repetiria a infância?
Mesmo para eu comprar os bilhetes amanhã,
Que depois de amanhã é que está bem o espectáculo...
Antes, não...
Depois de amanhã terei a pose pública que amanhã estudarei.
Depois de amanhã serei finalmente o que hoje não posso nunca ser.
Só depois de amanhã...
Tenho sono como o frio de um cão vadio.
Tenho muito sono.
Amanhã te direi as palavras, ou depois de amanhã...
Sim, talvez só depois de amanhã...

O porvir...
Sim, o porvir...

will be summoned by a notice in the paper...
But a notice in tomorrow's paper...
Today I'd like to sleep, I'll compose tomorrow...
For today, I wonder what show could recreate my childhood?
Even if it meant buying tickets tomorrow,
since the day after would do for the show...
No sooner...
The day after tomorrow I shall have the public posture that I'll
rehearse tomorrow.
The day after tomorrow I shall at last be what I could never be today.
Not until the day after tomorrow...
I'm tired the way a stray dog is cold.
I'm very tired.
Tomorrow I'll tell you the words, or the day after...
Yes, perhaps not until the day after...

The time to come...
Yes, the time to come...

Gazetilha

Dos Lloyd Georges da Babilónia
Não reza a história nada.
Dos Briands da Assíria ou do Egipto,
Dos Trotskys de qualquer colónia
Grega ou romana já passada,
O nome é morto, inda que escrito.

Só o parvo dum poeta, ou um louco
Que fazia filosofia,
Ou um geómetra maduro,
Sobrevive a esse tanto pouco
Que está lá para trás no escuro
E nem a história já historia.

Ó grandes homens do Momento!
Ó grandes glórias a ferver
De quem a obscuridade foge!
Aproveitem sem pensamento!
Tratem da fama e do comer,
Que amanhã é dos loucos de hoje!

Feuilleton

Of ancient Babylon's Lloyd Georges,
history has breathed its last.
The Egyptian or Assyrian Briand,
the Trotskys in colonial quarters
of the Greek or Roman past—
their names, though written once, are gone.

Only some muddle-headed poet
or philosophizing loon,
a geometer, old and doddering,
survives near-nothingness, pulls through it
and exits that recess of gloom
whereof the books no longer sing.

O mighty heroes of the Moment!
O you seething glories great,
from whom the dark oblivion flies!
Prosper for now and think not of it!
Mind your fame and eat your meat,
for tomorrow is the prize
of today's fools and nobodies!

Apontamento

A minha alma partiu-se como um vaso vazio.
Caiu pela escada excessivamente abaixo.
Caiu das mãos da criada descuidada.
Caiu, fez-se em mais pedaços do que havia loiça no vaso.

Asneira? Impossível? Sei lá!
Tenho mais sensações do que tinha quando me sentia eu.
Sou um espalhamento de cacos sobre um capacho por sacudir.

Fiz barulho na queda como um vaso que se partia.
Os deuses que há debruçam-se do parapeito da escada.
E fitam os cacos que a criada deles fez de mim.

Não se zangam com ela.
São tolerantes com ela.
O que eu era um vaso vazio?

Olham os cacos absurdamente conscientes,
Mas conscientes de si-mesmos, não conscientes deles.

Olham e sorriem.
Sorriem tolerantes à criada involuntária.

Alastra a grande escadaria atapetada de estrelas.
Um caco brilha, virado do exterior lustroso, entre os astros.
A minha obra? A minha alma principal? A minha vida?

Jotted Note

My soul broke apart like an empty vase.
It fell excessively far down the stairs.
It fell right out of the careless housemaid's hands.
It fell and broke into more bits than there was china in the vase.

Nonsense? Impossible? Who can say?!
I have more feeling now than when I felt myself.
I am a strewing of shards across a mat that needs a shake.

I made a noise as I fell like a vase shattering.
The gods above lean over the stair-rail,
staring down at the shards the maid has made of me.

They are not cross with her.
They are tolerant with her.
What was I for an empty vase?

They look upon the absurdly conscious shards—
conscious of themselves, not conscious of them.

They look and they smile.
They smile tolerantly at the unintending maid.

The stairway is spread wide with a carpet of stars.
A shard, turned glossy side up, shines out among the spheres.
My work? My chiefest soul? My life?

Um caco.
E os deuses olham-no especialmente, pois não sabem porque ficou ali.

One shard.

One the gods look upon especially, wondering why it ever got there.

Aniversário

No tempo em que festejavam o dia dos meus anos,
Eu era feliz e ninguém estava morto.
Na casa antiga, até eu fazer anos era uma tradição de há séculos,
E a alegria de todos, e a minha, estava certa com uma religião qualquer.

No tempo em que festejavam o dia dos meus anos,
Eu tinha a grande saúde de não perceber coisa nenhuma,
De ser inteligente para entre a família,
E de não ter as esperanças que os outros tinham por mim.
Quando vim a ter esperanças, já não sabia ter esperanças.
Quando vim a olhar para a vida, perdera o sentido da vida.

Sim, o que fui de suposto a mim-mesmo,
O que fui de coração e parentesco,
O que fui de serões de meia-província,
O que fui de amarem-me e eu ser menino,
O que fui — ai, meu Deus!, o que só hoje sei que fui...
A que distância!...
(Nem o acho...)
O tempo em que festejavam o dia dos meus anos!

O que eu sou hoje é como a humidade no corredor do fim da casa,
Pondo grelado nas paredes...
O que eu sou hoje (e a casa dos que me amaram treme através das
                                                    minhas lágrimas),
O que eu sou hoje é terem vendido a casa,

Birthday

Back when they used to celebrate my birthday,
I was happy and no one was dead.
In our old house, my birthday was a tradition going back centuries,
and everyone's joy, and mine, fit into some sort of religion.

Back when they used to celebrate my birthday,
I enjoyed the great healthiness of not understanding a thing,
of being clever to my family,
and having none of the hopes that others had for me.
When I got round to having hopes, I no longer knew how to be hopeful.
When I got round to having a look at my life, I had lost my sense of life.

Yes, what I was supposed to be to myself,
what I was from heart and kinship,
what I was from evenings in the semi-countryside,
what I was from being loved as a boy,
what I was—oh, my God!, what I never knew I was till now…
So far away!…
(I can't even find it…)
Back when they used to celebrate my birthday!

What I am today is like the damp in the corridor at the end of the house,
growing sprouts in the walls…
What I am today (and the house of the ones who loved me trembles
                                                    through my tears),
what I am today is how they have sold the house

É terem morrido todos,
É estar eu sobrevivente a mim-mesmo como um fósforo frio...

No tempo em que festejavam o dia dos meus anos...
Que meu amor, como uma pessoa, esse tempo!
Desejo físico da alma de se encontrar ali outra vez,
Por uma viagem metafísica e carnal,
Com uma dualidade de eu para mim...
Comer o passado como pão de fome, sem tempo de manteiga nos dentes!

Vejo tudo outra vez com uma nitidez que me cega para o que há aqui...
A mesa posta com mais lugares, com melhores desenhos na louça, com
                                                              mais copos,
O aparador com muitas coisas, — doces, frutas, o resto na sombra
                                                      debaixo do alçado —,
As tias velhas, os primos diferentes, e tudo era por minha causa,
No tempo em que festejavam o dia dos meus anos...

Pára, meu coração!
Não penses! Deixa o pensar na cabeça!
Ó meu Deus, meu Deus, meu Deus!
Hoje já não faço anos.
Duro.
Somam-se-me dias.
Serei velho quando o for.
Mais nada.
Raiva de não ter trazido o passado roubado na algibeira!...

O tempo em que festejavam o dia dos meus anos!...

and all died off,
how I have outlived myself like a match gone cold…

Back when they used to celebrate my birthday…
So dear to me, like a person, that time!
How my soul physically longs to find itself there again,
by a journey both metaphysical and carnal,
with a duality between myself and me…
To eat up the past like the bread of hunger, too quick to feel the
$$\text{butter it in my teeth!}$$

I see it all over again with a clarity that blinds me to what is here…
The table laid with more places, nicer patterns on the china, more glasses,
the sideboard loaded with things—sweets, fruits, the rcst in shadow
$$\text{under the cabinet—,}$$
the old aunts, the different cousins, and all there for me,
back when they used to celebrate my birthday…

Stop it, my heart!
No thinking! Leave that in the head!
Oh my God, my God, my God!
I no longer have birthdays.
I last.
I tack on days.
When I'm old I'll be old.
That's all.
Maddening that I didn't carry the past away in my pocket!…

Back when they used to celebrate my birthday!…

Trapo

O dia deu em chuvoso.
A manhã, contudo, esteve bastante azul.
O dia deu em chuvoso.
Desde manhã eu estava um pouco triste.
Antecipação? tristeza? coisa nenhuma?
Não sei: já ao acordar estava triste.
O dia deu em chuvoso.

Bem sei: a penumbra da chuva é elegante.
Bem sei: o sol oprime, por ser tão ordinário, um elegante.
Bem sei: ser susceptível às mudanças de luz não é elegante.
Mas quem disse ao sol ou aos outros que eu quero ser elegante?
Dêem-me o céu azul e o sol visível.
Névoas, chuvas, escuros — isso tenho eu em mim.
Hoje quero só sossego.
Até amaria o lar, desde que o não tivesse.
Chego a ter sono da vontade de ter sossego.
Não exageremos!
Tenho efectivamente sono, sem explicação.
O dia deu em chuvoso.

Carinhos? afectos? São memórias...
É preciso ser-se criança para os ter...
Minha madrugada perdida, meu céu azul verdadeiro!
O dia deu em chuvoso.

Boca bonita da filha do caseiro,
Polpa de fruta de um coração por comer...

Rag

The day went rainy.
The morning, though, was quite clear.
The day went rainy.
Since morning I felt a bit sad.
Anticipation? Gloominess? Nothing at all?
I don't know: I woke up already feeling sad.
The day went rainy.

I am well aware: the half-light of the rain is elegant.
I am well aware: sunshine is oppressively vulgar when one is elegant.
I am well aware: being sensitive to changes in the light is not elegant.
But who told the sun or anyone else that I wanted to be elegant?
Give me blue sky and a visible sun.
Fog, rain, gloom—that much I've got in me.
All I want today is calm.
I would even love a home, so long as I didn't have one.
I actually feel sleepy, I want peace so badly.
Let us not exaggerate!
I do feel sleepy, with no explanation.
The day went rainy.

Tenderness? Affection? Just memories…
One must be a child in order to get them…
My lost dawn, my true blue sky!
The day went rainy.

Pretty lips of the caretaker's daughter,
fruity pulp of a heart uneaten…

Quando foi isso? Não sei...
No azul da manhã...

O dia deu em chuvoso.

When was that? I don't know…
Sometime in the clear blue morning…

The day went rainy.

Ah, um soneto...

Meu coração é um almirante louco
Que abandonou a profissão do mar
E que a vai relembrando pouco a pouco
Em casa a passear, a passear...

No movimento (eu mesmo me desloco
Nesta cadeira, só de o imaginar)
O mar abandonado fica em foco
Nos músculos cansados de parar.

Há saudades nas pernas e nos braços.
Há saudades no cérebro por fora.
Há grandes raivas feitas de cansaços.

Mas — esta é boa! — era do coração
Que eu falava... e onde diabo estou eu agora
Com almirante em vez de sensação?...

Ah, a sonnet...

My heart is a demented admiral,
long since retired from the briny waters,
who manages, in pieces, to recall
those days, whilst round and round the house he potters...

And with his motion (I shift slightly, too,
in my chair, just from visualizing it)
the sea he left behind comes into view
in his old muscles, tired of having quit.

A yearning works his limbs to do their part.
A yearning simmers through his brain and out.
A rage runs deep, begot of lethargy.

But—goodness me!—the matter was my heart...
and what the devil have I got on about
with admirals where feelings ought to be?...

QUERO ACABAR ENTRE ROSAS, PORQUE AS AMEI NA INFÂNCIA.
Os crisântemos de depois, desfolhei-os a frio.
Falem pouco, devagar.
Que eu não oiça, sobretudo com o pensamento.
O que quis? Tenho as mãos vazias,
Crispadas flebilmente sobre a colcha longínqua.
O que pensei? Tenho a boca seca, abstracta.
O que vivi? Era tão bom dormir!

I wish to end up among roses, for I loved them as a child.
The chrysanthemums later on, I tore the petals off cold-heartedly.
Speak slowly, sparely.
Don't let me hear, least of all with my thoughts.
What have I wished? My hands are empty,
ruefully clutching my long-lost quilt.
What have I thought? My mouth is dry, abstracted.
What have I lived? It would be so nice to sleep!

Magnificat

Quando é que passará esta noite interna, o universo,
E eu, a minha alma, terei o meu dia?
Quando é que despertarei de estar acordado?
Não sei. O sol brilha alto,
Impossível de fitar.
As estrelas pestanejam frio,
Impossíveis de contar.
O coração pulsa alheio,
Impossível de escutar.
Quando é que passará este drama sem teatro,
Ou este teatro sem drama,
E recolherei a casa?
Onde? Como? Quando?
Gato que me fitas com olhos de vida,
Quem tens lá no fundo?
É Esse! É esse!
Esse mandará como Josué parar o sol e eu acordarei;
E então será dia.
Sorri, dormindo, minha alma!
Sorri, minha alma, será dia!

Magnificat

When will this inward night, the universe, end,
and I, my soul, have my day?
When shall I ever awaken from being awake?
I don't know. The sun shines on above,
too bright to look at.
The stars blink on coldly,
too many to count.
The heart throbs on blankly,
too secret to hear.
When will this theaterless drama be done,
or this dramaless theater,
and I get to go home?
Where? How? When?
Cat staring up at me with eyes of life,
who have you got in there?
It is He! It is he!
Like Joshua he will command the sun to stop and I shall awake;
and then it will be day.
Smile in your sleep, my soul!
Smile, my soul, it will be day!

Pecado original

Ah, quem escreverá a história do que poderia ter sido?
Será essa, se alguém a escrever,
A verdadeira história da humanidade.

O que há é só o mundo verdadeiro, não é nós, só o mundo;
O que não há somos nós, e a verdade está aí.

Sou quem falhei ser.
Somos todos quem nos supusemos.
A nossa realidade é o que não conseguimos nunca.

Que é daquela nossa verdade — o sonho à janela da infância?
Que é daquela nossa certeza — o propósito à mesa de depois?

Medito, a cabeça curvada contra as mãos sobrepostas
Sobre o parapeito alto da janela de sacada,
Sentado de lado numa cadeira, depois de jantar.

Que é da minha realidade, que só tenho a vida?
Que é de mim, que sou só quem existo?

Quantos Césares fui!

Na alma, e com alguma verdade;
Na imaginação, e com alguma justiça;
Na inteligência, e com alguma razão —
Meu Deus! meu Deus! meu Deus! —

Original Sin

Ah, who will write the history of what might have been?
That would be, if anyone were to write it,
the true history of humanity.

That which is, is only the actual world—not us, only the world;
we are that which is not, and therein lies the truth.

I am who I have failed to be.
We are all the ones we have supposed we could be.
Our reality is that which we never attain.

Where's that old truth of ours—the dream at our childhood window?
Where's that old certainty of ours—the intention on the table later on?

I ponder, bowing my head against my hands
folded over the high rail of the balconette,
sitting sideways in a chair, after supper.

What's become of my reality, when I've nothing but my life?
What's become of me, when I'm only the one I exist as?

How many Caesars have I been!

In my soul, and rather truthfully;
in my imagination, and rather justly;
in my mind, and rather rightly—
My God! My God! My God!—

Quantos Césares fui!
Quantos Césares fui!
Quantos Césares fui!

How many Caesars have I been!
How many Caesars have I been!
How many Caesars have I been!

Dactilografia

Traço, sozinho, no meu cubículo de engenheiro, o plano,
Formo o projecto, aqui isolado,
Remoto até de quem eu sou.

Ao lado, acompanhamento banalmente sinistro,
O tic-tac estalado das máquinas de escrever.

Que náusea da vida!
Que abjecção esta regularidade!
Que sono este ser assim!

Outrora, quando fui outro, eram castelos e cavalarias
(Ilustrações, talvez, de qualquer livro de infância),
Outrora, quando fui verdadeiro ao meu sonho,
Eram grandes paisagens do Norte, explícitas de neve,
Eram grandes palmares do sul, opulentos de verdes.

Outrora...

Ao lado, acompanhamento banalmente sinistro,
O tic-tac estalado das máquinas de escrever.

Temos todos duas vidas:
A verdadeira, que é a que sonhamos na infância,
E que continuamos sonhando, adultos, num substrato de névoa;
A falsa, que é a que vivemos em convivência com outros,
Que é a prática, a útil,
Aquela em que acabam por nos meter num caixão.

Typewriting

Alone in my engineer's cubicle, I draw up the plan,
work out the blueprint here in isolation,
secluded even from who I am.

Off to the side, a drearily sinister accompaniment,
the sputtering click-clack of the typewriters.

This nauseating life!
This degrading regularity!
So dull, being like this!

Long ago, when I was someone else, there were castles and knights,
(illustrations, perhaps, from some children's book),
long ago, when I was true to my dream,
there were great northern landscapes explicit with snow,
there were great southern palm-forests lush with greenery.

Long ago...

Off to the side, a drearily sinister accompaniment,
the sputtering click-clack of the typewriters.

We each have two lives:
the true one, the one we dream of in childhood,
and still dream of as adults, in an underlayer of mist;
the false one, the one we experience alongside other people,
the practical, useful one,
the one where we end up bunged in a coffin.

Na outra não há caixões, nem mortes,
Há só ilustrações de infância:
Grandes livros coloridos, para ver mas não ler;
Grandes páginas de cores para recordar mais tarde.
Na outra somos nós,
Na outra vivemos;
Nesta morremos, que é o que viver quer dizer.
Neste momento, pela náusea, vivo na outra...

Mas ao lado, acompanhamento banalmente sinistro,
Se, desmeditando, acordo,
Ergue a voz o tic-tac estalado das máquinas de escrever.

In the other life there are no coffins, no deaths,
only children's illustrations:
big colorful books, to look at but not read;
big colored pages to remember later on.
In the other life we are ourselves,
in the other life we live;
in this one we die, and that's what living means.
At this moment, with my nausea, I am living in the other one…

But off to the side, a drearily sinister accompaniment,
If, by ceasing to meditate, I waken,
the sputtering click-clack of the typewriters raises its voice.

Dobrada à moda do Porto

Um dia, num restaurante, fora do espaço e do tempo,
Serviram-me o amor como dobrada fria.
Disse delicadamente ao missionário da cozinha
Que a preferia quente,
Que a dobrada (e era à moda do Porto) nunca se come fria.

Impacientaram-se comigo.
Nunca se pode ter razão, nem num restaurante.
Não comi, não pedi outra coisa, paguei a conta,
E vim passear para toda a rua.

Quem sabe o que isto quer dizer?
Eu não sei, e foi comigo...

(Sei muito bem que na infância de toda a gente houve um jardim,
Particular ou público, ou do vizinho.
Sei muito bem que brincarmos era o dono dele.
E que a tristeza é de hoje.)

Sei isso muitas vezes,
Mas, se eu pedi amor porque é que me trouxeram
Dobrada à moda do Porto fria?
Não é prato que se possa comer frio,
Mas trouxeram-mo frio.
Não me queixei, mas estava frio,
Nunca se pode comer frio, mas veio frio.

Tripe Oporto Style

One day, in a restaurant, outside space and time,
I had love served to me as cold tripe.
I said politely to the kitchen missionary
that I would rather have it hot,
since tripe (and it was Oporto style) is never eaten cold.

They got flustered with me.
One can never be right, even in a restaurant.
I didn't eat it, didn't order anything else, paid the bill,
and took a walk all the way down the street.

Who knows what any of this means?
I don't, and I'm the one it happened to…

(I know full well that in everyone's childhood was a garden,
private or public, or the neighbor's.
I know full well that its owner was our playing there.
And that sadness belongs to today.)

I know this many times over,
but why, if I asked for love, did they bring me
cold Oporto-style tripe?
It isn't a dish that can be eaten cold,
but they brought mine cold.
I made no fuss, but it was cold,
can never be eaten cold, but it came cold.

Poema em linha recta

Nunca conheci quem tivesse levado porrada.
Todos os meus conhecidos têm sido campeões em tudo.

E eu, tantas vezes reles, tantas vezes porco, tantas vezes vil,
Eu tantas vezes irrespondivelmente parasita,
Indesculpavelmente sujo,
Eu, que tantas vezes não tenho tido paciência para tomar banho,
Eu, que tantas vezes tenho sido ridículo, absurdo,
Que tenho enrolado os pés publicamente nos tapetes das etiquetas,
Que tenho sido grotesco, mesquinho, submisso e arrogante,
Que tenho sofrido enxovalhos e calado,
Que quando não tenho calado, tenho sido mais ridículo ainda;
Eu, que tenho sido cómico às criadas de hotel,
Eu, que tenho sentido o piscar de olhos dos moços de fretes,
Eu, que tenho feito vergonhas financeiras, pedido emprestado sem pagar,
Eu, que, quando a hora do soco surgiu, me tenho agachado
Para fora da possibilidade do soco;
Eu, que tenho sofrido a angústia das pequenas coisas ridículas,
Eu verifico que não tenho par nisto tudo neste mundo.

Toda a gente que eu conheço e que fala comigo
Nunca teve um acto ridículo, nunca sofreu enxovalho,
Nunca foi senão príncipe — todos eles príncipes — na vida...

Quem me dera ouvir de alguém a voz humana
Que confessasse não um pecado, mas uma infâmia;
Que contasse, não uma violência, mas uma cobardia!

Poem in a Straight Line

I've never met anyone who has been knocked down.
All my acquaintances have been champions in everything.

Whereas I, so often lousy, so often slovenly, so often vile,
so often an unanswerable leech,
an inexcusable slob,
I who so often haven't bothered to wash myself,
I who so often have been foolish, absurd,
who have publicly tangled my feet in the carpets of etiquette,
who have been grotesque, small-minded, craven and priggish,
who have taken slights and held my tongue,
who, when I have not held my tongue, have made all the more fool
                                                    of myself;
I who have been the laughingstock of hotel maids,
I who have felt the porters' winking,
I who have committed financial disgraces, have borrowed and not repaid,
I who, when the time has come for fisticuffs, have cowered
outside any chance of fisticuffs;
I who have suffered anguish over foolish little things,
I have confirmed that for all this I have no equal in this world.

Everyone I've met, who speaks to me,
has never once acted the fool, never taken a slight,
never been less than a prince—princes every one—in his life…

How I long to hear someone's human voice
confessing not a sin, but an infamy;
recounting, not any violence, but some cowardice!

Não, são todos o Ideal, se os oiço e me falam.
Quem há neste largo mundo que me confesse que uma vez foi vil?
Ó príncipes, meus irmãos,

Arre, estou farto de semi-deuses!
Onde é que há gente no mundo?

Então sou só eu que é vil e erróneo nesta terra?

Poderão as mulheres não os terem amado,
Podem ter sido traídos — mas ridículos nunca!
E eu, que tenho sido ridículo sem ter sido traído,
Como posso eu falar com os meus superiores sem titubear?
Eu, que tenho sido vil, literalmente vil,
Vil no sentido mesquinho e infame da vileza.

No, they are all the Ideal, when I hear them and they speak to me.
Who in this wide world will admit to me that he has ever been vile?
O princes, my brothers,

blast it all, I'm sick of demigods!
Where in the world are people?

What, am I the only one on this earth who is vile and flawed?

Women may not have loved them,
they might have been made cuckolds—but never fools!
And I, who have been a fool without being a cuckold,
how can I address my superiors without stammering?
I who have been vile, literally vile,
vile in the small, embarrassing sense of villainy.

O SONO QUE DESCE SOBRE MIM,
O sono mental que desce fisicamente sobre mim,
O sono universal que desce individualmente sobre mim —
Esse sono
Parecerá aos outros o sono de dormir,
O sono da vontade de dormir,
O sono de ser sono.

Mas é mais, mais de dentro, mais de cima:
É o sono da soma de todas as desilusões,
É o sono síntese de todas as desesperanças,
É o sono de haver mundo comigo lá dentro
Sem que eu houvesse contribuído em nada para isso.

O sono que desce sobre mim
É contudo como todos os sonos.
O cansaço tem ao menos brandura,
O abatimento tem ao menos sossego,
A rendição é ao menos o fim do esforço,
O fim é ao menos o já não haver que esperar.

Há um som de abrir uma janela,
Viro indiferente a cabeça para a esquerda
Por sobre o ombro que a sente,
Olho pela janela entreaberta:
A rapariga do segundo andar de defronte
Debruça-se com os olhos azuis à procura de alguém.
De quem?,

THE SLEEP THAT DESCENDS UPON ME,
the mental sleep that physically descends upon me,
the universal sleep that individually descends upon me—
this sleep
may appear to others the sleep of slumbering,
the sleep of sleepiness,
the sleep that sleep is.

But it is more, more from within, more from above:
it is the sleep that summarizes all disillusion,
the sleep that recapitulates all despair,
the sleep that there is a world with me in it,
without my having had a hand in that at all.

The sleep that descends upon me
is nevertheless like any sleep.
There is an ease, at least, to weariness,
a calm, at least, in exhaustion,
surrender at least means the end of an effort,
the end at least means no longer having to hope.

There's a sound of a window opening,
indifferently I turn my head to the left
over my shoulder which can feel it,
and look through the half-opened window:
the girl across on the second story
leans out with her blue eyes searching for someone.
For who?,

Pergunta a minha indiferença.
E tudo isso é sono.

Meu Deus, tanto sono!...

wonders my indifference.
And that is all sleepiness.

My God, so sleepy!…

AFINAL, A MELHOR MANEIRA DE VIAJAR É SENTIR.
Sentir tudo de todas as maneiras.
Sentir tudo excessivamente,
Porque todas as coisas são, em verdade, excessivas
E toda a realidade é um excesso, uma violência,
Uma alucinação extraordinariamente nítida
Que vivemos todos em comum com a fúria das almas,
O centro para onde tendem as estranhas forças centrífugas
Que são as psiques humanas no seu acordo de sentidos.

Quanto mais eu sinta, quanto mais eu sinta como várias pessoas,
Quanto mais personalidades eu tiver,
Quanto mais intensamente, estridentemente as tiver,
Quanto mais simultaneamente sentir com todas elas,
Quanto mais unificadamente diverso, dispersadamente atento,
Estiver, sentir, viver, for,
Mais possuirei a existência total do universo,
Mais completo serei pelo espaço inteiro fora,
Mais análogo serei a Deus, seja ele quem for,
Porque, seja ele quem for, com certeza que é Tudo,
E fora d'Ele há só Ele, e Tudo para Ele é pouco.

Cada alma é uma escada para Deus,
Cada alma é um corredor-Universo para Deus,
Cada alma é um rio correndo por margens de Externo
Para Deus e em Deus com um sussurro soturno.

Sursum corda! Erguei as almas! Toda a Matéria é Espírito,
Porque Matéria e Espírito são apenas nomes confusos
Dados à grande sombra que ensopa o Exterior em sonho

IN THE END, THE BEST WAY OF TRAVELING IS TO FEEL.
To feel everything in every way.
To feel it all excessively,
for all things are, in truth, excessive
and all reality is an excess, a violence,
an extraordinarily clear hallucination
lived by all of us together with the fury of our souls,
the center towards which tend the strange centrifugal forces
that are our human psyches in their sensory accord.

The more I feel, the more I feel as different persons,
the more personhoods I hold,
the more fiercely, stridently I hold them,
the more simultaneously I feel with them all,
the more unifiedly varied, manifoldly aware
I am, feel, live, become,
the more I shall possess the total existence of the universe,
the more whole I shall be throughout all space,
the more I shall resemble God, whoever he may be,
for whoever he may be, surely he is All,
and nothing outside Him but Himself, and All to Him but little.

Each soul is a ladder to God,
each soul is a corridor-Universe leading to God,
each soul is a river that runs through margins of the External
to God and in God with a sullen susurrus.

Sursum corda! Lift up your souls! All Matter is Spirit,
for Matter and Spirit are but confounded names
given to the great shadow that steeps the Exterior in dream

E funde em Noite e Mistério o Universo Excessivo!
Sursum corda! Na noite acordo, o silêncio é grande,
As coisas, de braços cruzados sobre o peito, reparam
Com uma tristeza nobre para os meus olhos abertos
Que as vê como vagos vultos nocturnos na noite negra.
Sursum corda! Acordo na noite e sinto-me diverso.
Todo o Mundo com a sua forma visível do costume,
Jaz no fundo dum poço e faz um ruído confuso,
Escuto-o, e no meu coração um grande pasmo soluça.

Sursum corda! Ó Terra, jardim suspenso, berço
Que embala a Alma dispersa da humanidade sucessiva!
Mãe verde e florida todos os anos recente,
Todos os anos vernal, estival, outonal, hiemal,
Todos os anos celebrando às mancheias as festas de Adónis
Num rito anterior a todas as significações,
Num grande culto em tumulto pelas montanhas e os vales!
Grande coração pulsando no peito nu dos vulcões,
Grande voz acordando em cataratas e mares,
Grande bacante ébria do Movimento e da Mudança,
Em cio de vegetação e florescência rompendo
Teu próprio corpo de terra e rochas, teu corpo submisso
À tua própria vontade transtornadora e eterna!
Mãe carinhosa e unânime dos ventos, dos mares, dos prados,
Vertiginosa mãe dos vendavais e ciclones,
Mãe caprichosa que faz vegetar e secar,
Que perturba as próprias estações e confunde
Num beijo imaterial os sóis e as chuvas e os ventos!

and smelts into Night and Mystery the Excessive Universe!
Sursum corda! In the night I awake, the silence is vast,
things, their arms crossed over their chests, regard
with a noble sorrow my gaping eyes,
which see them as dim darkling figures in the black night.
Sursum corda! I awake in the night and feel varied.
All the World with its visible form of wont
lies at the bottom of a well and makes a confounded noise,
I hearken to it, and in my heart a great amazement whimpers.

Sursum corda! O Earth, suspended garden, cradle
which rocks the manifold soul of successive humanity!
Green mother blossoming every year anew,
every year vernal, aestival, autumnal, hiemal,
every year honoring lavishly the feasts of Adonis
in a rite preceding all signification,
a great worship riotous over the mountains and valleys!
Great throbbing heart in the naked breasts of volcanoes,
great voice awakening in cataracts and oceans,
great drunken Bacchante of Motion and Change,
in a heat of growth and bloom cleaving open
thy very body of earth and stone, thy body submitted
to thine own eternal overturning will!
Unanimous doting mother of the winds, the seas, the meadows,
giddy mother of the squalls and cyclones,
fickle mother who makes thrive and wither,
who disturbs her very seasons and confounds
by an immaterial kiss the suns and the rains and the winds!

Sursum corda! Reparo para ti e todo eu sou um hino!
Tudo em mim como um satélite da tua dinâmica íntima
Volteia serpenteando, ficando como um anel
Nevoento, de sensações reminiscidas e vagas,
Em torno ao teu vulto interno, túrgido e fervoroso.

Ocupa de toda a tua força e de todo o teu poder quente
Meu coração a ti aberto!
Como uma espada trespassando meu ser erguido e extático,
Intersecciona com meu sangue, com a minha pele e os meus nervos,
Teu movimento contínuo, contíguo a ti própria sempre.

Sou um monte confuso de forças cheias de infinito
Tendendo em todas as direcções para todos os lados do espaço,
A Vida, essa coisa enorme, é que prende tudo e tudo une
E faz com que todas as forças que raivam dentro de mim
Não passem de mim, não quebrem meu ser, não partam meu corpo,
Não me arremessem, com uma bomba de Espírito que estoira
Em sangue e carne e alma espiritualizados para entre as estrelas,
Para além dos sóis de outros sistemas e dos astros remotos.

Tudo o que há dentro de mim tende a voltar a ser tudo.
Tudo que há dentro de mim tende a despejar-me no chão,
No vasto chão supremo que não está em cima nem em baixo
Mas sob as estrelas e os sóis, sob as almas e os corpos
Por uma oblíqua posse dos nossos sentidos intelectuais.

Sou uma chama ascendendo, mas ascendo para baixo e para cima,
Ascendo para todos os lados ao mesmo tempo, sou um globo

Sursum corda! I regard thee and I am all a hymn!
All of me as a satellite to thy innermost dynamic
snakes about, becoming like a misty ring
of vague reminisced sensations
round thy turgid, fervorous figure within.

Fill up with all thy strength and all thy fiery might
my heart opened unto thee!
Like a sword piercing through my ecstatic risen being,
intersect with my blood, with my skin and my nerves
thy continuous motion, contiguous unto thyself forever.

I am a great tangle of forces imbued with the infinite
tending in every direction towards everywhere in space,
Life, that enormous thing, is what holds all of me together,
and keeps all the forces that rage within me
from exceeding myself, from breaking my being, from splitting my body,
from hurling me out like a Spirit-bomb bursting
into blood and flesh and soul all spiritualized among the stars,
out past the suns of other systems and the spheres beyond.

Everything within me tends towards becoming everything again.
Everything within me tends towards dumping me to the ground,
the vast supreme ground that is neither above nor below
but under the stars and suns, under our souls and bodies
by way of a slanting possession of our intellectual senses.

I am a rising flame, but I rise both downwards and upwards,
I rise every way at once, I am an orb

De chamas explosivas buscando Deus e queimando
A crosta dos meus sentidos, o muro da minha lógica,
A minha inteligência limitadora e gelada.

Sou uma grande máquina movida por grandes correias
De que só vejo a parte que pega nos meus tambores,
O resto vai para além dos astros, passa para além dos sóis,
E nunca parece chegar ao tambor donde parte...

Meu corpo é um centro dum volante estupendo e infinito
Em marcha sempre vertiginosamente em torno de si,
Cruzando-se em todas as direcções com outros volantes,
Que se entrepenetram e misturam, porque isto não é no espaço
Mas não sei onde espacial de uma outra maneira-Deus.

Dentro de mim estão presos e atados ao chão
Todos os movimentos que compõem o universo,
A fúria minuciosa e dos átomos,
A fúria de todas as chamas, a raiva de todos os ventos,
A espuma furiosa de todos os rios, que se precipitam.
E a chuva como pedras atiradas de catapultas
De enormes exércitos de anões escondidos no céu.

Sou um formidável dinamismo obrigado ao equilíbrio
De estar dentro do meu corpo, de não transbordar da minh'alma.
Ruge, estoira, vence, quebra, estrondeia, sacode,
Freme, treme, espuma, venta, viola, explode,
Perde-te, transcende-te, circunda-te, vive-te, rompe e foge,
Sê com todo o meu corpo todo o universo e a vida,

of explosive flames seeking God and scorching
the crust of my senses, the wall of my logic,
my frozen, limiting intelligence.

I am a great machine powered by great chains,
only able to see the part of them fixed round my drums,
the rest runs out past the stars, beyond the suns,
and never seems to arrive at the drum where it started...

My body is the center of a stupendous infinite wheel
forever turning giddily about itself,
steering past other wheels on all sides,
which interpenetrate and merge, for this is not in space,
but a spatial elsewhere in some other God-way.

Within me is held and fastened to the ground
every motion that makes up the universe,
the meticulous fury belonging to the atoms,
the fury of every flame, the rage of every wind,
the furious foam of every surging river.
And the rain like pebbles fired from catapults
by mighty armies of dwarves hidden in the sky.

I am an awesome dynamism compelled to the equilibrium
of being within my body, of not overflowing my soul.
Roar, burst, smite, crack, boom, clatter,
crash, quake, foam, gust, breach, blast,
begone, transcend yourself, surround yourself, experience yourself,
                                                    break free and fly,
become with all of my body all the universe and life,

Arde com todo o meu ser todos os lumes e luzes,
Risca com toda a minha alma todos os relâmpagos e fogos,
Sobrevive-me em minha vida em todas as direcções!

burn with all of my being every flame and light,
strike with all of my soul every flash and fire,
outlive me in my life in every direction!

NOTES

Idle sun of useless days As Fernando Cabral Martins observed (F. Pessoa, *Ficções do Interlúdio*, p. 254), this poem was published by the author with the title "Canção" ["Song"] in *Ilustração Portuguesa* (1922), later untitled in *Athena* (issue 3, 1924), and finally again with the same title in *Cancioneiro – Salão dos Independentes* (1930). In this anthology, Casais Monteiro cites the 1924 edition.

Excerpts of Two Odes (Evidently the ending of two odes) "Come, most ancient selfsame Night" and "Ah the dusk hour, the fall of night, the lighting of the lights all across the great cities" are generally published as two fragments of a single poem: "Excerpts of Two Odes (Evidently the endings of two odes)," a title extracted from a version handwritten by Fernando Pessoa. In *Revista de Portugal* (issue 4), the source used by Casais Monteiro, both poems had appeared together with the title "Two Poems," probably assigned by the publisher of the journal. Casais Monteiro dismissed the title "Two Poems" and opted to publish them separately.

DATES OF THE POEMS AND SOURCES INDICATED BY A. CASAIS MONTEIRO

Ó naus felizes, que do mar vago
Obras Completas de Fernando Pessoa, Lisboa,
Ática, I [Obras Completas, I]

Impressões do crepúsculo
29.3.1913 • A Renascença, 1, 1914

Hora absurda
04.07.1913 • Exílio, 1, 1916

Chuva oblíqua
08.03.1914 • Orpheu, 2, 1915

Como a noite é longa!
04.11.1914 • O Globo, 28, 01.08.1944

Bate a luz no cimo
04.11.1914 • O Globo, 28, 01.08.1944

Saber? Que sei eu?
04.11.1914 • O Globo, 28, 01.08.1944

Vai redonda e alta
04.11.1914 • O Globo, 28, 01.08.1944

Chove? Nenhuma chuva cai...
01.12.1914 • O Globo, 28, 01.08.1944

Passos da cruz
Centauro, 1, 1916

Súbita mão de algum fantasma oculto
14.03.1917 • Obras Completas, I

Intervalo
Momento, 8, 1935

Onde pus a esperança, as rosas
16.02.1920 • Presença, série II, 2, 1940

Natal
Contemporânea, 6, 1922

Canção
Folhas de arte, 1924

Leve, breve, suave
Athena, 3, 1924

Pobre velha música!
Athena, 3, 1924

Sol nulo dos dias vãos
Athena, 3, 1924

Trila na noite uma flauta. É de algum
Athena, 3, 1924

Manhã dos outros! Ó sol que dás confiança
Athena, 3, 1924

Dorme sobre o meu seio
Athena, 3, 1924

Ao longe, ao luar
Athena, 3, 1924

Ela canta, pobre ceifeira
Athena, 3, 1924

O menino da sua mãe
Contemporânea, série III, 1, 1926

Marinha
Presença, 5, 1927

Qualquer música...
Presença, 10, 1928

Depois da feira
Presença, 16, 1928

Tenho dó das estrelas
[Revista] Mensagem, 1, 1938

Natal... Na província neva
Notícias Ilustrado, 30.12.1928

Aqui na orla da praia, mudo e contente do mar
10.08.1929 • Obras Completas, I

Contemplo o lago mudo
04.08.1930 • Revista de Portugal, 4, 1938

Dá a surpresa de ser
10.09.1930 • Obras Completas, I

Não: não digas nada!
05/06.02.1931 • Obras Completas, I

O andaime
Presença, 31-32, 1931

Hoje que a tarde é calma e o céu tranquilo
01.08.1931 • Obras Completas, I

Quem bate à minha porta
23.05.1932 • Revista de Portugal, 4, 1938

Na sombra do Monte Abiegno
03.10.1932 • Obras Completas, I

Autopsicografia
Presença, 36, 1932

Não sei se é sonho, se realidade
30.08.1933 • Obras Completas, I

Não sei que sonho me não descansa
10.10.1933 • Obras Completas, I

Foi um momento
09.05.1934 • Presença, série II, 2, 1940

Cessa o teu canto!
09.05.1934 • Presença, série II, 2, 1940

Neste mundo em que esquecemos
09.05.1934 • Presença, série II, 2, 1940

Montes, e a paz que há neles, pois são longe...
09.05.1934 • Presença, série II, 2, 1940

Onda que, enrolada, tornas
09.05.1934 • *Obras Completas*, I

O céu, azul de luz quieta
Presença, 53-54, 1938

Dizem?
Obras Completas, I

Glosa
[Revista] *Mensagem*, 1, 1938

Assim, sem nada feito e o por fazer
[Revista] *Mensagem*, 1, 1938

de *Mensagem*
   Ulisses; D. João, Infante de Portugal;
   D. Sebastião, Rei de Portugal; O Infante
   D. Henrique; O Mostrengo; Noite
   Fernando Pessoa, *Mensagem*, Lisboa,
   Parceria António Maria Pereira, 1934.

Gomes Leal
Cancioneiro, 1930

O último sortilégio
Presença, 29, 1930

Iniciação
Presença, 35, 1932

Liberdade
16.03.1935 • *Seara Nova*, 526, 11.09.1937

O corvo
Athena, 1, 1924

Annabel Lee
Athena, 4, 1925

Ulalume
Athena, 4, 1925

Hino a Pã
Presença, 33, 1931

«O Guardador de Rebanhos» (V, IX, X, XX,
XVIII, XXXII, XXXIX, XLVI, XLVIII, XLIX)
Athena, 4, 1925

   O oitavo poema de «O Guardador de
   Rebanhos» (VIII)
   Presença, 30, 1931

O penúltimo poema
Presença, 31-32, 1931

«Poemas Inconjuntos»
Athena, 5, 1925

Odes. Livro Primeiro
Athena, 1, 1924

Outras Odes
   Não só vinho, mas nele o olvido, deito
   Presença, 6, 1927

   Quanta tristeza e amargura afoga
   Presença, 6, 1927

   A nada imploram tuas mãos já coisas
   Presença, 6, 1927

O rastro breve que das ervas moles
Presença, 10, 1928

Já sobre a fronte vã se me acinzenta
Presença, 10, 1928

Quando, Lídia, vier o nosso Outono
Presença, 31-32, 1931

Ténue, como se de Éolo a esquecessem
Presença, 31-32, 1931

Para ser grande, sê inteiro: nada
Presença, 37, 1933

Dois excertos de odes
30.06.1914 • *Revista de Portugal*, 4, 1938

Soneto já antigo
Contemporânea, 6, 1922

Lisbon revisited (1923)
Contemporânea, 8, 1923

Lisbon revisited (1926)
Contemporânea, série III, 2, 1926

Tabacaria
15.01.1928 • *Presença*, 39, 1933

Escrito num livro abandonado em viagem
Presença, 10, 1928

Apostila
11.04.1928 • *Notícias Ilustrado*, 21.05.1928

Adiamento
14.04.1928 • *Solução Editora*, 1, 1928

Gazetilha
Presença, 18, 1929

Apontamento
Presença, 20, 1929

Aniversário
15.10.1929 • *Presença*, 27, 1930

Trapo
Presença, 31-32, 1931

Ah, um soneto...
Presença, 34, 1932

Quero acabar entre rosas, porque as amei na infância
Descobrimento, 1, 1932

Pecado original
07.12.1933 • *Obras Completas*, II

Dactilografia
19.12.1933 • *Presença*, série II, 1, 1939

Dobrada à moda do Porto
Obras Completas, II

Poema em linha recta
Obras Completas, II

O sono que desce sobre mim
28.08.1935 • *Presença*, 52, 1938

Afinal, a melhor maneira de viajar é sentir
Obras Completas, II

APPENDICES

Meu presado Camarada:

     Muito agradeço a sua carta, a que vou responder
immediata e integralmente. Antes de, propriamente, começar,
quero pedir-lhe desculpa de lhe escrever neste papel de copia.
Acabou-se-me o decente, é domingo, e não posso arranjar outro. Mas mais vale, creio, o mau papel que o addiamento.

     Em primeiro logar, quero dizer-lhe que nunca eu
veria "outras razões" em qualquer coisa que escrevesse, dis-
cordando, a meu respeito. Sou um dos poucos poetas portugue-
zes que não decretou a sua propria infallibilidade, nem to-
mou qualquer critica, que se lhe faça, como um acto de lesa-
divindade. Além disso, quaesquer que sejam os meus defeitos
mentaes, é nulla em mim a tendencia para a mania da persegui-
ção. Áparte isso, conheço já sufficientemente a sua indepen-
dencia mental, que, se me é permittido dizel-o, muito appro-
vo e louvo. Nunca me propuz ser Mestre ou Chefe - Mestre,
porque não sei ensinar, nem sei se teria que ensinar; Chefe,
porque nem sei estrellar ovos. Não se preoccupe, pois, em
qualquer occasião, com o que tenha que dizer a meu respeito.
Não procuro caves nos andares nobres.

     Concordo absolutamente comsigo em que não foi
feliz a estreia, que de mim mesmo fiz com um livro da natureza de "Mensagem". Sou, de facto, um nacionalista mystico, um
sebastianista racional. Mas sou, áparte isso, e até em contra-
dicção com isso, muitas outras coisas. E essas coisas, pela
mesma natureza do livro, a "Mensagem" não as inclue.

     Comecei por esse livro as minhas publicações
pela simples razão de que foi o primeiro livro que consegui,
não sei porquê, ter organizado e prompto. Como estava prompto, incitaram-me a que o publicasse: acceitei. Nem o fiz,
devo dizer, com os olhos postos no premio possivel do Secretariado, embora nisso não houvesse peccado intellectual de
maior. O meu livro estava prompto em Setembro, e eu julgava,
até, que não poderia concorrer ao premio, pois ignorava que
o praso para entrega dos livros, que primitivamente fôra a-
té fim de Julho, fôra alargado até fim de Outubro. Como, porém, em fim de Outubro já havia exemplares promptos da "Mensagem", fiz entrega dos que o Secretariado exigia. O livro
estava exactamente nas condições (nacionalismo) de concorrer.
Concorri.

     Quando ás vezes pensava na ordem de uma futura
publicação de obras minhas, nunca um livro do genero de "Mensagem" figurava em numero um. Hesitava entre se deveria começar por um livro de versos grande - um livro de umas 350
paginas -, englobando as varias sub-personalidades de Fernando
Pessoa elle-mesmo, ou se deveria abrir com uma novella poli-
ciaria, que ainda não consegui completar.

First page of the letter sent to Adolfo Casais Monteiro.
Photo: National Library of Portugal

Letter from Fernando Pessoa on the Genesis of the Heteronyms

Post Office Box 147
Lisbon, January 13, 1935

My dear Comrade:

I am very grateful for your letter, which I will respond to immediately and in full. Before properly beginning, I would like to apologize to you for writing on this copy paper. I am out of decent paper, it is Sunday, and I cannot get more. But better, I think, bad paper than delay.

In the first place, I want to tell you that I have never found "other motives" in anything I have written, disagreeing about myself. I am one of the few Portuguese poets who has not decreed himself infallible, and does not take any criticism made to him as an act of lèse-divinity. Besides, whatever my mental defects may be, the tendency towards a mania of persecution is void in me. That aside, I am sufficiently aware of your mental independence, which, if I may say so, I greatly approve of and praise. I have never made myself out to be a Master or Chief—a Master, because I cannot teach, nor do I know if I would have anything to teach; a Chief, because I cannot even scramble eggs.[1] Do not fret, therefore, at any moment, over what you have to say about me. I do not look for basements on the upper floors.

I agree with you completely that the debut I made of myself with a book of the nature of *Message* was infelicitous. I am, in fact, a mystic nationalist, a rational Sebastianist. But I am, besides that, and even in contradiction with it, many other things. And those things, because of the nature of the book, *Message* does not include.

---

1. The Portuguese word *chefe*, translated here as "chief," also means "chef." [Translator's Note]

I have started my publications with this book for the simple reason that it was the first book I managed, who knows why, to have organized and ready. Since it was ready, I was encouraged to publish it: I agreed. I did not do so, I should say, with my eyes on a possible Secretariat prize, although that would not have been a major intellectual sin. My book was ready in September, and I did not even believe I could compete for the prize, being unaware that the deadline for the submission of books, which initially had been the end of July, had been extended to the end of October. Since, however, at the end of October there were already copies of *Message* ready, I submitted those requested by the Secretariat. The book had exactly the conditions (nationalism) for competition. I entered.

When I used to think about the order of future publication of my works, I never pictured a book such as *Message* as number one. I hesitated over whether I should begin with a long book of verse—a book of 350 pages or so—encompassing the various subpersonalities of Fernando Pessoa himself, or should open with a police novella, which I never managed to complete.

I agree with you, I said, that the debut I made of myself with the publication of *Message* was not felicitous. Precisely because that facet—somewhat secondary—of my personality had not ever been sufficiently manifested in my collaborations in journals (except in the case of the "Mar Português" ["Portuguese Sea"] part of the same book)—precisely for that reason it was appropriate that it appear, and right away. This coincided, without my planning or premeditating it (I am incapable of practical premeditation), with one of the critical moments (in the original sense of the word) of remodeling the national subconscious. What I did by chance and was completed through correspondence, had been precisely hewn, with Square and Compass, by the Great Architect.

(Let me interrupt. I am not mad or drunk. I am, however, writing straight ahead, as quickly as the typewriter allows me, and I am employing the phrases that come to me, without looking at what literature is in them. Imagine—and you will do well to imagine, because it is true—that I am simply talking to you.)

I will respond directly now to your three questions: (1) future publication plan for my works, (2) genesis of my heteronyms, and (3) occultism.

With *Message* published under the conditions I mentioned, it being a unilateral manifestation, here is how I intend to proceed. I am now completing a fully remodeled version of "O Banqueiro Anarquista" ["The Anarchist Banker"]; this should be ready soon and I expect, as soon as it is, to publish it immediately. If I do so, I will translate that piece immediately into English, and see if I can publish it in England. The way it should turn out, it has potential in Europe. (Do not take this sentence in the sense of an immanent Nobel Prize.) Then—and now I will properly respond to your question, which refers to poetry—I intend, during the summer, to assemble that large volume of sort poems by Fernando Pessoa himself, and see if I am able to publish it by the end of this year. That will be the volume you are awaiting, and it is the one I want done myself. That one, then, will have all the facets, except the nationalist one, which *Message* has already manifested.

I have referred, as you have seen, to Fernando Pessoa only. I am not thinking of Caeiro, Ricardo Reis, or Álvaro de Campos. I cannot do any of that, in the sense of publishing, not until (see above) I am given the Nobel Prize. And yet—I think sadly—I have put into Caeiro all my power of dramatic depersonalization, into Ricardo Reis all my mental discipline, dressed in the music that is his own; in Álvaro de Campos I have put all the emotion that I do not give to myself or to life. To think, my dear Casais Monteiro, that all these must be, in the sense of publication, surpassed by Fernando Pessoa, impure and simple!

I believe I have answered your first question.

If I have been remiss, let me know in what. If I can respond, I will. I have no other plans, for now. And, knowing what it is my plans lead toward, that is reason to say, *Thank God*!

I will move on now to your question about the genesis of my heteronyms. I will see if I can answer it thoroughly.

Let me begin with the psychiatric part. The origin of my heteronyms is the deep streak of hysteria that exists in me. I do not know if I am simply hysterical, or if I am more properly a hystero-neurasthenic. I am inclined to this second hypothesis, because in me are phenomena of abulia that hysteria, properly speaking, does not include in the list of its symptoms. Be that as it may, the mental origin of my heteronyms lies in my constant and organic tendency towards depersonalization and dissimulation. These phenomena— luckily for me and for others—have been mentalized in me; I mean, they are not manifested in my practical, exterior life in contact with others; they make an inward explosion and I experience them alone with myself. If I were a woman—in women hysteric phenomena break out in seizures and the like— every poem by Álvaro de Campos (the most hysterically hysterical part of me) would be an alarm to the neighbors. But I am a man—and in men hysteria assumes primarily mental aspects; thus it all comes out in silence and poetry…

This explains, *tant bien que mal*, the organic origin of my heteronymism. I will now tell you the direct story of my heteronyms. Let me begin with the ones who have died, some of whom I no longer remember—those who lie lost in the distant past of my almost forgotten childhood.

Since I was a child I have had the tendency to create around myself a fictitious world, to surround myself with friends and acquaintances who have never existed. (I do not know, of course, if they really have never existed, or if it is I who do not exist. In these as in all matters, we should not be dogmatic). For as long as I have known myself as what I call myself, I can remember detailing mentally, with figure, movements, character, and history, various unreal figures who were to me as visible and as much my own as the things of what we call, perhaps unfairly, real life. This tendency, which has come to me ever since I can remember being a self, has always followed me, changing a bit the type of music it charms me with, but never altering the manner of its charm.

I remember, thus, what seems to me to have been my first heteronym, or rather, my first nonexistent acquaintance—a certain *Chevalier de Pas* from age six, on whose behalf I wrote letters from him to myself, and whose figure, now fully faded, still captivates that part of my affection that he touches with yearning. I remember, with less clarity, another figure, whose name escapes me now but who was also a foreigner, and was, I am not sure in what, a rival of the Chevalier de Pas… Do such things happen with all children? Without a doubt—or perhaps. But I experienced them to such a degree that I still do, remembering them so clearly that it takes effort to remind myself that they were not real.

This tendency to create around me another world, the same as this one but with different people, never left my imagination. It has had various phases, among which this one, which happened to me as an adult. A witticism occurred to me, absolutely alien, for some reason or another, to who I am, or to who I suppose I am. I spoke it, immediately, spontaneously, as if it were some friend of mine, whose name I made up, whose history I added, and whose figure—face, height, clothes, and mannerisms—I immediately saw before me. And thus I acquired, and propagated, various friends and acquaintances who never existed, but who still today, nearly thirty years later, I hear, feel, see. I repeat: I hear, feel, see... And I miss them.

(Having started speaking—and typing to me is speaking—I can hardly find the brakes. Enough of bothering you, Casais Monteiro! I will get into the genesis of my literary heteronyms, which is, after all, what you wanted to know about. In any case, what has been said above gives you the story of the mother who bore them.)

Around 1912, if I am not mistaken (I cannot be by much), I had the idea of writing a few poems with a pagan character. I sketched out a few things in irregular verse (not in the style of Álvaro de Campos, but in a style of half-regularity), and gave up. However, there had been sketched for me, in a barely pictured half-light, a faint portrait of the person who was writing them. (Unbeknownst to me, Ricardo Reis had been born.)

A year and a half, or two years, later I decided one day to play a joke on Sá-Carneiro—to invent a bucolic poet, a complicated type, and introduce him to him, I no longer remember how, in some sort of reality. I spent several days developing the poet but nothing came of it. One day when I had finally given up—it was the 8th of March, 1914—I ensconced myself in a high room, and, taking a pen, began to write, standing, the way I write whenever I can. And I wrote thirty-some poems in a row, in a kind of ecstasy whose nature I will never be able to define. It was the triumphal day of my life, and I will not ever get another like it. I opened with a title, "The Keeper of Flocks." And what followed was the appearance of someone in me, to whom right away I gave the name Alberto Caeiro. Forgive me the absurdity of the phrase: my master had appeared in me. That was the immediate sensation I had. And so much so that, once those thirty-some poems were written, I immediately took another sheet of paper and wrote, in succession, the six poems that make up "Slanting Rain," by Fernando Pessoa. Immediately and completely... It was the return from Fernando Pessoa as Alberto Caeiro to Fernando Pessoa as himself only. Or rather, it was Fernando Pessoa's reaction against his nonexistence as Alberto Caeiro.

Alberto Caeiro having appeared, I then attended to finding him— instinctively and subconsciously—some disciples. I pulled out of his false paganism the latent Ricardo Reis, discovered his name, and adjusted him to himself, for at this point I now *saw* him. And, suddenly, by an opposite derivation from that of Ricardo Reis, a new individual came to me impetuously. In a burst, at the typewriter, without interruption or emendation, out came the "Ode Triunfal" ["Triumphal Ode"] of Álvaro de Campos—the Ode with that name and the man with the name he has.

I formed, then, a nonexistent *coterie*. I cast it all in molds of reality. I graded their influences, learned of their friendships, heard within myself their arguments and differences of opinion, and in all this it seemed that I, the creator of it all, was the one least there. It all seemed to take place independently of me. And it seems that it still does. If I ever am able to publish the aesthetic argument between Ricardo Reis and Álvaro de Campos, you will see how they are different, and how I am not in the material at all.

When we were publishing *Orpheu*, we needed, at the last hour, to put together something to fill out the page count. I suggested then to Sá-Carneiro that I write an "old" poem by Álvaro de Campos—a poem from how Álvaro de Campos would have been before meeting Caeiro and falling under his influence. And that was how I wrote "Opiário" ["Opiarium"], in which I tried to put all the latent tendencies in Álvaro de Campos, as would later be revealed, but without yet any trace of contact with my master Caeiro. It was, of the poems I have written, the one which gave me the most work, due to the double strength of depersonalization that I had to develop. But, in the end, I think it didn't come out badly, and that it gives us Álvaro in the bud...

I think I have explained the origin of my heteronyms. If however there is any point on which you need a more lucid clarification—I am writing quickly, and when I write quickly I am not very lucid—say so, and I will gladly give you one. And, it is true, a true hysterical complement: when writing certain passages of "Notes for the recollection of my master Caeiro," by Álvaro de Campos, I have wept real tears. This is to let you know whom you are dealing with, my dear Casais Monteiro!

A few more notes on this matter... I *see* before me, in the colorless but real space of dream, the faces, the movements of Caeiro, Ricardo Reis, and Álvaro de Campos. I have constructed their ages and lives. Ricardo Reis was born in 1887 (I don't remember the day and month, but I have them somewhere) in Porto, is a doctor, and currently lives in Brazil. Alberto Caeiro was born in 1889 and died in 1915; he was born in Lisbon, but lived almost all his life in the country. He had no profession and almost no education. Álvaro de Campos was born in Tavira, on the 15th of October, 1890 (at 1:30 in the afternoon, Ferreira Gomes tells me; and it is true, as the horoscope for that time of day is right). He, as you know, is a naval engineer (educated in Glasgow), but now he is here in Lisbon without employment. Caeiro was of medium height, and, although quite frail (he died of tuberculosis), he did not look as frail as he was. Ricardo Reis is a little, but not much, shorter, stronger, but lean. Álvaro de Campos is tall (1.75 meters, 2 centimeters taller than I), thin and tending to stoop a bit. All of them with short hair—Caeiro blond and pale, blue eyes; Reis vaguely swarthy with dull brown hair; Campos between pale and swarthy, a vaguely Portuguese Jewish look, but hair straight and normally parted on the side; a monocle. Caeiro, as I said, had next to no education— only primary school; his father and mother died young, and he was able to stay hoe, living off some small income. He lived with an old aunt, a great-aunt. Ricardo Reis, educated at a Jesuit high school, is, as I said, a doctor; he has lived in Brazil since 1919, as he voluntarily expatriated himself because he was a monarchist. He is a Latinist by education from others, and a semi-Hellenist by self-education. Álvaro de Campos had an ordinary high school education; then he was sent to Scotland to study engineering, first mechanical and then naval. On a holiday he took a trip to the East, from which came "Opiário." He learned Latin from an uncle from Beira who was a priest.

How do I write on behalf of these three?... Caeiro by pure and unanticipated inspiration, without knowing or even guessing what I was going to write. Ricardo Reis, after some absent-minded deliberation, which suddenly becomes encapsulated in an ode. Campos, when I feel a sudden impulse to write and do not know what to write. (My semi-heteronym, Bernardo Soares, who happens in many ways to resemble Álvaro de Campos, always appears when I am tired or drowsy, with my qualities of reason and inhibition somewhat suspended; his prose is a constant daydream. He is a semi-heteronym because, while his personality is not mine, it is not different from mine, but simply a mutilation of it. He is me minus my reasoning and affectivity. His prose, except for the subtlety my reasoning gives mine, is the same as it, and his Portuguese entirely the same; whereas Caeiro wrote badly in Portuguese, Campos passably but with some lapses, like saying "such as me" instead of "such as I," etc. Reis writes better than I do, but with a purism I consider excessive. What is hardest for me is to write prose by Reis—still unpublished—or by Campos. The simulation is easier, as it is more spontaneous, in verse.)

At this point you must be wondering what cruel fate made you fall, by reading, right into a madhouse. In any case, the worst part of all this is the incoherence with which I am writing. I repeat, however: I am writing as if I were talking to you, so that I can write back immediately. Otherwise, months would go by before I managed to write.[2]

I still must respond to your question regarding occultism. You ask me if I believe in occultism. Put that way, the question is not quite clear; however, I understand your meaning and will respond to it. I believe in the existence of worlds superior to ours and of inhabitants of those worlds, in experiences of various grades of spirituality, growing subtler all the way to a Supreme Being, who presumably created this world. It may be that there are other Beings, likewise Supreme, who have created other universes, and that those universes coexist with ours, overlappingly or not. For these reasons, and others too, the Extreme Order of Occultism, that is, the Masonic Order, avoids (except the Anglo-Saxon Freemasons) the expression "God," given its theological and popular implications, and prefers to say "Great Architect of

---

2. This letter, as inserted by Adolfo Casais Monterio in the edition by Editorial Confluência [and, earlier, in the journal *Presença* (issue 9), June 1937], omitted the following two paragraphs, on occultism, respecting the postscript in which Fernando Pessoa requested and justified its non-publication. However, beginning with the work *Páginas de Doutrina Estética by Fernando Pessoa*, edited by Jorge de Sena for Editorial Inquérito, the text of the letter has been published in full.

the Universe," which leaves blank the question of whether he is creator, or mere Governor of the world. Given these levels of beings, I do not believe in direct communication with God, but, according to our spiritual refinement, we may communicate with progressively higher beings.

There are three paths to the occult: the magical path (including practices such as spiritism, intellectually at the level of witchcraft, which is also magic), this path being extremely dangerous, in all senses; the mystical path, which is not strictly dangerous, but is uncertain and slow; and what is called the alchemical path, the most difficult and most perfect of all, for it entails a transmutation of one's own personality that *prepares* one, without great risks, but rather with defenses that the other paths lack. As for my "initiation" or not, I can tell you only this, although I do not know whether it responds to your question: I do not belong to any Initiating Order. The citation, as an epigraph to my poem "Eros e Psique" ["Eros and Psyche"], of a passage (translated, as the Ritual is in Latin) of the Ritual of the Third Degree of the Knights Templar of Portugal, indicates merely—which is a fact—that I was allowed to leaf through the Rituals of the first three degrees of that Order, defunct, or dormant, since around 1888. If it were not dormant, I would not cite the passage from the Ritual, as passages from Rituals are not to be cited (indicating the origin) in any work.

Thus I believe, my dear comrade, to have responded, albeit with certain incoherencies, to your questions. If there are others you wish to ask, do not hesitate to do so. I will answer as I can and to the best of my ability. What may happen, and I will apologize for this in advance, is that I do not respond so quickly.

Your comrade who greatly appreciates and admires you embraces you,

Fernando Pessoa

Besides the copy I normally make for myself, when I type, of any letter that involves explanations on the order of those that this one contains, I have made a supplemental copy, both in case this letter is misdelivered, and in case it may be necessary to some other end. This copy is available to you anytime.

One more thing. It may be that, for some study, or another similar purpose, you need in the future to quote some passage of this letter. You are permitted in advance to do so, *but with one reservation*, and I ask your permission to emphasize it. The paragraph about occultism, on page 7 of my letter, is not to be reproduced in print. Hoping to respond as clearly as possible to your question, it purposely goes a bit beyond the limits inherent to this material.

This is a private letter, and for that reason I did not hesitate in doing so. Nothing should keep you from reading that paragraph to whomever you wish, as long as that other person also obeys the condition of not reproducing in print what is written in that paragraph. I believe I can rely on you to that negative end.

I remain in debt to you as far as a long-owed letter about your latest books. I maintain what I believe I told you in my previous letter: whenever (I believe it will not be until Februrary) I spend a few days in Estoril, I will get that correspondence in order, as I am in debt, in that matter, not only to you, but also to several other people.

It occurs to me to ask again something I have asked you before, which you did not answer: did you receive my pamphlets of poetry in English that I sent you awhile back?

"For my government," as is said in business language, I would ask that you indicate as quickly as possible that you have received this letter. Thank you.

F. Pessoa

Notes for the recollection of my master Caeiro

I met my master Caeiro in exceptional circumstances—as are all circumstances in life, and especially those which, being nothing in and of themselves, turn out to mean everything in their results.

I left my Scottish degree in naval engineering nearly three-quarters done; I set sail for the Orient; on the return, disembarking in Marseilles, and feeling awfully bored with carrying on, I came over to Lisbon by land. A cousin of mine brought me to Ribatejo one day for a stroll; I knew a cousin of Caeiro's and had done business with him; I found myself with the man who would become my master at his cousin's house. There is no more to tell, for it was short, like all fertilizations.

I still find, with a clear soul, that the tears of memory do not abscond, for my vision is not external... I see him before me, and I may forever see him as I first saw him. First, his blue eyes like an unfearing child's; then, his cheekbones already a bit prominent, his color a bit pale, and his strange Grecian air, that came from within and was a calmness, and not from without, for it was neither and expression nor a feature. His hair, practically lush, was blond, but turned in a dim light turned brown. His height was average, tending towards tall, but hunched, without high shoulders. His movements were plain, his smile was the way it was, his voice was even, issuing with the tone of someone who seeks nothing but to say what he is saying—neither loud nor soft, clear, free of intentions, of hesitations, of bashfulness. His blue eyes could never stop staring. If anything seemed strange to my observation, it was that his brow, though not high, was powerfully white. I repeat: it was its whiteness, seeming more so than the paleness of his face, that held majesty. His hands a bit slender, but not very; the palms were wide. The expression of his mouth, the last thing to notice—as if speaking were, to this man, less than existing— was the kind of smile attributed in poetry to beautiful inanimate objects, simply because they are pleasant—flowers, wide fields, sunlit waters—a smile at existing, and not at speaking with us.

My master, my master, gone so soon! I see you again in the shadow that I am in myself, in the memory I keep of my own deadness...

453

During our first conversation… How it happened I don't know, he said, "There's a young man here you'd enjoy getting to know, Ricardo Reis: he's very different from you." And then he added, "everything is different from us, and that's why it exists."

That sentence, spoken like an old saw from his home, seduced me with a shock, like the shock of all first possessions, entering me through the foundations of my soul. But, unlike material seduction, the effect on me was of suddenly receiving, in all my sensations, a virginity I had not had before.

*

Once, referring the straightforward conception of things that characterized Caeiro's sensibility, I mentioned to him with friendly wickedness that Wordsworth designates someone as insensible with the phrase:

A primrose by the river's brim
A yellow primrose was to him,
And it was nothing more.

And I translated (omitting the exact translation of "primrose," since I don't know the names of flowers or plants), saying in Portuguese, "A yellow flower by the river was a yellow flower to him, and it was nothing more."

My master Caeiro laughed. "That simpleton saw it right: a yellow flower really isn't anything but a yellow flower."

But, suddenly, he reconsidered.

"There is one difference," he added. "It depends on whether you take the yellow flower as one of many yellow flowers, or as a yellow flower on its own."

And then he said, "What this English poet meant was that to that man the yellow flower was an ordinary experience, or something familiar. Now, that's not quite right. Every thing we see, we always ought to see for the first time, because it really is the first time we're seeing it. And so each yellow flower is a new yellow flower, even if you call it the same as yesterday. We're not the same anymore, and neither is the flower. Even the yellow can't be the same anymore. It's too bad we don't exactly have the eyes to know that, because then we'd be happy."

My master Caeiro was not a pagan: he was paganism. Ricardo Reis was a pagan, António Mora is a pagan, I am a pagan; even Fernando Pessoa would be a pagan, if he weren't so tightly wound inside. But Ricardo Reis was a pagan in character, António Mora is a pagan in intellect, I am a pagan in outrage, that is, in temperament. In Caeiro there was no explanation for paganism, but a consubstantiation of such.

I shall define this in the way that undefinable things are defined—through the cowardice of example. One of the most vividly striking things in comparing ourselves with the Greeks is the lack of a concept of the infinite, the repugnance for infinity, among the greeks. Now, my master Caeiro had in him that same unconception. I shall recount, very accurately I think, the arresting conversation in which he reveals this to me.

He was mentioning to me, rather elaborating on what he says in one of his poems from *The Keeper of Flocks*, that somebody had used to call him a "materialist poet." Not finding the expression fair, since my master Caeiro is not definable with any fair expression, I told him nevertheless that the attribution was not altogether absurd. And I explained to him, more or less correctly, about classical materialism. Caeiro listened to me with a pained-looking attention, then said to me abruptly, "But that's all very stupid. That's something for priests who have no religion, and so no excuse."

I was astonished, and I pointed out to him several similarities between materialism and his own doctrine, minus its poetry. Caeiro protested.

"But what you're calling poetry is everything. It's not even poetry: it's seeing. Those materialist folks are blind. You say they say space is infinite. Where in space did they see that?"

I replied, disoriented, "But don't you conceive of space as infinite? Can't you conceive of space as infinite?"

"I don't conceive of anything as infinite. How am I supposed to conceive of something as infinite?"

"Man," I said, "imagine a space. Beyond that space is more space, past that there's more, and past that, and past, and past… It doesn't end…"

"Why not?" said my master Caeiro.

I underwent a mental earthquake. "Say it ends," I shouted. "What then?"

"If it ends, then there isn't anything," he answered.

This type of argument, cumulatively childish and feminine, and therefore unanswerable, tangled up my mind for a few moments.

"But is that what you understand?" I let out at last.

"Understand what? Something having limits? I'd better! If it doesn't have limits it doesn't exist. Existing means that there's something else, and so everything is limited. What's hard to understand about something being something, and not being something else farther off too?"

At this point I felt in my flesh that I was arguing not with another man, but with another universe. I made one last attempt, a detour I felt obliged to view as legitimate.

"Look, Caeiro... Take numbers... Where do numbers end? Let's take any number—34, for instance. After that we have 35, 36, 37, 38, and so on with nowhere to stop. There is no number so big that there isn't a bigger number..."

"But those are just numbers," protested my master Caeiro.

And then he added, looking at me with formidable childlikeness, "What in Reality is 34?"

*

There are sudden phrases, deep because they come from somewhere deep, that define a man, or, rather, with which a man defines himself, without definition. I have not forgotten the one in which Ricardo Reis once defined himself to me. We were discussing lying, and he said, "I detest lies, for a lie is an inaccuracy." All of Ricardo Reis—past, present, and future—was plain to see.

My master Caeiro, since all he ever said was what he was, could be defined by any phrase of his, written or spoken, especially after the period that begins halfway through "The Keeper of Flocks". But, out of so many phrases that he wrote and are in print, out of so many he spoke to me that I have related or not, the one which contains the greatest simplicity is one he said to me once in Lisbon. We were discussing something having to do with one's relationship to oneself. And out of the blue I asked my master Caeiro, "Are you happy with yourself?" And he replied, "No, I'm just happy." It was like the voice of the earth, everyone and no one.

*

I never saw my master Caeiro sad. I don't know if he was sad when he died, or in the days leading up. I could have found out, but the truth is I have never dared to ask those who saw him die anything about his death or how it came to him.

In any case, it was one of my life's anguishes—one of those true anguishes in the midst of so many fictitious ones—that Caeiro died without me by his side. It's stupid but it's human, and that's the way it is.

I was in England. Even Ricardo Reis was not in Lisbon; he was back in Brazil. Fernando Pessoa was there, but it was as if he weren't. Fernando Pessoa feels things but doesn't touch them, not even on the inside.

Nothing consoles me from not having been in Lisbon that day, except what consolation I get from spontaneous thoughts of my master Caeiro. No one can be inconsolable with the memory of Caeiro around, or of his poetry; and even the idea of nothingness—the most harrowing of any that can be sensibly thought—has, in his work and in the recollection of my dear master, something high and luminous about it, like the sun on the snowy caps of unattainable peaks.

Álvaro de Campos

Bibliographical Table

Born in Lisbon, on June 13, 1888. Educated at the High School in Durban, Natal, South Africa, and at the (English) University of the Cape of Good Hope. There awarded the Queen Victoria prize for English style in 1903—the first year that prize was given.

What Fernando Pessoa writes belongs to two categories of works, which we may call orthonymous and heteronymous. It cannot be said that they are anonymous or pseudonymous, because they truly are not. Pseudonymous work is by the author in his own person, except the name assigned; heteronymous work is by the author outside his own person, from an individual completely fabricated by him, as would be the speeches of any character in any play he wrote.

The heteronymous works of Fernando Pessoa are written under, so far, three people's names—Alberto Caeiro, Ricardo Reis, Álvaro de Campos. These individuals ought to be considered as distinct from their author. Each one forms a kind of drama; and all of them together form another drama. Alberto Caeiro, who is considered to have been born in 1889 and died in 1915, has written poems with one certain orientation. He has had as disciples—coming, as such, from various aspects of that orientation—the other two: Ricardo Reis, considered to have been born in 1887, who isolated in his work, stylizing it, the intellectual and pagan side; Álvaro de Campos, born in 1890, who in his work isolated the emotional side so to speak, which he called "sensationist," and which—linking it to various influences, among which predominates, although below that of Caeiro, that of Walt Whitman—produced various complications, generally of scandalous and provocative character, especially for Fernando Pessoa, who in any case has no remedy but to write them and publish them, however much he disagrees with them. The works of these three poets form, as stated, a dramatic set; and the intellectual interaction of their personalities has been duly studied, as well

---

From the "Bibliographical Table," written by Fernando Pessoa himself and inserted, for the first time, in issue 17 of *Presença* (December 1928), Adolfo Casais Monteiro published only an excerpt in the edition of this anthology edited by Editorial Confluência (1945). In the present edition, the Table is republished in its complete form.

as their personal relationships. All this will appear in biographies yet to be written, accompanied, when they are published, by horoscopes and, perhaps, photographs. It is a drama in people, instead of acts.

(Whether these three individuals are more or less real than Fernando Pessoa himself—that is a metaphysical problem, which he, absent from the secret of the Gods, and ignoring therefore what reality is, will never. be able to solve.)

Fernando Pessoa has published, orthonymously, four pamphlet of English poetry: *Antinous and 35 Sonnets*, together, in 1918, and *English Poems I-II and English Poems III*, also together, in 1922. The first poem from the third of these pamphlets is a recasting of the "Antinous" of 1918. He has published, additionally, in 1923, a manifesto, *Sobre Um Manifesto de Estudantes* [On a Students' Manifesto], in support of Raul Leal, and, in 1928, a pamphlet, *Interregno. Defesa e Justificação da Ditadura Military em Protugal* [Interregnum. A Defense and Justification of the Military Dictatorship in Portugal], which the government agreed to publish. None of these texts is definitive. From an aesthetic point of view, the author prefers, therefore, to consider these works as only approximately existent. No heteronymous writing has been published in a pamphlet or book.

Fernando Pessoa has collaborated significantly, always on the occasion of friendly requests, on journals and other publications of various characters. What of him has been scattered among those is, overall, of even less public interest than the pamphlets cited above. There are, however, with reservations, the following exceptions:

As for the orthonymous works: the static drama "O Marinheiro" ["The Mariner"] in *Orpheu 1* (1915); "O Banqueiro Anarquista" ["The Anarchist Banker"] in *Contemporânea 1* (1992); the poems "Mar Português" ["Portuguese Sea"] in *Contemporânea 4* (1922); a small collection of poems in *Athena 3* (1925); and, in volume 1 of the Lisbon newspaper *Sol* (1926), the precise and moving narration that is "O Conto do Vigário" ["The Vicar's Tale"].

As for the heteronymous works: the two odes—"*Ode Triunfal*" and "*Ode Marítima*" ["Triumphal Ode" and "*Maritime Ode*"]—by Álvaro de

Campos in *Orpheu 1* and *2* (1915), "Ultimatum" by the same, in the only issue of *Portugal Futurista* (1917); the book of *Odes*, by Ricardo Reis, in *Athena 1* (1924); and the excerpts of poems by Alberto Caeiro in *Athena 4* and *5* (1925).

The rest, orthonymous or heteronymous, either is of no interest, or only of passing interest, or needs refining or redefining, or are short compositions, in prose or verse, that it would be difficult to remember and tedious to enumerate once remembered.

From the point of view of publicity, so to speak, it is, however, worth mentioning a few articles in *A Águia*, from 1912, especially due to the upset caused by the announcement made in them of the "next appearance of the super-Camões." With the same intent may be cited the set that was published in *Orpheu*, given the inordinate scandal that resulted from that publication.

Those are the only two cases of any writing by Fernando Pessoa reaching the attention of the public.

Fernando Pessoa does not intend to publish—at least not for a long while—any book or pamphlet. Having no public to read them, he may be excused from pointlessly spending money he does not have on that publication; and, to get any publisher to spend pointlessly, it would take an apprenticeship for the process to which the wistful Manuel Peres Vigário gave his name, indirectly cited above.

The *Pessoa* of Casais Monteiro

an essay by
Eduardo Lourenço

We still have not had from Casais Monteiro's pen that complete Pessoa whom we will always lack if bad fortune is unwilling to bring him into existence. But we have had occasionally, as a negative, a full sketch of that Pessoa of his whom we so need. In the series of "approximations" that have been his successive studies dedicated to the author of "Maritime Ode," most of polemical origin, in the elevated sense of the term, a Pessoa is portrayed like no other, except in what, as a public echo of him, no one can remember the origin of. Luckily, the image of Pessoa, notwithstanding the national tradition of cliché and stereotyped glory, is still being forged. It is not difficult to recognize in the disturbed magma—but no longer disturbing—the contributions made by a few towards the future statue in which it will someday (already here) be nearly impossible to recognize the one who, to others and to himself, barely but so vertiginously existed. They are reflections, mostly, from people who exist corporeally and socially with a self-satisfaction alien to any "sudden hand of some unseen phantasm" and this enviable splendor will make them apt to govern the world or their grandfather's bank. As such we will pass over them in silence, Fernando Pessoa being in them a cultural pretext, low or high it hardly matters, but not a life, in any case not that luminous blind life that in him was embossed with night and storm. Casais Monteiro's Pessoa does not belong to this family, and he has written nearly all of his "approximations" to save him from eventually belonging to it. It is not too late to see Pessoa living in them and that Casais Monteiro's view of Poetry and its place in human existence is brought to bear through him, since in Casais Monteiro's critical work his constant interest in Pessoa is situated in a broader and more general attempt to understand poetic reality in and of itself.

The poetic and cultural comprehension of Pessoa by Casais Moneiro distinguishes itself from all the rest by its *personal* character, we might even

---

This essay was composed in the 1960s, the manuscript of which is held in the National Library of Portugal. Transcribed, annotated, and published in 2018 by Pedro Sepúlveda. *Cf.* P. Sepúlveda, "Um ensaio inédito de Eduardo Lourenço sobre o *Pessoa* de Casais Monteiro", *Colóquio/Letras*, 197 (January 2018). In the following pages are also included, in translation, the footnotes from this publication.

say *familiar*, if the term did not evoke—at least in Portugal...—a comfort, an ease, a sweetness that are not those of the now long and not extinct monologue of Casais Monteiro in Fernando Pessoa's company. I am not sure that Casais Monteiro and Pessoa are what is often called kindred spirits. By examining his Pessoa we will have the chance to elucidate a point in close connection with this question. Now, what is clear to those familiar with Casais Monteiro's poetic and mental itinerary is that he was, out of all the men of his generation who have given their own testimony, the one who most intensely *experienced* Fernando Pessoa. It would not be unfair to suppose that without his encounter with Casais Monteiro's world Pessoa would not quite be who he is. We understand this, it goes without saying, in the same sense in which Paul Valéry understood it, in a sentence quoted by Casais Monteiro in one of the most colorful and provocative critical essays[1] of our half-century: "Not Verlaine, not Mallarmé, not Rimbaud would have been who they were without having read *Les Fleurs du Mal* at a formative age." Casais Monteiro likewise took illumination from his reading of Pessoa's poetry, as he himself confessed. And what suddenly opened before him, never again to be shut, was the horizon of a *specifically modern* world, a world already sensed and anticipated, at once nearby and uplifting. The sap that arose from there would nourish the creator whilst the critic would find in it the angel he would battle tirelessly, in his never-finished attempt to capture the essence of that *modernity* of which he, like no one else, was son, brother, and secret enemy. It was not, to be sure, mere chance that Fernando Pessoa came by his hand to stroll "across the whole breadth of the street." The effects of this *Anthology* of Fernando Pessoa are now visible, though incalculable, but the great clearing they opened in the national poetic consciousness on their appearance in 1942,[2] they had opened earlier in the mind of Casais Monteiro, leaving in him an indelible trace, the first great *full* reflection of the most significant poetic appropriation of the world in this twentieth century.

Everyone knows that the cultural fixation—chiefly poetic—around Pessoa and Sá-Carneiro is the work of the *Presença* generation. We prefer

---

1. *Cf.* A.C. Monteiro. *Considerações Pessoais.* Lisboa: INCM, 2004.
2. *Cf.* F. Pessoa. *Poesia*, A.C. Monteiro (introd. and sel.), 2 vols. Lisboa: Editorial Confluência, 1942.

this picture of things to the more debatable one of "discovery," although in what is in literature the essential world of life that nourishes life, the term "discovery" is appropriate and even carries a double meaning, as is perhaps always the case. By discovering, those few youths became discovered, who first saw the quality of "masters" in eccentric, socially obscure poets. However, if we actually read their readings—which were always plural, even as much as they did not appear so externally—we will find in them no experiences of that quality. And this is important for understanding how "modernity" and "modernism" did not and do not mean the same thing for a José Régio, a Gaspar Simões, a Casais Monteiro, who, each from his own perspective, knew sooner than others that he had been *sensitized* to new poetic or cultural values. It would be unfair—but not altogether illogical—to judge Gaspar Simões's relationship with Pessoa solely through his belated assessment and biography of the Poet,[3] referred to by Casais Monteiro as "the most sensational failure, not only in the G[aspar] S[imões]'s career but in contemporary criticism." Indeed, the modernist adventure appears as a purely culturological object, when viewed from the outside or submerged in a biographical pathos profoundly alien to the deep and serious spiritual adventure embodied therein. There are pages one would think had been written by the same philistines against whom Sá-Carneiro and Pessoa rebelled. Most shocking, however, is Gaspar Simões's objective good conscience and goodwill, since in its intention this work of terrible misunderstanding of Pessoa's universe is truly hagiographical. The young Gaspar Simões, nevertheless, managed to be sensitive—although the poetic content kept to the shadows—to a "childhood voice" he discovered in Pessoa's world. All shrouded, though, in Freudian mists, all basically translated into merely psychological complications with no deeper personal appropriation. Moreover, as this encounter for him was not a source of poetry, his case would be of no interest were it not for the rather extraordinary circumstance of his having publicly taken charge, so to speak, of Fernando Pessoa.

Quite different is Régio's case. When the author of *Jacob e o Anjo* [Jacob and the Angel] finds Pessoa his critical lucidity—extreme in him—is sensitive

---

3. *Cf.* J.G. Simões. *Vida e Obra de Fernando Pessoa: História de Uma Geração.* 2 vols. Lisboa: Bertrand, 1950.

to the novelty, the originality of his poetry and even more so to Sá-Carneiro's. But to Régio Pessoa was not tantamount to a revolution. Régio views Pessoa from his own world, not as a thunderstruck adolescent, but as a poet touching another poet's garden wall. Régio's spiritual relationship to Pessoa always had—and will have more and more—a critical coordinate. Régio found himself much more disarmed by Sá-Carneiro. It was with him that he had certainly the most exalted and crucifying experience: that of finding a "double" who had in some way anticipated him. His powerful personality, however, even before that encounter was already grappling with a more archaic world, carved out by other gods and, to some extent, protected by its very extremism from Sá-Carneiro's fatal venture. As for Pessoa's, or some of it, it would always strike him as *somewhat intellectual* when compared with that of his deceased friend. In sum, Régio never encountered, experienced, or appropriated the modernist adventure as a *mythic experience*, at the same time a brilliant formal revolution destroying old canons and a revolution of depth, the roaring echo of a world and of men in it for whom the ways of the soul had become "suddenly untraversable."

Younger, a philosophy student—and this is significant—Casais Monteiro, gifted in analysis and dialectic, certainly without a structured view of life or else already sensitive to the endless difficulty of such a proposition, would experience, and with a fulness without precedent, except in subsequent generations, that *mythic experience*. His merit—and it was not minor—was experiencing it before anyone else. It was to him that Fernando Pessoa appeared in the form of a supreme *undiscipliner of souls*, to use the excellent title from Jorge de Sena, who, in his own turn, personally, would recreate that same mythic experience. In other words, what for others, for one reason or another, remained in some way external, in Casais Monteiro took root, became life and enlivened him, making him for us, as a poet, and perhaps even as a critic, an exponent, but never entirely a prisoner, of *modernist mythology*, that is, of a certain cultural practice and a certain figure of the poet and of poetry and its place in the world which, without reference to Pessoa or Sá-Carneiro—Casais Monteiro's cultural awareness is extraordinarily broad and diverse—have in them and in what they signify a brilliant exemplification.

The fact that Casais Monteiro "lived" the modernist experience—and beyond that, quite simply, the modern experience, for it to open unto itself—signifies the opposite of passivity. As in all authentic "encounters" there must be two to encounter each other or the encounter itself, if decisive, will provoke true duality. At the same time, however, it will erase the indifference, *the distance*, at a level where it is not registered in other contemporaries of his. To live, to have lived, is more or less the same as to "comprehend," but any possible "comprehension" will arise from then on marked by what has been, beyond a cultural and intellectual experience, a source of profound vital and historical emotion. Thus everything that Casais Monteiro writes about Pessoa bears the mark of non-neutrality and even passion, without which nothing is really worthwhile. Simply, this "passion" is itself a complex of intellectual, ethical, even metaphysical choices, in sum, a translation into the plane of will or combative understanding of a personal vision that conveys as "reasons" the conception of life. The revelation of the "modern" is thus naturally "dialectic" or dialogic, to avoid confusion, Casais Monteiro having seen and experienced Modernism according to the perspective inherent to his conception of life or, as things never have such precision, in inner conflict with it.

This last observation is important lest we think of Casais Monteiro's attempts at "comprehension"—and his criticism in general—as originating from or in service of some *philosophy*, in the strict or even approximate sense that can and should be given to the word. The comprehension of Pessoa by Casais Monteiro is not of the same type as that of Antero by António Sérgio, nor, it goes without saying, that which became common in the form of neo-realism. Between pure impressionism, which it is in its ingenuousness or unconsciousness, and dogmatic criticism, in any of its forms, Casais Monteiro's comprehension is *without dogmas but not without principles*, perhaps, in its most subtle, complex, and ductile formulation out of those existing among us, *because no other criterion is given but that of learning what in the works is irreducible and even altogether unlearnable, creatures belonging to a single man among men by the testimony even of that work.*

Thus summarized, Casais Monteiro's critical atitude enters the Caudine Forks of generality. Absolutely opposite critics, if questioned on their critical intention, may present a similar "respect" for the "works," a submission of principle to the *uniqueness* they convey. Especially today when that crucial tune has become commonplace. However, situated dialectically and historically in the whole of *Portuguese criticism*, the attitude configured by Casais Monteiro—which in its "intention" is that of his whole generation—has an undeniable specificity. We are not speaking of *taste*—ultimately *the truth of criticism*, which in that generation was, as a general rule, unequalled—but of principles themselves. Recent generations, who now have barely read them—and this is fatal—would like to imagine that in this chapter, as in others, *the attitude called Presencist* is a dry branch on a dead tree. Putting aside the fact that they themselves have not countered it with anything superior (quite the contrary), such an attitude holds, now as then, *as a generic attitude towards Art*, an exemplary value. It is not idle to repeat it in an era when a confusion of taste that seemed impossible after the passing of Régio and Casais Monteiro publicly installs once again the realm of mediocrity, at the same time that simple judgments of social efficacy replace the anguished, difficult, perhaps *unattainable* preoccupation *with exclusively literary value* that oriented and constituted the Presencist literary attitude.

It will be said that one way or another, with good or bad criticism, as a function of absurd or just principles, the *valuable work* will always have the strength to radiate and impose itself, little matter the blindness or privileged light of a single day. This is not the case. It is in the light of the living that the dead are resurrected, in the light of the present that the eternal battles are waged. From the *critical* point of view the Presencist generation was, and is, exemplary for having experienced and theorized, not only classically, on Art in general, *but on Artistic Creation as a general human problematic*. That is to say—and this is related closely to the subject of this article—this generation assumed *in the critical plane* the reflection of the revolution that in the plane of creation represents the poetic making of the *Orpheu* generation. To be precise, the poetry of Sá-Carneiro and Pessoa *is man in question, totally and radically*; and this Art in which man finds himself so absolutely in question—and whose panoramic is confused in the end with "modern art"—the Presencists made a *vital subject*, it mattering little to us now if one or the other of them did so at times in a banal or degraded form.

Does this mean that they assumed, from the critical point of view, the same problematicity inherent in the poetic making of *Orpheu*?

This is the decisive question already partly answered. In another essay we have had occasion to situate the distinct levels of problematicity in the generations of *Orpheu* and *Presença* with respect to the same works. We wrote then that the adventure of *Orpheus* is *ontological*—from the "literary" point of view *tragic*—while that of *Presença* is predominantly *psychological* and *dramatic*.[4] In the critical plane such a distinction seems not to fit, since it is commonly said that the *Orpheus* generation was not *critical*. It is not without interest to highlight that this opinion comes from *Presença* itself and that no perspective of "literary history" or "genres" appears to justify it. Let us be clear, though. On the one hand, Fernando Pessoa was—is—an extraordinary critic—the assertion is not excessive and only to the eyes of Gaspar Simões will it seem bizarre—to make nothing or little of his complacent or unreal "criticisms" of this one or that one (what about the ingenious ones?); on the other hand, *the most profound critical reality* (in the sense of consciousness not merely of the "poetic" in general but of such or such poet) is included in the very poems from which no one has yet extracted it. Let us not say of "Ultimatum" that its "scandalous" appearance made it visible as a "negative act" but that it is *a literary course* with the speed of lightning. Very well: *this criticism*, not made explicit, but so present, is to the same degree *revolutionary* as the poems and there is between it and the general Presencist criticism a difference of the same type as that highlighted in the works. In Pessoa's criticism, or rather in his "poetics" it is Art that is in question. It seems almost the same. There is a chasm between the two formulas, the same that separates the victims or survivors of an earthquake from those who come to live there later in spite of them.

As the Presencist criticism was above all *literary* we will put from here on the word Literature where we have put Art, the considerations of principle holding for both. Moreover, one of the contributions of *Presença* was that of

---

4. Essay written in December of 1958 and published under the title "Presença ou A Contra-Revolução do Modernismo," in the supplement "Cultura e Arte" of *O Comércio do Porto* (14 and 28 of June, 1960). An edited version was published, with the title *"Presença* ou A Contra-Revolução do Modernismo Português,"* in *Revista do Livro* (Rio de Janeiro, July 1961), later included in the volume *Tempo e Poesia*, published for the first time in 1974.

making commonplace among us the reference to the *creative act* or *creation* as a support and unity of worlds until then *sociologically* sealed. We will say, then, that Presencist criticism is simultaneously *man as a literary problem and Literature as a human problem.* This means for us that from the perspective of this criticism *man* appears as more problematic than Literature, in sum, that here *man is in some way more real than his own empirical or historical appearance.* On another occasion we have interpreted this attitude in too negative a sense by designating it as mythification of Literature. There is some of that in Presencism, its *gods* or supreme references belonging in general to the *literary horizon,* but it is necessary to complete this appraisal by saying that, in turn, Literature is that magical reality *because it is the place of de-mythifications, of the authenticity of the image of men.* The famous "subjectivism" of *Presença,* if it exists—and everything is always "the subjective" of someone...—would have here its point of application and self-overcoming. The conscience of the human mystery, the unassailable subjectivity of man, ascends to overcome it from within itself in the mirror of Literature. But this literature is, for its own turn, a source of subjectivity and of a perplexity to the second power, for not everything that takes its form truly *exists.* To determine the *degrees* of that *existence,* which may be nonexistence, that is the tremendous, the impossible and nonetheless banal and natural *critical temptation.* No generation in Portugal has known it like this one, for only this one gave itself *as a norm* to distinguish what is living from what is in function of *exclusively literary values.*

It is easy to accuse this purpose or that intention of being utopian or idealistic. What is difficult is to replace it with another. It is not even an argument to demonstrate that *in practice* Presencist criticism is far from obeying that exclusively literary criterion. In practice, all critical theorization is a source of identical contradiction, except for cases of incurable blindness to values. It is this fatality that makes one think and there may be in it the beginnings of wisdom. Presencist criticism was right, and continues to be so, in refusing other criteria than the *literary* as a horizon of judgment, but it goes beyond its powers and everyone's by presupposing a *clarity,* or an access to that criterion, which in reality do not exist.

They do not exist, we say, because they are always existing. It is the fiction of their absence that is unsustainable and there is some of that in the

Presencist conviction that a critical attitude is guided by nothing but the pure idea of *literature as such*. To show how in *practice* the criticism of Régio, of Gaspar Simões, and of Casais Monteiro convey a much more heavily laden and impure substance would be child's play. Here we are concerned with principles. In their polemical intention and obstinate and salutary reference to *literature*—that is, the ideal motion in the order of immanence—the Presencist generation encloses an undeniable truth. Two philosophies, quite different, have given a grandiose and pertinent expression to the idea of the *irreducibility of art in general* and, as a consequence, to the idea that creation can only be comprehended or judged by a critic who is, at the same time, from the same family as the creators. This was the cultural condition of the men of *Presença* and few have been so like the author of this Pessoan *Anthology*, who will be for others the bridge to their relationship with Fernando Pessoa.

Eduardo Lourenço

ACTIVE BIBLIOGRAPHY OF FERNANDO PESSOA

Works referenced for the production of this edition

PESSOA, F., (1942). *Obras Completas de Fernando Pessoa. Poesias.* Lisboa: Ática. Vol. I.

___, (1944). *Obras Completas de Fernando Pessoa. Poesias de Álvaro de Campos.* Lisboa: Ática. Vol. II.

___, (1945). *Poesia.* A.C. MONTEIRO (ed.), 2nd ed. Lisboa: Editorial Confluência.

___, (1996). *Correspondência (1923-1935).* M.P. SILVA (ed.). Lisboa: Assírio & Alvim.

___, (1997). *Poemas de Fernando Pessoa.* J. DIONÍSIO, I. CASTRO and L. PRISTA (eds.). Lisboa: Imprensa Nacional Casa da Moeda. Vol. I, books 1–3.

___, (1998). *Ficções do Interlúdio (1914-1935).* F.C. MARTINS (ed.). Lisboa: Assírio & Alvim.

___, (2006). *Poesia do Eu.* R. ZENITH (ed.). Lisboa: Assírio & Alvim.

___, (2014). *Obra Completa de Álvaro de Campos.* J. PIZARRO and A. CARDIELLO (eds.) Lisboa: Tinta-da-China.

___, (2015). *Poemas de Alberto Caeiro.* I. CASTRO (ed.). Lisboa: Imprensa Nacional Casa da Moeda.

___, (2016). *Obra Completa de Ricardo Reis.* J. PIZARRO and J. URIBE (eds.). Lisboa: Tinta-da-China.

Fernando Pessoa in English

PESSOA, F., (1988a). *Always Astonished: Selected Prose.* E. HONIG (trans.). San Francisco: City Lights Books.

___, (1988b). *Self-Analysis and Thirty Other Poems.* G. MONTEIRO (trans.). Lisboa: Fundação Calouste Gulbenkian.

___, (1998a). *Fernando Pessoa & Co.: Selected Poems.* R. ZENITH (trans.). New York: Grove Press

___, (1998b). *Poems of Fernando Pessoa.* E. HONIG and S. BROWN (trans.). San Francisco: City Lights Books.

___, (2004). *Selected Poems.* D. BUTLER (trans.). Dublin: Dedalus Press.

___, (2006). *A Little Larger Than the Entire Universe: Selected Poems.* R. ZENITH (trans.). New York: Penguin Books.

___, (2007). *Message; Mensagem.* J. GRIFFIN (trans.). Exeter: Shearsman Books & Menard Press.

___, (2008). *Forever Someone Else: Selected Poems.* R. ZENITH (trans.). Lisboa: Assírio & Alvim.

___, (2017). *The Book of Disquiet: The Complete Edition.* M.J. COSTA (trans.). New York: New Directions.

___, (2020a). *The Complete Works of Alberto Caeiro.* M.J. COSTA (trans.). New York: New Directions.

___, (2020b). *Message.* A.A. LOURENÇO (ed.); Martin EARL (trans.). Lisboa: Shantarin [Lisboa Poets & Co].

ESSAYS ON FERNANDO PESSOA

CASTRO, M.G. (ed.), (2013). *Fernando Pessoa's Modernity Without Frontiers: Influences, Dialogues and Responses.* Oxford: Tamesis.

JACKSON, K. D., (2010). *Adverse Genres in Fernando Pessoa.* Oxford: Oxford University Press.

KLOBUCKA, A. and M. SABINE (eds.), (2007). *Embodying Pessoa: Corporeality, Gender, Sexuality.* Toronto: University of Toronto Press.

KOTOWICZ, Z., (2008). *Fernando Pessoa: Voices of a Nomadic Soul.* Exeter: Shearsman Books.

MONTEIRO, G., (1982). *The Man Who Never Was: Essays on Fernando Pessoa.* Providence: Gavea-Brown.

___, (1998). *The Presence of Pessoa: English, American, and Southern African Literary Responses.* Lexington, KY: University Press of Kentucky.

___, (2000). *Fernando Pessoa and Nineteenth-Century Anglo-American Literature.* Lexington, KY: University Press of Kentucky.

SADLIER, D., (2009). *An Introduction to Fernando Pessoa: Modernism and the Paradoxes of Authorship.* Gainesville: University Press of Florida.

SANTOS, I.R., (2003). *Atlantic Poets: Fernando Pessoa's Turn in Anglo-American Modernism.* Hanover, NH: University Press of New England.

ZENITH, R., (2021). *Pessoa: A Biography.* New York: Liveright / W.W. Norton.